FUCHSIAS

THE COMPLETE GUIDE

NEW EDITION

❧ EDWIN GOULDING ❧

Timber Press • Portland, Oregon

Acknowledgements

I would like to acknowledge the debt of gratitude owed to the following people, some of whom played a large part in the first edition of *Fuchsias, The Complete Guide.* Some have contributed to the production of this second edition.

First, Alison M. Jones is to be thanked for her excellent line drawings and paintings. My brother Graham Goulding, my daughter Linda J. Morris and my late aunt Miss F. M. Abbott helped me immeasurably. My son Timothy J. Goulding has given invaluable assistance, not least with the computer technology required for such a large task. Timothy Auger of B.T. Batsford contributed much to the success of the first edition of this book.

In The Netherlands help has been received from many friends. Khoen and Rhea Loe, the late Mia Goedman-Frankema and her husband Ton, the family Appel and Mr J. v. d. Hee offered great support. Herman de Graaff con- tributed the Foreword to the first edition of the book. Friends in the Dutch Fuchsia Society have given their assistance freely. Latterly, my friend Martin Beije has been a tower of strength in so many different ways.

In the United Kingdom Brian Kimberley has shown that skill and enthusiasm in fuchsia growing are alive and flourishing. Dr Leslie Blaber has given his help and advice to me in so many ways: I am especially grateful to him for contributing the Foreword to this second edi- tion. To Brian C. Morrison I owe a huge debt for his friendship and support, from the book's inception. Lastly, to the staff of B.T. Batsford I would like to extend my thanks: Tina Persaud has made all the hard work pleasurable. The sec- ond edition of this book is dedicated to Pauline and to my fuchsia friends.

Edwin J. Goulding, 2001

This new edition first published in North America 2002

ISBN 0-88192-554-3

A CIP record for this book is available from the Library of Congress.

Printed and bound in Spain
For the publishers

Timber Press, Inc.
The Haseltine Building
133 S.W. Second Avenue, Suite 450
Portland, Oregon 97204, U.S.A.

Contents

Illustrations

Paintings

Photographic Plates

Line drawings

Foreword to the First Edition

That the love of fuchsias once again flourished, after the craze for them during the Victorian Age, was due to English enthusiasts. Fuchsia pioneers like the Reverend Dr Brown and his sister, Mrs Margaret Slater, whom I was honoured to meet at a fuchsia conference in Holland, spring to mind. On the continent, albeit much later and fed by material and knowledge from England, a fuchsia revival also took place. Thirty years after its foundation in 1965 the Nederlandse Kring van Fuchsiavrienden (Dutch Circle of Fuchsia Friends), with six thousand members, has grown to be one of the largest societies in the world. In Holland the love of fuchsias has a new face.

Growing plants for competitive shows, as the English enthusiasts are renowned for doing, did not take off here in Holland. Many fuchsia lovers were satisfied with putting together large collections of fuchsias as garden decorations. Frequently, people pursued this so intensely that they caused previously pleasant gardens to be overrun by fuchsias. Other growers wanted something different, and this led to a more scientific approach towards fuchsias as a hobby.

This is how a group of people in Holland came to occupy themselves in searching for methods of describing fuchsia cultivars in a scientific way that would make precise determination possible. Descriptions can play an important part in the future in helping to determine whether a new hybrid can be classified as different from existing cultivars.

To make accessible for cultivation as much new genetic material as possible, an extensive collection of species was put together. Obviously, this effort did not go unrewarded. In less than ten years members of the Dutch Hybridizing Group developed cultivars with completely new colours, flower shapes and even flowering habits.

Due to the somewhat isolated geography of the United Kingdom, part of this development was missed by British enthusiasts. Their clear lead did not prevent them from being overtaken. From an outsider's viewpoint it is easy to come to the conclusion that often the only changes taking place when new British books are produced are the names of their newest introductions.

Luckily, people such as Edwin Goulding regularly left their island to follow developments on the European continent, and reported on them on their return. Edwin researched everything and retained all that was best. He displays the wisdom of Merlin, as I try to do, in the naming of new introductions. In this book he merges the new continental influences with traditional English knowledge. The result is a modern 'Fuchsia bible' in which amateurs and professionals, beginners and experts, will be able to find many answers to their questions.

Herman J. de Graaff
1995

Foreword to the Second Edition

The popularity of fuchsias is still increasing around the world. One has only to look at the large number of web sites to see the enthusiasm in the most unlikely places; from Norway in the north to Australia and South Africa in the south, the USA in the West and Japan in the east. The reasons for growing fuchsias can vary from the showman who grows them for exhibition to the gardener who delights in plants that flower from early summer to the first frost either in the garden or in containers. In addition, there are those who have a more serious interest in the science of the genus. I attended the Millennium Fuchsia convention in Seattle last year and was privileged to meet enthusiasts from all corners of the earth who manage to grow fuchsias under the most extreme of climatic conditions.

Edwin Goulding's book contains valuable advice and information for all growers whatever their particular enthusiasm for growing fuchsias, and this second edition covers all the most recent advances in both the horticultural and scientific aspects of the genus *Fuchsia*. One of the biggest advances has been in the introduction of new types of cultivars, due in no small part to Edwin himself and to the Dutch hybridists. Many of these advances have been as a result of using as parents the much wider range of species *Fuchsia* now in cultivation. This has resulted in new colours and flower types and resistance to heat – a big advantage with the threat of global warming.

One of the challenges facing us today is to rediscover species of *Fuchsia* that have been lost to cultivation, or that are as yet undiscovered, before their native habitat is lost in the destruction of the cloud forest. This involves scientists who must authenticate the species and allocate an accession number that relates to the specific information of the collector, the date and the precise location of the habitat. This accession number should always be on the label of a genuine species as it validates its authenticity. Unfortunately, both professional and amateur growers fail in this respect and the authenticity of the plant is then in question.

There is a large minority of plants in cultivation that are labelled as species but which have been shown to be hybrids especially in sections *Quelusia, Encliandra* and *Schufia* and particular species such as *F. fulgens* in section *Ellobium*. There are many reasons for this but unless more care is taken to maintain proper labelling, eventually most of our authentic species will disappear and our bloodstock for creating new types of cultivar will be degraded. Fortunately, there are fuchsia growers who maintain collections of species. However, the question of authenticity of these species remains. New techniques, such as DNA fingerprinting, will facilitate the process of authentication once a standard fingerprint has been obtained for each species.

Whether you grow fuchsias for fun or professionally (not mutually exclusive), this comprehensive book will be invaluable, with up-to-date information on what fuchsias to grow, where and how to grow and propagate them. If you are more technically minded or would like to know more about the plants we love, then you need look no further than between the covers of this book.

Dr Leslie Blaber
2001

Preface

Books on fuchsias usually fall into one of two groups. The first produces a list of cultivars and describes them in words or pictures. The second concentrates on the cultivation of fuchsias. This book, for the first time, bridges the gap between these two groups. It aims to be a good read and a valuable reference source on the genus.

Pictures speak louder than words for most people and special attention has been paid to the quality of those that have been included. New ways of looking at fuchsias and their culture are combined with the most up-to-date hybrids and the most unusual species. Top-quality paintings take their place with photographs of fuchsias, most of which cannot be seen elsewhere.

Pictorial references are given for many other well-established fuchsias. A chromosome reference section is also provided. The Bibliography gives details of publications of value to fuchsia growers. The list of species shows which are in cultivation, which are in jeopardy in the wild, what each one looks like and how to cope with their foibles when grown. Practical problem-solving methods are described in easy format.

Cultural information is current and comprehensive. The subject of growing for exhibition is tackled in the sure knowledge that more people will display their fuchsias in their gardens than on the show bench. Other, public displays are recognized for their importance in bringing fuchsias before an ever-widening audience. In this book, for the first time, stopping dates are given for those who want vast quantities of flowers on a specific day for a special purpose.

Lastly, the international nature of fuchsia growing has been recognized. Membership of fuchsia clubs worldwide is greater than that for any other garden plant. To those who can envisage the exciting possibilities that fuchsias offer in the years to come, this book seeks to build a firm base of knowledge.

This fascinating genus has a longer flowering season than virtually all others. It has fewer faults and is amenable to growth. Fuchsias are rewarding to beginners and absorbing to experts. They have given me so much pleasure over the years. I hope this is apparent as you read the book. Perhaps this satisfying flower will enhance your future gardening years too.

Edwin J. Goulding

CHAPTER 1

Fuchsias in History

The history of the fuchsia in cultivation is of relatively short duration, dating as it does from around AD1700. Prior to this, species fuchsias (wild) had been restricted to two widely separated regions within the Southern Hemisphere where they had existed since prehistoric times, when the ancient super-continent on which they had their homes fragmented. Fuchsias have two natural homes, namely South America and New Zealand. The range of species found in the second of these two territories is small and genetically quite distinct from those fuchsias that inhabit South America. There, they are found from Chile and Peru in the south, across the Panamanian isthmus and into Mexico in the north. It is noticeable that most wild fuchsias in South America grow close to the western seaboard. The atmosphere is much more humid there and this may account for the large range of species that flourish in the region.

Within the Mayan and Inca civilizations, fuchsias seem to have had little economic or cultural importance. Pottery decorations do not include illustrations of them, as one might expect. With the sack of the Inca civilization by Spanish conquistadors, Europeans were introduced for the first time to the riches of South America. The many new plants that collectors found there were not the least among those treasures that would significantly affect the modern world. At first, plant-hunting expeditions concentrated their efforts on those subjects that could be grown for food. There was also a substantial interest in plants that had a medicinal value. (The fuchsia has no such uses.) Many of the other plants from

this continent, such as the potato and the tomato, have made a vast economic impact since their discovery. This huge influx of new plants stretched the old method of plant identification and classification beyond breaking point, and was largely responsible for the introduction of modern methodology in plant naming. We shall return to this later.

The first recorded fuchsia was discovered by Père Plumier, a French Catholic priest, from the order of Minims. He was on a plant-hunting expedition through what is now the Dominican Republic when he found the plant now called *F. triphylla*. Unfortunately, all his plant specimens were lost in a shipwreck in 1695. Drawings of the plant, however, appeared in his *Nova Plantarum Americanum Genera* (1703), and were labelled '*Fuchsia triphylla flore coccinea*'. He named his discovery after a famous Doctor of Medicine, Leonhart Fuchs, who had occupied the chair of Medicine at Tübingen University from 1536 to 1566: medicine and botany had been closely associated since the days of ancient Greece. Fuchs had written several books, among them a Latin herbal in which he described plants from his native Germany. Like many books of his day, his *De Historia Stirpium* (1542) was illustrated with superb woodcuts. The same technique was used by Plumier in 1703 to show the first fuchsia.

The person responsible for the new and much simpler system of botanical classification with which we are familiar was Carl von Linné (1707–78), known in the Latinized version as Carolus Linnaeus. He was the son of a Swedish pastor and studied medicine at Lünd University.

Note: References to fuchsia species, variants and synonyms are abbreviated in the conventional manner.
References to species will be by abbreviation to *F*. The species begins with a lower case letter, for example *F. magellanica*.
Subspecies will be referred to by the abbreviation subsp. as *F. encliandra* subsp. *microphylloides*. Varieties will be shortened to var. Where two or more names have been given to a single plant, these synonyms will be abbreviated to syn., such as *F. lampadaria* (syn. *F. magdelanae*).

Later, at Uppsala University, he took up teaching and developed his interest in botany. Linnaeus expounded his idea of binomial nomenclature in his work *Species Plantarum* (1753). The chaos that had previously reigned, disappeared with the introduction of this simple idea and fuchsias were able to take a settled place within the new system of classification. *F. triphylla* became just one of over a hundred species to be discovered and classified in the years up to 2001.

The first species fuchsia was introduced to London in around 1788. By this time, current tastes demanded that many exotic and decorative plants were imported for the gardens of the well-to-do. In those days of sailing ships, plant importation was an exacting and expensive business; long distances and extensive travelling times presented formidable obstacles. Rats, salt water and humid conditions made the movement of seed very difficult. It was more common for mature plants to be shipped and, even with these, losses were colossal. Special provision had to be made on board ship to give specimens periodic air and water. Only later, with ideas that were put forward by Nathaniel Bagshaw Ward and published by Sir William Jackson Hooker in the *Companion to the Botanical Magazine* (1836), could plants be safely grown and transported within a closed environment.

It is likely, in spite of suggestions to the contrary, that the first fuchsia arrived in England as a fully grown plant. Such a likelihood is due to the fact that it is a shrubby, deciduous plant, which means that the fuchsia would have travelled most easily during its winter rest. One Captain Firth is credited with giving the first fuchsia plant to the Royal Botanic Gardens at Kew. Shortly afterwards, James Lee, a nurseryman from Hammersmith, began to sell plants that he had propagated, at twenty guineas each. Lee put about a strongly emotional story about the acquisition of his fuchsia. He explained that he had seen this strange flowering plant standing in the window of a widow's house. Her son, an ordinary seaman, was supposed to have given it to her; Lee said he had paid her eight guineas for it. This, the first fuchsia in the British Isles, was probably *F. magellanica*, but there was much confusion in the early years between *F. coccinea* and *F. magellanica* and this makes early records difficult to interpret.

During the early 1800s many new fuchsia species were brought from South America. Herbalists and their plant collections were a thing of the past. In their place came enthusiasts for ornamental gardens with concerns for perspective, vista, emotional appeal, and dependence on colour and form in planting material. Gardening as we know it had arrived. The trend was carried to its extreme in France but developed more slowly elsewhere. Many imported exotic plants were thought to require hothouse conditions; such buildings were provided at great expense. Fuchsias were kept in hothouses for many years before it was realized that the expense was unnecessary. (Wood (1950) gives an excellent analysis of this early history for those wishing to pursue the fine details of this story.) For our purposes, *F. triphylla* did not appear in England until 1882, when Henderson's of St John's Wood presented one to Kew.

The introduction of increasing numbers of fuchsia species from South America produced a correspondingly greater interest in hybridizing them. Attempts were made to broaden the range of colours, adapt the shape and size of bloom, and particularly to introduce double corollas. One landmark in fuchsia breeding occurred when 'Venus Victrix' was introduced by Gulliver of Herstmonceux in 1840. This fuchsia was a genuine breakthrough in its day, combining white tubes and sepals with violet corollas, clearly showing its *F. magellanica* origins.

James Lye, who was born in 1830, is probably the best-known early British hybridist. The many fuchsias he introduced were notable for having long white tubes, white sepals with green tips, and pink, rose or red petals in single corollas. His introductions were superior in vigour and size to many others of his time. His earliest-recorded introduction was 'Loveliness' (1869), which is grown to this day. His last raisings included 'W. R. Mould' (1897), which is not now in existence. He also became famous for spectacular fuchsia pillars that he contrived to grow more than 3 metres tall. James Bright, his son-in-law, continued the family tradition and became the most famous exponent of his day in the art of growing fuchsia pillars. He also produced some outstanding seedlings of his own. Double fuchsias were common by his time; one of his, named 'Pink Pearl' (1919), is still grown. Tubes, sepals and corollas were increasing in size, shape and diversity of colouring.

The modern theory of genetics had not been widely disseminated by the time that James Lye was producing cultivars like 'Loveliness' (1869), 'Beauty of Swanley' (1875) and 'Lye's Unique' (1886). The Augustinian monk Father Gregor Mendel first formulated the theory from his experiments with garden peas (1865). His ideas were not generally accepted, however, until about 1900. Their application to fuchsia hybridizing has been slow to catch on, perhaps due to a lack of economic impetus. (This subject is dealt with in more detail in the chapter on hybridizing.)

It would be easy to assume because of the vast amount of literature from this source that the British Isles was the mainspring of all early fuchsia-breeding activity. This was not so. In France, Courselles raised 'Corymbiflora Alba' (1847), sometimes referred to nowadays as *F. boliviana* var. 'Alba'. It had very long white tubes, short white sepals and rosy red petals. Flowers were produced in terminal racemes like those of *F. triphylla*. The well-known fuchsia 'Fascination' was bred by M. Lemoine in France and introduced under the name 'Emile de Wildeman' (1905). In Belgium, Cornellisen was hard at work: his ever-popular 'Mme Cornellisen', introduced in 1860, has become one of the best-known hardy fuchsias. Also in France, Felix Porcher published the first book devoted to fuchsias, entitled *Le Fuchsia; son histoire et sa culture*. The second edition appeared in 1848 and listed 520 cultivars. It also gave instructions on the cultivation of fuchsias. It proved popular and further editions appeared over the following 26 years.

In Germany special attention was paid to the breeding of *triphylla* types. These were frost-shy but relatively heat-resistant and eminently suitable for bedding out during the summer months. Rehnelt introduced 'Heinrich Henkel' in 1897. Bonstedt followed this with 'Traudschen Bonstedt' and 'Göttingen' in 1905. He also released 'Koralle' and 'Gartenmeister Bonstedt' in 1905. It is possible that he used *F. triphylla* as one of their parents, or perhaps *F. fulgens*, which had been found in 1828, and maybe 'Lye's Unique'. The original parents probably died within a few years, so that all hybridizing of this type of fuchsia ceased. Bonstedt may well have used *F. splendens*, which had been found in 1832, as one of the parents of 'Bornemann's Beste', which was released before the outbreak

of the First World War, but no other progeny appeared from this cross. He bred 'Mary' in 1894 but, again, no further developments arose from this line.

The fuchsia's advance in popularity has not been without setbacks. During the First and Second World Wars, emphasis was placed upon the production of food from plants – for example, from the tomato – and fuchsia cultivation suffered as a result. Most fuchsias were grown in greenhouses and conservatories; because of this they were particularly susceptible to whitefly attack at a time when adequate controls were unavailable. In spite of the work by people such as Wood, who concentrated on hardiness within his hybridizing programme, it was many years before fuchsias regained their pre-war popularity in Britain.

In America a national society, The American Fuchsia Society, was formed in 1929. Fuchsias had been imported from Mr H. A. Brown's nursery at Chingford, England. These plants formed the basic stock on which future hybridists would build. Great emphasis was placed on whites and pastel shades, and most attention was paid to their heat tolerance. Fuchsia blooms increased dramatically in size. Some, like 'Texas Longhorn' (1960, released by Fuchsia-La) were as much as 20 cm (8 in) across the span of their open sepals. The breeding of plants with enormous corollas was made possible by the increase in the number of chromosomes among some hybrids. Tiered corollas and marbled hues began to appear. Edward Paskesen, among the most famous of hybridists, was known especially for his work with orange doubles such as 'Eternal Flame' (1971) and 'Bicentennial' (1976). Raymond Hodges produced a wide range of types, such as 'Lillibet' (1954) with its marbled pink corollas and lantern-like buds, and 'Carmel Blue' (1956) with its white tubes and sepals and dark blue petals. Muriel Waltz is best remembered for her 'Tennessee Waltz' (1951). Robert Castro has fuchsias like 'Zeigfield Girl' (1966) to his name. Hugh and Bessie Hazard gave us gems like 'Chang' (1946). In recent years, Annabel Stubbs has become famous for her large doubles with striking colours and shapes: 'Seventh Heaven' (1981), 'Nancy Lou' (1971), 'Pink Marshmallow' (1971), 'Snowfire' (1978) and 'Gay Parasol' (1979) are notable among them.

The British Fuchsia Society was formed in

1938. Great emphasis was placed on the hardiness of new releases. It was fortunate that *F. magellanica* had been used so widely as a parent, as its progeny were by far the hardiest of the genus. Mr W. P. Wood, at one time President of the Society, and author of *A Fuchsia Survey* (1950) concentrated his efforts in this direction. Among his raisings were 'Mrs W. P. Wood' (1949), a pale pink single, and 'Margaret' (1949), which has red tubes and sepals with violet, two-tiered corollas. Another stalwart was Mr H. A. Brown who, as Dr H. A. Brown, was elected to the presidency of the Society in 1975. Among his releases was 'Phyllis' (1938), which is popular to this day.

Interest in hybridizing has spurred an awareness of the breeding possibilities offered by the broad range of species that are generally unavailable, and therefore unused as a source of genetic material. Also, very few of the available species have made any significant impact on the development of fuchsias until recently. John Wright, the British hybridist, is credited with some of the first breakthroughs of note. His 'Whiteknight's Amethyst' (1980) was the result of a cross between *F. magellanica* var. *molinae* and *F. excorticata*. 'Whiteknight's Cheeky' (1980) was produced by crossing *F. procumbens* onto 'Whiteknight's Ruby', which was itself a cross between *F. triphylla* and *F. procumbens*.

John Wright produced a series of seedlings between 1983 and 1985. These species crosses were prefixed with 'Lechlade': the range of their variability was great. They were:

'Lechlade Apache' (1984) – *F. simplicicaulis* x *F. boliviana*

'Lechlade Chinaman' (1983) – *F. splendens* x *F. procumbens*

'Lechlade Debutante' (1984) – *F. paniculata* x *F. lampadaria* (syn. *F. magdelanae*)

'Lechlade Fire-Eater' (1984) – *F. triphylla* x *F. denticulata*

'Lechlade Gorgon' (1985) – *F. arborescens* x *F. paniculata*

'Lechlade Maiden' (1985) – (*F. splendens* x *F. fulgens*) x *F. denticulata*

'Lechlade Marchioness' (1985) – (*F. splendens* x *F. fulgens*) x *F. splendens*

'Lechlade Potentate' (1984) – *F. splendens* x *F. lampadaria* (syn. *F. magdelanae*)

'Lechlade Rajah' (1984) – *F. boliviana* x *F. excorticata*

'Lechlade Rocket' (1984) – *F. lampadaria* (syn. *F. magdelanae*) x *F. fulgens*

'Lechlade Tinkerbell' (1983) – *F. arborescens* x *F. thymifolia* subsp. *thymifolia*

'Lechlade Violet' (1984) – *F. paniculata* x *F. colensoi*

The Dutch Fuchsia Society has a distinguished history and in recent years its members have concentrated much of their attention on acquiring and using lesser-known species in well-documented hybridizing programmes. This followed the lead given by John Wright in England. Notable among those working in this field is Herman de Graaff, who so kindly contributed the foreword to the first edition of this book. What has attracted the greatest notice is the area of their work that concentrates on the New Zealand species. This has provided a spate of aubergine-coloured blooms such as 'Zulu Queen' (de Graaff, 1987), 'Haute Cuisine' (de Graaff, 1988) and 'Maori Pipes' (de Graaff, 1987). The programme undertaken by Henk Waldenmaier has been less publicized but has produced numerous progeny. His efforts have concentrated on the orange colouring and on the use of *F. magdalenae* (syn. *F. lampadaria*). Among his gems are 'Walz Fluit' (1988), (*F. magdalenae* x *F. fulgens* var. *grandiflora*) x 'Golden Glow'. He also produced one of the brightest oranges to date in 'Walz Mandoline' (1989): here the crosses are (*F. magdalenae* x *F. fulgens* var. *grandiflora*) x 'Bicentennial'. Two other unusual fuchsias were created by Mrs Felix in 1987: *F. fulgens* var. *gesneriana* x *F. colensoi* gave us 'Rina Felix', while 'Tarra Valley' came from *F. colensoi* x *F. splendens*. Both have green tubes and sepals with plum-coloured corollas.

Ornamental or variegated foliage has increased over the years, mainly as a result of sports (naturally occurring mutations) that have occurred in varieties and hybrids under cultivation. *F. magellanica* has several well-known foliage sports such as *F. magellanica* var. *macrostema* 'Variegata' and *F. magellanica* var. *macrostema* 'Aurea' which have red and purple flowers. *F. magellanica* var. *molinae* produced 'Sharpitor' and 'Enstone'. Well-known fuchsias such as 'Tom West' (Miellez, 1853) and 'Golden Marinka' (Weber, 1955) were raised from cutting material, not from seed. 'Celebration' (Goulding, 1985) is one of the few fuchsias to be raised, with its variegation, from the seedling stage.

Fig. 1 An informal garden setting with fuchsias: wall planting, tubs and a standard.

The development of upward- and outward-flowering fuchsias has seen spasmodic advances in this century. The first of these plants, 'Bon Accord', was raised by Crousse in France in 1861. Attempts to develop this idea achieved little of consequence, until 'Estelle Marie' was produced by Newton in America in 1973. Growth was short-jointed and stiffly upright. The single saucer-shaped blooms had white tubes and sepals, with pale lilac corollas. As many as eight flowers are carried in each leaf joint once blooming starts. 'Linda Goulding' (Goulding, 1981) has white tubes, sepals and petals, with a hint of pink; anthers are ruby red. 'Excalibur' (Goulding, 1983) has pink tubes, sepals and petals; the corollas also carry small petaloids within their cups and these give them a ruffled appearance. 'Pink Fantasia' was bred by Webb in 1989 and, although its red and violet flowers are intensely bright, it is chiefly significant for its heat and drought tolerance. Perhaps the best-known in this group is 'Look East' raised by Paul Heavens in 1987. Its large saucer-shaped blooms are white and violet. Unfortunately, it is neither easy to obtain nor to grow. There remains great scope for the breeding of bedding fuchsias that display their flowers prominently when viewed from above, as they must if they are planted in the garden border.

Advances in hybridizing and the recognition that a wider genetic pool is available and essential suggest that the time is ripe for a renewed interest in fuchsias in their native habitats. Massive road-building programmes and an upsurge in travel increases this sense of urgency. In South America, the demand for industrialization threatens indigenous species. Vast tracts of natural landscape, including cloud forests that are the home of so many species fuchsias, are being rapidly destroyed. With the destruction in food habitats, fuchsia pollinators such as humming birds and wild bees are placed under mounting pressure. It is essential that before drastic and irreversible change occurs, detailed studies are carried out on all the species fuchsias based upon living plants in their native environments, rather than upon the pressed and dried herbaria specimens of the past. Too often, the demise of a wild species goes almost unnoticed. If this has been true of animals, it is

much more so of plants like fuchsias that appear to have little or no economic importance.

Fuchsia societies have sprung up in such diverse places as Australia, South Africa, Germany, Belgium, the United States of America, Great Britain, France, Denmark, New Zealand, Norway, Austria, Switzerland and Sweden. A wide appreciation of the plant's potential as ornamental and long flowering is now general. Fuchsias are more popular than any other garden flowering plant, even than such traditional favourites as roses, chrysanthemums and geraniums. Thousands of enthusiasts have joined local and national clubs, taken part in shows, read books and grown their fuchsias in a multiplicity of ways. Fuchsias are proving themselves as popular as they are versatile. It remains to be seen what we, the fuchsia-growing public of today, do to advance the future of the genus. Could we, for example, use further species in a deliberate attempt to introduce immunity from certain pests and diseases? We already know that *triphylla* types are less susceptible to rusts and mites. Could we breed a new range of flowering houseplants that will tolerate low light levels and central heating systems? Encliandras have a great potential here. Fuchsia-growers everywhere are just waking up to the possibilities inherent in this varied genus. Fuchsias have an interesting history and a fascinating future.

Note: Moves are under way to rationalize and clarify the naming of many fuchsias currently described as variants of species. 'Lumping' of those related to *F. magellanica* and *F. fulgens* is likely to see the greatest change in nomenclature. Until these changes are formalized, names used are the conventional ones.

CHAPTER 2

Types of Fuchsias

There are many different ways of subdividing fuchsias. The diversity of the genus *Fuchsia*, in colour and form, combined with an exceptionally long flowering season, guarantees its popularity.

Quelusia, the section from which the 'common' fuchsia is derived, is quite small, containing only eight species. Flowers are held in the upper leaf axils and the majority have red tubes and sepals, with four violet petals in each corolla. There are eight stamens and one stigma to each flower. Pollinators like birds, moths and bees are attracted to them. The dominant feature that has been exploited by gardeners in the United Kingdom is their relative frost hardiness. Some species, such as *F. glazioviana*, also possess remarkable resistance to all known pests and diseases, but such features have yet to be utilized by fuchsia hybridists.

COLD-TOLERANT

Gardeners buying fuchsias choose those plants they feel are best suited to their own needs. They envisage the exact location within their garden or yard that requires filling and they pick plants to fill particular places and purposes. It may be that they have a permanent herbaceous border in which they wish to place cold-resistant, or hardy, fuchsias. With this in mind, the average nurseryman groups hardies so that they are easy to find and to choose from. Some markets, such as the South African one, will profit from large plants ready for instant gardens; others, like the United Kingdom, will supply predominantly small and cheap cuttings that can be grown-on by customers. Earliness of flowering is of paramount importance to a fuchsia living permanently out-of-doors.

HEAT-TOLERANT

At the other extreme, many people select fuchsias to withstand heat and drought. The triphyllas are the most easily recognized of this type. They adapt easily to patio-style gardening and tubs. Their flamboyant appearance adds an air of exoticism to any garden. Triphyllas do not flower in their leaf axils, but produce terminal racemes of long, tapered flowers. Most of this length is found in their tubes and none currently available have long sepals or petals. Flowers are usually long-lived and, because most produce little pollen, triphyllas always look clean and tidy with the minimum of care. Hanging baskets provide equally attractive homes for these continuous and prolifically flowering fuchsias.

APETALOUS

Fuchsias from the Hemsleyella section have no petals. Furthermore, they flower just as the days start to lengthen if they are kept reasonably warm. When they do bloom, it is usual for them to have little or no foliage present. Their tubes are long and funnelform and come in a wide range of colours. In many respects they resemble orchids more than fuchsias to look at. *F. procumbens* is the only other species fuchsia outside section Hemsleyella to produce apetalous flowers. Hybridists are now working with those available in cultivation, but they are still regarded by many enthusiasts as mere collectors' items. Most have long thin branches, and tuberous roots. They require a heated greenhouse to thrive and flower in the United Kingdom. Apetalous fuchsias have unusual shapes and colours when compared with other fuchsia sections.

SINGLE BLOOMS

Single flowers – that is, those with four petals in the corolla – are the norm among species. Among hybrids their forms are many and their colours varied. Some, such as 'Ann Roots', have large bell-shaped skirts. 'Citation' has cup-shaped corollas. 'Impudence' has saucer-shaped corollas. 'Mary Fairclo' has cornet-shaped corollas.

Sepal positions vary considerably, from below the horizontal, as in *F. magellanica* var. *macrostema* 'Aurea', to completely recurved and covering the tube and ovary, as in 'Capt. Al Sutton'. 'Curly Q' has tightly rolled sepals, while 'Whirlaway' has widely spreading and twisting sepals. The position of sepals can make a great difference to the amount of floral colour seen by onlookers.

DOUBLE BLOOMS

Double flowers have more petals and some, such as 'Wally Yendell' and 'Suffolk Punch', can have as many as eighty petals and petaloids in each corolla. Sometimes corollas have a rosette conformation like 'Scarborough Rosette'. Others have two-tiered skirts. 'Alison Ruth Griffin' has orchid-shaped corollas.

Size is only one part of a double's appeal; weather resistance and lack of bruising are equally important to the pristine plant. The range of colours to be found among modern doubles is truly remarkable. Nevertheless it is being constantly extended and improved.

The largest double-flowered fuchsias will usually be grown at eye level because of the weight of their blooms. Most have a spreading habit that leads to their beauty being spoilt if they are planted directly into the garden border. Fuchsias such as 'Ron Chambers Love' will be at their best in baskets, wall-pockets or tubs. Truly pendulous growth is quite hard to find and is not dependent upon the size of flowers produced. Of the species, *F. procumbens* is the only one with this feature. Some hybrids, like 'Barry M. Cox' and 'Mancunian', exhibit the characteristic to their advantage.

SUMMER BEDDING

Fuchsias in this group are usually capable of giving a good show when planted in the border. Most will withstand a small amount of frost, but they usually flower too late in the season to be worth the trouble as hardies. Upward- and outward-flowering fuchsias, such as 'Walz Jubelteen' and 'Pink Fantasia', are often more heat- and drought-tolerant than average; they are also clearly visible to anyone looking down at them. Short, strong pedicles help to display fuchsia flowers most clearly near each plant's periphery. Blooms might be singles or doubles.

MINIATURES

Encliandras form another section of fuchsias that is now more widely recognized. Their tiny flowers are carried in the leaf axils on fine fern-like foliage. The leaves are often attractive in their own right; modern introductions may be variegated or metallic in hue. Like the triphyllas, they are largely resistant to most pests or diseases. The majority of them flower at their best in the shorter daylight hours, so long as temperatures are kept above freezing, and they provide a wide range of colours. Encliandras have above-average heat and cold tolerance, a fact belied by their appearance. They can be used as houseplants, especially with reasonable light, even when central heating is used. Bonsai and large conservatory specimens can equally easily be created from them. Interestingly, the smallest flowers are usually female (pistillate) only, larger flowers being those with male and female parts present (perfect), a condition called gynodioecy. Multiflowering is still rare among encliandra hybrids. Doubleness is unknown but seems achievable. It would help to increase the size of bloom.

PANICULATES

The section Schufia is now being used extensively by hybridists. *F. arborescens* and *F. paniculata* carry their blooms in terminal panicles that look more like lilac than conventional fuchsias. Their individual flowers are small, like encliandras, but this is more than compensated for by large numbers of them. Modern hybrids such as 'Wapenveld's Bloei' will often carry more flowers than foliage. This group of fuchsias provides statuesque conservatory-style tub plants, many, like 'Dymph Werker van Groenland', being capable of producing specimens 3 metres tall. They can also be used on sheltered patios and in borders when the danger of frosts has passed. As a group, they dislike extremes of temperature and humidity. Their colour range is still rather limited, but it is expanding rapidly.

FEATURES FOR DEVELOPMENT

Size can be so unusual that it impresses even when flowers have only four petals. 'Très Long' has blooms that are longer and thinner than the average pen. 'Big Slim' also has exceptionally long tubes although its sepals and corollas are more bulbous in outline. 'Texas Longhorn', on the other hand, is known principally for the spread of its sepals.

Spoonbill petals are a common feature among chrysanthemums but are only now being developed in fuchsias such as 'Nettala'. This novel characteristic is also to be seen in 'Delta's Drop' and 'Delta's Prelude'. A wider colour range will add greatly to their appeal.

Lace-edged petals appeal to many gardeners. 'Martin's Double Delicate' and 'Dorothy M. Goldsmith' have a darker edge (lace-edge) to each petal: true zonal separation of petal colours is still a rarity among fuchsias, such as 'Look East', although it is common among plants like auriculas.

Almost black corollas are to be found on 'Gruss aus dem Bodethal'. Hybrids produced from New Zealand crosses often have very dark petals and a good example of these 'aubergines' is 'Delta's Night'. Another feature of these crosses is their tendency to have 'port wine' blotches on their leaves; these are not a symptom of any pest or disease but are a cultural feature most commonly acquired from *F. excorticata*.

Yellow is another colour being sought by hybridists. 'Martin's Choice' (1999), produced by Martin Beije, is the first hybrid to display and to retain this characteristic in its corollas. Fully double, totally yellow fuchsias remain several generations away. Fortunately, 'Martin's Choice' is fertile, so more visually attractive hybrids are a distinct possibility. Fuchsia hybridists still have many opportunities to exploit their favourite plant to the full. Novel features and new markets are waiting to be found and developed.

Multiflowering (more than one bloom being produced from each leaf axil) is commonest among upward – and outward – flowering, summer bedding, fuchsias. There is no reason why it cannot be achieved with even the largest doubles.

Bicoloured triphyllas, especially ones with white tubes and sepals and violet corollas are highly desirable as, indeed, are double terminal-flowering hybrids. As a group, the range of colours in triphyllas is expanding and their habits of growth are steadily improving.

CHAPTER 3
Soils, Fertilizers and Potting Procedures

Garden soils are unsuitable for sieving and/or to use with pot-grown fuchsias, even when peat is added. The presence of soil pests and diseases and the variable nature and availability of nutrients make their use, unless sterilized, unwise. This is not to say that any special care needs to be taken once fuchsias are well-grown and ready for permanent planting in well-prepared sites. However, garden soils vary in their constituents and texture. Sometimes there is a large variation between one part of a plot and another. Sandy soils, formed by the fragmentation of rocks, can contain rock particles of a size and quantity to encourage drainage. As particle size decreases, drainage lessens and it is easy for water to stagnate. Soils that are too sandy are usually very short of moisture during the hot months of the year. Those that are composed principally of clay, should be used with care or should be avoided, as fuchsias prefer large particles, free drainage and high soil oxygen levels. Clay soils are frequently referred to as colder than sandy soils and this probably means that growth is slower to recommence at the start of each growing season.

Humus is advantageous in opening up the soil structure when clay is predominant. It also helps to make nutrients more freely available. Flat fibres, like those of reed peat or grass mowings, do little to improve soil structure. Moss peat, spent mushroom compost, stacked horse and cattle manure, leaf mould or even bracken debris can help to provide ideal conditions for fuchsia culture. There is some evidence that bracken mould should not be used on ground where food crops are grown, but for ornamental crops it seems to have many assets.

While soil has its problems, most of the proprietary composts have gone through stringent quality-control procedures and can be used for growing fuchsias without qualms. The only satisfactory way to decide which is the best compost when presented with a choice of products is to set up comparative trials. Cuttings of the same cultivars struck at the same time and in the same place but using different composts will show widely differing results. Some composts are satisfactory for a short time, then settle into an airless and compressed state with steadily declining benefits. Heavier composts are often most useful when plants are grown in pots out-of-doors, as they provide some stability. Lighter, soil-less composts are best used for hanging pots and baskets, where increased weight can be a positive disadvantage.

The presence of fertilizers within compost is of little help to plants that are liquid-fed. The major elements usually found in composts will be well-known to most gardeners. Nitrogen is the fertilizer that helps to create foliage. During sunny weather its use can be increased for pot-grown fuchsias, to compensate for conditions that would otherwise tend to stunt growth and promote flowering. Nitrogen is usually available in highly soluble forms and is therefore available to plants at a very early stage. Phosphates are most helpful in the production of root growth and in promoting the general health of fuchsias. Some phosphates are less soluble than others and an examination of the analysis printed on any fertilizer bag or bottle will show whether insoluble elements are present. When fuchsias are pot-grown, insoluble elements build up in the compost and inhibit the availability of other chemicals to the plants. Potassium is often called 'artificial sunlight'. It has a slightly slower action than some nitrogenous fertilizers and is often used during the flowering season to help promote the development of blooms and intensify their colours. The majority of garden soils will be short of each of the major nutrients; where permanent planting is to be undertaken, it is worth analysing the soil before adding fertilizers at the appropriate rates.

Trace elements are not usually a problem with outdoor plants, but pot-grown fuchsias may well benefit from some supplementation. Chelated elements are readily available and are often used for plants such as rhododendrons. When it is felt there might be an advantage in using such supplements, a little and often is preferable to once-a-year dosing. The constant use of fertilizers, an obvious necessity for pot-grown fuchsias, steadily moves the root environment towards acidity. Eventually, this will affect the plants adversely. Calcium can be added to the compost in soluble form to compensate for this. Chalk is less soluble than hydrated lime, but it is slower to disperse, so it is also available over a longer period and is therefore of greater use to plants. Not all of the calcium will be used by plants. Pot-grown fuchsias will lose some of each element (not just calcium) by natural leaching from the soil during watering.

There are other ways of feeding fuchsias that are less popular because they are generally less precise. Granular feeds, such as those that were used in John Innes' fertilizers, and National Growmore, are less commonly used than in the past. Slow-release, or resin-coated, fertilizers are most useful when applied to large fuchsia plants that are to be marketed in flower later in the growing season. Their action is not as predictable as some other methods of feeding, but guarantees the presence of some fertilizer to the plants even after they have been sold and planted.

Liquid feeding is the most precise method and is the one preferred for raising fuchsias commercially. A range of specialized feeds is also available to amateurs who wish to grow exhibition plants to a high standard. During prolonged sunny spells, higher nitrogen feeds can be given. When the weather is dull, higher potash levels can be applied. Foliar feeds are widely available but are not the most popular products with fuchsia growers. Soft, wet foliage during the darker months can help to promote botritis, while sprays used in hot weather can easily lead to leaf burn. This is not to say that such feeds have no part to play in fuchsia culture but, rather, that they need to be used with care.

One of the best ways to create one's own growing medium is the use of composting bins. These can be a boon to the keen amateur who wishes to provide ideal conditions for fuchsias. Coarse peat or bracken mould can make up half such a bin's constituents. Sifted soil may be used for up to a quarter of the total bulk. Mushroom compost is best applied up to 15 per cent and seaweed up to 10 per cent. The whole heap is then constructed in sandwich form (in layers) using small amounts of each product and finishing with a sprinkling of sulphate of ammonia to top it off. If the heap is dry, water can also be added to moisten the whole bin. After six months it can be thoroughly turned, left for a further six months and then turned again. The heap is then ready to be used.

Bins can be made of wooden palings, or readily available concrete coalbunkers can be used. Wire mesh can also be placed around corner posts, but weeds might grow freely if the sides are not carefully lined inside with black polythene sheeting. Compost heaps of this type are best made in sandwich form with a very open and fluffy texture. Do not tread the heap down, as this will make it more airless and prevent the breakdown of its constituents, especially the seaweed.

There is a wide choice of pot types available to growers. It makes commercial sense to propagate and grow fuchsias in square pots, as these maximize the bench space and keep the warmth on propagating benches evenly distributed. Pots about 5.8 cm (2 in) square can be used to provide an almost perfect product for sale, and they allow for a reduction in the labour associated with potting on from thimble pots. Round pots are still most readily available and come in a variety of types. At the cutting stage, less root space is available for each square metre of propagating bench with these pots. At the point of sale, larger round pots of fuchsias in flower are probably more aesthetically pleasing.

Whereas the average amateur will fill individual pots with compost, this is uneconomical for fuchsia nurseries. Propagating benches are normally laid out with pots before compost is screeded across and then watered into place. The same technique can also be used at a later stage, provided that the pots are square and fit closely together. It might be worthwhile, commercially, creating a special frame in which several large batches of pots can be filled at one time, before cuttings or young plants are potted and grown on.

Amateurs often pot up their fuchsias one at a time. A reliable way of providing the best conditions at this stage is to fill the new, larger pot with compost. A small pot, of the same size as that from which the cutting or young plant is to be taken, is fitted into the centre of this compost to create a hole of exactly the right size for the incoming fuchsia. The same technique is

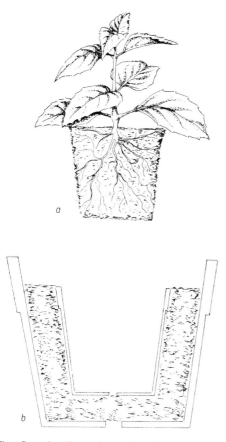

Fig. 2 Rooted cutting ready to go into a larger pot:
a A strong cutting with well-formed roots, taken out of
*   its pot.*
b: Double potting to prepare a hole of the correct size
*   for the small rooted plant. The inside pot is removed,*
*   leaving the surrounding compost, just prior to*
*   potting on.*

used for fuchsias taken from big pots and put into still larger ones. The best results are obtained if compost is placed into the larger pot in a damp state: this makes watering unnecessary for some time and helps to prevent the settling of the soil that at this stage is associated with watering through a can. A further way of avoiding losses at the potting-on stage is to raise the incoming fuchsia perhaps 6 mm (0.25 in) above the surrounding soil. This helps to keep the surface (and the plant's lower leaves) dry, thereby reducing the incidence of fungal disorders.

Standards can be difficult to pot on single-handedly. By creating a hole in the centre of the compost in the larger pot, it is possible to lift the

whip or standard from its old pot and lower it into its new position. More firming than is usual for other fuchsias might be needed to hold the stem and cane in an upright position, but it is best if this can be avoided.

Lopsided plants can be corrected at the potting-on stage. Beginners are often tempted to lift stems and then to press plants firmly into the desired position: in doing so, they break some of the fine roots and inhibit further growth. The best technique is to centre the main stem and branches in the new, larger pot. This might mean that the root ball is tilted steeply to one side or is at one side of the new pot, but this does not matter unduly. Once the compost has settled around the root ball and the plant has stood on the bench for a few days, its leaves will turn to take advantage of the available light and the fuchsia will look normal and well-shaped. The process by which foliage is drawn towards the light is called phototropism and the subject is dealt with more fully by Wilkins (1988) in his book called *Plantwatching.*

Double potting is one of those techniques employed by showmen in order to provide better conditions for their plants during the height of the growing season when days are long and sunshine can be fierce. The idea is simple. A plant in its ultimate pot (there is usually a maximum pot size restriction for competition plants) is placed inside a larger pot. The space between is usually filled with peat or something similar. This can then be wetted to raise air humidity around the foliage. Extra weight can be added to the pot if stones are placed in the bottom of the larger pot before double potting is undertaken. This helps to stabilize the plant and to prevent wind damage that might otherwise occur. One benefit of double potting in the later stages of growing a show plant is that the outer pot and the materials between the two pots act as insulators. This reduces the impact of the sun's heat on the side of the root ball at a time in the plant's development when it is least able to cope with extremes of weather. Wide, rather than deep, pots are best for the outer containers used for such purposes.

Coarse shrub peat is commonly used as a filler in double potting. The plants' watering needs become a little more difficult to assess and during dull, wet weather take care not to overwater. To prevent show plants from rooting through into the space between the two pots, central pots should be turned every week or so;

occasionally the plants and pots can be lifted and any adventitious roots rubbed off. Plants removed at the last moment and with large amounts of root removed as well are likely to become limp and suffer just when they need to look at their best for the judge. Perlite is sometimes used as a space filler and it has the advantage that it is a very good insulator, but its crumbly structure and light weight mean that the central plant and pot are more likely to move around in windy weather, which can cause damage. Sand has the distinct advantage that it is heavy. Some sands can become rather waterlogged to the detriment of the show fuchsia in the central pot and, as an insulator, sand is by no means as effective as some of its alternatives.

There are other techniques employed by competitors in the growing of their fuchsias. One of these is the process of sinking the fuchsia slightly lower in the compost each time it is potted on into a larger pot. This is obviously helpful if the plant has an unsightly short leg or is a standard with a stem that is marginally too long. Over a period of several months a reduction of about 7.6 cm (3 in) can be achieved. One disadvantage with this technique is that any young branches sunk in wet compost are more prone to botritis attacks. Watering from below, and keeping the soil surface rather dry, will help to prevent such problems arising. An advantage with this system, however, is that the plant gradually produces its branches nearer to the soil level. The branches gain extra support, when they come into full flower, as they are then able to rest on the pot sides. Thus the overall appearance of show plants can be radically but gradually altered without any setbacks to their development. Show fuchsias can look as if they have just been taken from the garden and in consequence they will have a more natural appearance.

A further technique employed by showmen, which has dubious advantages, is the process of cutting back the root ball of plants as they grow. This is usually to encourage the growth of large tops when pot size is severely limited. The idea is that the bottom half of the root ball is cut away and the space made available in the same pot is refilled with fresh compost. Sometimes, the plant and remaining root ball are dropped further into the pot before extra compost is added on top of the remaining soil and roots. An alternative that is sometimes used is to cut wedge-shaped sections from the root ball, but in this case it is not usual for more than 25 per cent of it to be removed at any one time.

Potting back is usually undertaken when fuchsias are to be pruned drastically and returned almost immediately into growth. Some show plants respond best when grown for two years, so that a sturdy framework can be constructed to support the weight of large numbers of blooms. As the fuchsia enters what would normally be its rest period, much of the root ball is cut away. Extra compost can also be teased away by hand before the fuchsia is replaced in a much smaller pot that is then filled with new compost. Warmth, protection and food then help the fuchsia to grow and allow a long growing season to be used.

Potting on is the term used when a fuchsia is placed in a series of steadily increasing pot sizes as the season progresses. Potting up describes taking fuchsias from trays or bare root situations and placing them into pots for the first time. Potting back has been described above, but it can be helpful in reducing the problems associated with pests such as vine weevil larvae, whose eggs are often laid in greatest numbers as the day length starts to wane. As well as teasing out old compost to remove any eggs or larvae of pests like vine weevil, it is wise to wash the soil away from the roots of plants as they enter their short-day rest phase. Treatment with nematodes (see Chapter 15) is most likely to be effective if carried out at this time.

Keen fuchsia growers are often acutely aware of the slightest changes to the foliage of their plants. The part of each plant that is hidden from immediate sight is just as important, if not more so. Marginal improvements to cultural expertise are usually made by experimentation with composts and specialized growing techniques. Again, it cannot be stressed too highly, especially at this point, that new methods are best tried out when other plants grown by more conventional or familiar methods can be used for comparison. This gives a measurable standard of improvement or change that can be assessed and finely tuned for the best results. The wealth of experience gained in this way can add to the pleasure and interest obtained from growing fuchsias. It also gradually increases the ratio of successes to failures, even when conditions beyond our control are not ideal.

CHAPTER 4

Propagation and Growing On

Rooting Media

Fuchsias have little economic importance, yet they are among the easiest of all plants to propagate from cuttings. Their demands are few and almost 100 per cent success is assured, given reasonable stock and environmental care. Vast numbers of cuttings are produced every year. Patio gardening and the plants' long flowering season have combined in recent years to promote fuchsias. Many thousands of different named fuchsias are available to those interested and involved in growing them, as well as an accompanying wealth of knowledge. Their propagation can be rewarding and fun.

The first consideration should be to choose the best compost. Soil-based composts used to be popular, but with mass-production these have proved less predictable in quality and less stable with age than most soil-less alternatives. Lawrence & Newell, in their publication (1939) based on work for the John Innes Institute, gave an accurate assessment of soil-based composts given ideal supplies and conditions. The pH of composts, as they age, normally moves towards acid, as the chemicals that are added in production change their structure or are used up. The ideal compost pH for fuchsias, for propagation and for adult growth, is in the region of neutral (pH 7.0), but there is considerable flexibility in this.

In the past, 'sterility' of soil-based composts has meant steam sterilization to kill pests, diseases and weeds. This is an expensive and difficult operation to carry out thoroughly. Chemical sterilization is also possible, but adequate aeration of the compost is essential following such treatment. Some time (dependent on the instructions given and the chemical used) must be allowed to pass before composts treated in this way are used for growing plants, and yet sterility is essential in soil used for propagation or pot use, in order to kill weeds, pests and diseases. Sterility is not the only factor of

importance in composts. The size of their particles affects such things as their drainage and their air-filled porosity. Clay particles are small and greasy in texture. On its own, clay produces an airless environment that is entirely unsuitable for fuchsia roots. Sand has a larger particulate size that is much better for gaseous exchange within the rooting medium. There is a popular misconception that sand is an important additive in any soil-less compost; this is not borne out in comparative trials. The subject of soils in relation to plants is dealt with in detail by E. Walter Russell in *Soil Conditions and Plant Growth* (1961).

Weight is the single largest drawback of modern soil-based composts. Tonnage in transportation is as important and costly as bagging and handling are at the propagating point. When commercial firms fulfil mail-order requests, costs can be nearly doubled by the choice of heavier composts. For this reason, peat-based composts are usually preferred to soil-based ones. Peat-based composts come in two basic types. The first is reed fibre, which is usually dark in colour and tends to settle into an airless and acid state more quickly than its alternative, moss. Moss fibres are springy and provide a more open and spongy texture that suits fuchsias better. Milling to a fine texture helps at the propagating stage: lumpy composts are unsuitable for cuttings. Nowadays most soil-less composts have a wetting agent added in order to reduce the need for watering. The majority of composts will have some nutrients and can be used for cuttings or for older plants. This matter is dealt with more fully in Chapter 3.

Perlite, a proprietary product made from volcanic ash, is frequently added to soil-less composts, principally to help with rewetting dry compost and also to open the texture. It is exceptionally lightweight and its water-absorbing capabilities great. Once saturated with moisture, Perlite releases it slowly into the surrounding compost, providing an even distribution of water. It helps to retain water during hot spells and guards against over-watering during dull, cold conditions. Vermiculite, another proprietary product, has properties similar to Perlite, but is now less commonly used for propagating fuchsias.

In the past, sand was used on its own for propagating plants. Fuchsias grew as successfully in sand as other subjects did, though it was not ideal. Reasonably coarse sharp sand, which had been washed to remove all contaminants, was preferred. Sand that contained salt was unsuitable, and considered too fine in texture. In practice, fuchsias will root adequately in many such substances (but better materials can be used). Comparative trials show that sand produces coarser and more succulent roots that are prone to breakage when the young fuchsias are transferred to pots.

Blocks are used increasingly for propagating plants. Formerly, these would have been made from pressed compost; nowadays they are made from products like rockwool, an inert and sterile rooting medium widely used in commercial horticulture. Experiments carried out on fuchsias grown in this medium have shown that although losses in this medium can be minimal, rooting takes about a week longer than in conventional composts. Cuttings can be kept for longer in rockwool at this stage before potting on becomes necessary. Watering needs, when cuttings are grown in this inert substance, can be a little more difficult to assess than would be the case with more conventional materials (except when automatic systems have been installed).

With the current emphasis on conservation, alternatives to peat are eagerly sought. There is an ever-greater need for suitable composts that can be manufactured from renewable resources. Trials have not yet shown that substitutes like coir and bark are adequate long-term replacements for peat in the propagation of fuchsias. As peat stocks become scarce, it will be interesting to see what substitutes will be produced in the future. Composts produced specifically for propagating purposes usually have a minimal nutrient content. Nitrogen is unhelpful in composts used for cuttings; potassium is also relatively unimportant, but phosphates encourage rooting. Other elements, including trace elements, come into their own when fuchsias have rooted and begun to grow.

Producing Cuttings

Nurseries grow large and bushy plants (mother plants) especially so they can take numerous of cuttings from them. Nurseries tend to be of two types: those that carry large numbers of plants of only a few cultivars, and those that carry a few plants of very many cultivars, which provide plants at higher prices for keen enthusiasts and collectors. Mother plants are generally grown outdoors during the hotter months of the year, so that their wood can ripen and their growth shorten. These bushy plants provide cutting material that is less susceptible to botritis than that from younger, more succulent plants. Big plants can be grown over several months and large numbers of cuttings cropped at any one time. The choice of cultivar also determines the amount of cuttings available from a plant. Fuchsias commonly used as mother plants include 'Beacon Rosa', 'Dollar Princess', 'Bealings', 'Display' and 'Alice Hoffman'. Greenhouse-grown fuchsias will almost always be grown on at a faster rate and may be less affected by pests and diseases. Stock protected in this way can also be persuaded to grow even faster by striking (rooting) more but smaller sections of the branches, such as leaf bud cuttings. Excessive heat during the summer months is to be avoided. Most fuchsias prefer air temperatures between 7°C (45°F) and 23°C (73°F). As a rule, when fuchsias are grown under glass during hot and bright conditions, the air humidity should be raised in line with the temperature. This is dealt with in more detail in Chapter 7.

Fuchsias will root at just about any time of year, but are most successful (in the United Kingdom) in the spring or autumn: adequate light levels then match temperatures. Successful rooting presumes that stock plants have been prepared in advance and that suitable cutting material can be found. Sales of cuttings are predominantly highest in the spring and usually remain high for up to five months. Thereafter, larger plants in flower can be sold selectively over perhaps four months. Cutting losses above 5 per cent are not commercially viable due to the fuchsia's relatively low sale price and profitability.

One reason for a deterioration of the success rate in striking cuttings is that, with the advance of longer days and consequently higher light levels, fuchsias start to flower. Branches that are blooming will not readily produce side shoots suitable for cuttings, even if the flowers are removed. Ripe wood is generally slower and less successful in rooting. When cuttings are required at the least suitable times of the year, there are a number of ways to improve the chances of successful rooting. First, trimming back flowering wood will promote new shoot production. Secondly, high nitrogen feeds will encourage leafy growth at the expense of flowering and ripening. It is also possible to take the tips from cuttings that have already rooted, as these are usually sappy and easy to strike. Once rooted cuttings have reached a height of about 7.5 cm (3 in), extra cutting material is likely to be available.

Mother plant production is best undertaken deliberately. Pests and diseases should be guarded against because propagating beds provide almost ideal conditions for the proliferation of problems. Large tubs or fully round hanging baskets will help to provide sufficient material to take cuttings. Pruning and shaping will help to create a sturdy and well-branched framework from which to remove cuttings. Prune when plants are rather dry so that their branches do not bleed and subsequently die back. When pruning, open the centre of each plant so that air movement can be maintained through the branches: dead and crossing stems should be removed. Straight cuts should be made just above leaf joints, or knuckles, with a pair of secateurs or a sharp knife.

Conventional fuchsia cuttings are about 7.5 cm (3 in) long with two full pairs of leaves and a growing tip. The lower leaves are trimmed off cleanly and a cut is made below the leaf joint using a keen blade or scissors. Hormone agents are rarely used for fuchsias, but cuttings are dipped in fungicides prior to insertion and water the compost watered before use with a fungicidal solution. The stem is then inserted about 1.3 cm (0.5 in) into the compost or rooting medium. Showmen often take cuttings with just one pair of leaves and a growing tip. These usually root rapidly and shape easily into sturdy and bushy subjects. A nodal cutting is one in which the stem is cut cleanly just below a joint with leaves: fuchsia cuttings root best if they are nodal ones, rather than the internodal cuttings that work best for some other plants.

Two techniques have been proved to give extra success in rooting cuttings at a commercial

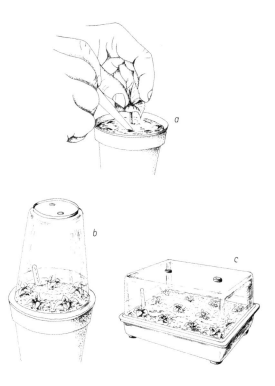

Fig. 3 Taking cuttings:
   a: Cuttings dibbed around the perimeter of a
      flowerpot.
   b: The same pot, filled with cuttings, labelled and
      covered with a clear plastic dome.
   c: Cuttings taken into a tray, also with a clear
      plastic cover.

level. Instead of severing straight across each cutting, just below a leaf joint, a diagonal slice is made through and below the joint. This allows extra water-absorbing surface and reduces the chance of calluses forming without roots. It speeds the rooting process and gives increased success especially in warm weather. The second beneficial technique involves reducing the length of the bottom leaves on each cutting by about a half. This helps to prevent cuttings from easing themselves out of the compost, by pressing downwards with their leaves, once they become turgid and ready to root; it is especially helpful when small cuttings are taken.

Side buds can be used for cuttings when material is scarce and there is an urgent need to increase stock. In this case, cut above and below a leaf joint and its two leaves. Make an elliptical cut around each bud, or split the stem cleanly down the middle to give one bud and leaf on each side of the stem. Press the cuttings into the rooting medium just far enough to maintain them in a vertical position. Ideally, upper leaf surfaces should face towards the light.

When cuttings are taken from shrubby garden fuchsias, it is possible to remove shoots from around the edge of a plant's stool. These should be shortened to about 15 cm (6 in) so that they do not dehydrate before rooting takes place, because of the lack of roots relative to shoots. When roots are already present, these can be preserved, although they are best shortened before planting. When they are absent, the heel can be tidied up with a sharp blade before dibbing the cutting into position. Sometimes such cuttings callus over but fail to produce roots: breaking the callus surface will help to allow roots to grow.

Layering is a technique that can be useful with more difficult subjects. Long branches are generally bent to ground level, where they are pegged into a pot filled with compost. It is usual to scrape the area where the branch touches the soil in order to encourage root formation. The compost should be kept moist. Alternatively, wrap the highest branches of a plant so that they produce roots (as with rubber plants). Wrap moist rockwool around a joint from which the leaves and flowers have been removed. Cover this with black polythene and seal it in position with adhesive tape. Rooting will normally take about six weeks and should be well advanced before the branch is severed from its parent. Reduce the newly rooted branch to no longer than 12.5 cm (5 in) when it is first potted up.

There is a popular misconception that branches with more than two leaves to a joint will root and make better standards than those having only two leaves. (This is untrue and can easily be proved by comparative trials.) More relevant to success is the position from which a cutting is taken. Shoots growing below the horizontal position rarely do as well as those that grow nearly vertically. So, though branches with whorls of leaves – which most commonly grow near the top of a plant or on whips – make good cuttings, this is because of their position. Hanging branches are more likely to carry flowers, and root (and subsequently grow) less easily than their vertical counterparts. Removing the blooms is not enough to guarantee success in rooting and

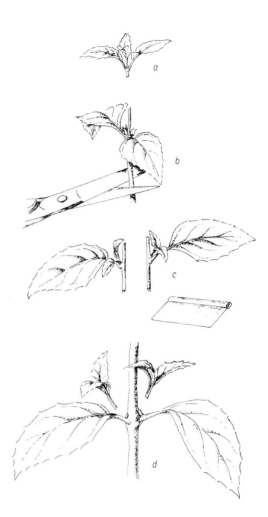

Fig. 4 Taking cuttings from a fuchsia stem:
   a: Tip cutting.
   b: A single node with two leaves.
   c: The stem divided to give nodal cuttings.
   d: Two more tip cuttings.

in growing. It is best if flowering branches are shortened back some three to four weeks before cutting material is required. High nitrogen feeds will then encourage regrowth and these shoots can be used for propagation purposes.

On occasion, in order to avoid losing a particular cultivar, it may be necessary to propagate from diseased or infected plant material. One successful way is to cut lengths of ripened stem to about 25 cm (10 in) in length. All leaves are removed and the branches dipped in weak fungicide. Lay the branches on the surface of moist compost on the propagating bench and cover them with black polythene for three weeks. When it can be seen that new shoots have started to form, the polythene is replaced with a clear sheet, through which light can enter. Moisture should be present at all times and, as each shoot starts to grow, a small slit can be made in the polythene cover so that the shoot can rise vertically through it. Roots will form after shoots have been made. Alternatively, the shoots can be struck as ordinary cuttings once chlorophyll is present in their leaves.

Factors in Rooting

Fuchsia cuttings without chlorophyll in the leaves will neither strike nor grow. Some coloration is essential in order that sunlight can act on the chloroplasts needed for plant growth. At times it is difficult to see this green pigmentation. Only when a fuchsia such as 'Enstone Gold' is placed against a branch with the bleached tones of de-pigmentation can the difference be seen clearly. If you are uncertain whether leaves lack chlorophyll, and will therefore die, try rooting them anyway; you have nothing to lose.

Cuttings require lower light levels than fully-grown plants. The latter easily become etiolated and unsightly. Very low light levels, however, fail to activate the rooting mechanism and soft-wood cuttings often rot quickly under such conditions. Hard-wood cuttings will tolerate low light levels for much longer and will frequently form roots when light levels improve after a long dull spell. Very high light levels are commonly associated with higher temperatures and dehydration in unrooted cuttings. The brightness of light is only one factor out of several. With the approach of longer days, blooming commences and rooting becomes more difficult. High nitrogen feed cannot be used on unrooted cuttings to compensate, as with other plants. Fuchsias are unable to use the full spectrum of light for growth and flower production, and are most successful in conditions of moderate light intensity and day length.

When it is impossible to avoid taking cuttings from flowering branches, remove all flowers before taking several cuttings from each branch. If even one of them forms roots and produces adequate shoots, a further cutting can be taken from the active tip. Stock can be gradually increased and improved thereafter.

Heating is a costly business and is likely to become even more expensive. It is imperative, therefore, that no wastage occurs. The nearer the temperature can be held to 17°C (63°F), the better cuttings will perform. Wide fluctuations in heat levels can damage or kill fuchsias most easily at the cutting stage. Persistently low temperatures are less damaging than violent swings between heat and cold. Thermostats help to provide optimum conditions for cuttings. It is easier to heat up propagating units than it is to reduce excessively high temperatures. Very hot conditions will rapidly desiccate unrooted cuttings unless they are provided with mist spray units. Some of the modern fibre insulating fleeces will allow light in while still inhibiting the accompanying rise in temperatures formerly associated with closed propagating units. For this reason, they are considered more effective than polythene sheeting for fuchsias on propagating benches during hot weather.

The subject of relative humidity is a complex one: humidity affects the propagating of fuchsias more than any other aspect of their growth. As air warms up, more moisture must be added to it to maintain the optimum level for plants. Small gauges can be purchased that give precise measurements for relative air humidity. In *The British Fuchsia Society Annual* (1981), Sherman gives an excellent assessment of the subject for fuchsia growers. In practice, air humidity needs to be high enough at the cutting stage for foliage of unrooted stock to remain fully charged with moisture. Sometimes leaves are limp instead of turgid, usually because more moisture is being lost from the leaves (by transpiration) than can be taken up through the bottom of the cut stem. Consequently, success rates will subsequently be retarded.

Soil moisture levels should also be kept high enough for the unrooted cuttings to absorb water as required. However, waterlogging of the compost can lead to a reduction of soil oxygen levels that is almost as harmful to the cuttings as too little water.

Propagation is a matter of experience, and what seems easy to the expert may be much harder for the beginner to achieve.

Professional Production Methods

Polythene sheeting has been widely used by commercial firms to propagate fuchsias on soil-warming systems. The greatest success with fuchsias appears to have been achieved when the polythene is allowed to lie on the foliage, so that the moisture level is kept high around each leaf. This is not always practicable, as labels are usually placed in the propagating bed at the same time as the cuttings. In spite of this, success rates are still excellent on well-prepared soil-warming systems covered with clear polythene. The same system has been widely adopted for propagating, especially during the darker days of the year when temperatures are lowest and there are advantages in retaining heat near the root zone in order to reduce costs.

Temperatures can rise steeply in sunlit periods, and at such times can be excessive under polythene covers. For this reason, it is common to avoid using polythene during hot weather, and to use mist propagating equipment instead or, more recently, fibre fleece. The advantages of polythene in the propagation of fuchsias on soil-warming systems are its low cost and ready availability. A marginal reduction in efficiency for some periods of the year is not such a disadvantage, given the seasonal nature of cutting distribution and sales.

Where fibre fleece is used to cover fuchsias on propagating beds, its best position is on the leaves or as near to them as possible. While the advantages in reducing excessive temperatures during sunny spells are obvious, winter benefits are less easy to see. They derive from the economy of buying only one type of cover, and in the protection from temperature drops that sometimes occur when heating systems are out of action on cold nights. Fibre fleece is used for insulation purposes with great success in many spheres. Placed on propagating beds during hot weather, the temperature is considerably cooler under fibre fleece than under polythene covers. This is probably because, while some heat convection takes place from below, radiant heat from above does not enter as easily. The material is now readily available and is quite cheap: it enjoys wide usage on out-of-season field crops. There is little price difference between fibre-fleece and polythene.

Soil-warming beds are easily constructed using electric cables and thermostats. The scope of this book does not allow an expanded section on this subject: it is dealt with fully in many books on propagation and nursery management. Electricity suppliers often produce growers' guides and these, together with literature supplied by manufacturers of soil-warming cables and thermostats, are useful. Gardening magazines often list suppliers and methods of construction for the amateur. In constructing soil-warming units, it is essential to erect the benches so that cuttings placed on the finished beds are at the best height for those working with them. The weight of wet sand normally used for enclosing the heating cable can be great, so strong materials and durable construction methods are required. Advantages in heat economy can be gained by lining the bottom and sides of the bench with polystyrene sheets so that heat rises only around the plants

Electric heat blankets are the modern equivalent of soil-warming beds. They are available in a variety of sizes. They are easy to lay out and to move as required. Bench construction will therefore be less costly and the benches do not need to be so strong. However, unlike soil-warming beds filled with damp sand, they do not retain heat in the event of an electrical problem. Hot water pipe systems went out of fashion for a time, but some modern versions are now available. These are usually based on flexible hosing that fits into polystyrene moulds. Soil-warming systems of any sort rarely maintain sufficient heat on their own; it is usually necessary to supply air heating at a reduced level in the greenhouses if cuttings are to be propagated during cold periods.

Once the benches have been constructed and put into operation, the choice of pot used can be of immense significance to success rates and costing. The majority of professional growers take their fuchsia cuttings into small pots about 3.7 cm (1.5 in) in diameter and about 4.3 cm (1.75 in) deep. There are advantages, however, in using pots in the region of 5.8 cm (2 in) across and deep in order to reduce holding problems and to avoid the need for potting up bare-rooted cuttings. Small wedge-shaped cells, made from pressed plastic, in sheets containing as many as 150 spaces for cuttings, are also used on a wide scale commercially; these prove most useful when a few cultivars with similar habits and vigour are due to be produced in a single batch. Some of the more conventionally shaped cells do not allow cuttings to be removed quickly and easily without damage.

Mist spray units are effective in producing cuttings during warm weather, but pose problems when stock is removed from the propagating benches for growing on, because the air humidity drops. Spray unit installation costs are hardly justified for fuchsias, though they would be for the hard-wood cuttings of many other plants. Where such units are available, they are of most use during bright, warm weather, and it is generally inadvisable to use them during prolonged cold and dark spells. Water is distributed through a series of partially overlapping circles (like shower heads); ideal fuchsia cutting production is difficult to achieve because of the variability of water distribution across the bench. The assembly and construction of mist propagating units are well documented. Suffice it to say that because water is heavy, solid construction is essential.

Mist spray units combine well with soil-warming beds, but are expensive to install. It is worthwhile examining the turnover and return from fuchsia cuttings before embarking on such methods. Of course, these variables will change in different parts of each country and across the world.

Methods for Amateurs

Amateurs frequently root their cuttings in small pots about 2.5 cm (1 in) across and pot them on rapidly once they are established. This allows for maximum turnover from small propagating areas, but is relatively labour-intensive. Another method often employed involves placing a small pot within a larger one and filling the space between the two with compost so that cuttings can be taken (put in) around the perimeter. A 7.5-cm (3-in) pot inside a 13.1-cm (5.25-in) pot gives adequate space, and the central pot can also be used for striking more cuttings. These pots are covered with firm plastic domes or, more cheaply, with clear polythene bags. The latter can be held above the cuttings by placing small canes around the edge or in the centre of each pot. A rubber band around the neck of the outer pot will keep the bag in position and maintain a humid atmosphere around the foliage.

In the past, rooting has been most successful for the amateur when cuttings were placed in wooden trays that were slightly deeper than their plastic seed tray equivalent. Wood is unlikely to become as hot as plastic during sunny weather. One advantage of tray propagation is that bush plants are produced with very low side shoots and this can be of most use if fuchsias are to be grown for exhibition. Plastic sheeting or rigid

domes can be used to cover trays with cuttings in them. Some literature advises that the inside surfaces are wiped free of moisture, but it is much more important that such items are kept clean and free of fungal spores.

Small, electric propagating units are now readily available, but some of these have no thermostatic control mechanism. It is therefore wise to ensure that the plants are never placed in direct sunlight where temperatures can rise to levels far too high for fuchsias. Such units have the advantages that they are small, relatively cheap and lightweight. This makes them ideal for elderly or disabled gardeners. Covers for such units are usually supplied with them. Safety in the greenhouse is essential: advice should be sought from suppliers and manufacturers on the best products and methods of installation.

Other Factors in Success

The majority of soft-wood fuchsia cuttings root within two to six weeks. At the height of the growing season, new roots will have formed, under ideal conditions, within a matter of days, but it is wise to wait a little longer before taking them off the propagating bench. Hard wood takes considerably longer and roots may appear slowly over many weeks in less favourable conditions. Soft wood grown very fast, being sappy, will normally develop a larger and stronger stem. This is partly because, as wood ages, it also ripens and with this ripening comes a degree of constraint upon further stem expansion. As a good general rule, the longer and softer the internodal spaces, the faster the rooting will be.

Larger leaves on an identical cultivar indicate that it is almost certainly growing more strongly and will therefore root more freely. Fuchsias such as 'Royal Velvet', which have large leaves and sappy growth, will always root and grow more easily than those with small leaves and woody branches, such as 'Eleanor Leytham'. Selection of the most suitable cultivars from among many with similar characteristics can make a considerable difference to propagating success, and therefore to the profitability of commercial enterprises.

Amateurs are often tempted to pull at cuttings to see if they are rooted. This is unwise, as it can destroy the newly forming root hairs and leave an airlock below cuttings when they are subsequently pushed back into the compost. When rooting has been in progress for a while, noticeable changes in the texture and colour of cuttings occur. These alterations are often first characterized by a gloss that appears on the growing point. With hairy leaves, such changes are generally associated with colour change, almost always a lightening in hue. This paler colour also appears on those fuchsias with smoother-textured leaves. At the same time as these changes in colour and texture occur, the growing tips will begin to elongate. The rate at which alterations happen will vary from one cultivar to another. It is unwise to disturb newly rooted cuttings until such changes are well established; this is usually at least a week after alterations are first visible.

Cuttings should be handled as little as possible. Inspection is obviously helpful and any material infected with botritis or rust should be removed. Once it has been decided to take them from the propagator, handling should be kept to the minimum. Healthy material should never be touched after diseased material, unless one's hands have been thoroughly washed first. Cuttings are best handled lightly by their leaves rather than by gripping their stems. Less damage is done if leaves tear than if stems are spoilt.

Flowers and buds should be removed as cuttings are prepared. When growth elongates, further buds will sometimes appear. These are best removed as well, if the energies of the small plants are not to be unnecessarily sapped. Stock from which cuttings are to be taken should be kept free from pests by careful inspection and, where necessary, by treatment with the appropriate insecticide. (This aspect of fuchsia culture is discussed more fully in Chapter 15.) Leaves that are affected with fuchsia rust should be removed: very small and immature shoots are usually the last to be infected and there is often enough foliage left to propagate from even the most affected branches. Of course, it is not ideal to use such material for cuttings, but sometimes, rather than losing stock, this can be done (see pages 25–26). Cuttings and propagating benches can be treated with suitable fungicides to reduce early problems.

After removing plants from the propagating area, it is wise to provide them with conditions that are as near as possible to those in which they have been raised. Normally this means lower air humidity but only slightly less warmth. Most growers uncover the cuttings for several days prior to their removal from the propagating bench. Inspection of the roots of young cuttings will, ideally, show masses of fibrous white roots. The perfect cutting will have roots almost equal in proportion to the foliage when it is removed from its nursery station. Evenly distributed roots provide a useful guide to the texture and moisture levels present in composts. Cuttings in small pots will require potting on earlier than those in large containers. Stunting and increased losses occur within a matter of days if attention to detail stops once propagation has been achieved.

Special Cases

Some fuchsias are worth propagating for their special features even though it is difficult to take and root cuttings from them. One example is 'Nellie Nuttall'. In such cases, where flowering predominates over growth, extra care has to be taken. Removing all flowers from mother plants, increasing the nitrogen in their liquid feed, cutting back to encourage regrowth and allowing adequate root space will all help. Some times of the year will prove better than others; these are generally periods when light levels are not too intense and humidity levels are reasonably high. Better stock can sometimes be obtained from another grower.

Encliandras are relatively difficult to propagate during the dull months of the year, when days are at their shortest. This is normally their flowering time and, because their blooms are very small, they tend to drop onto the propagating bench. In an ideal scenario the flowers would be stripped from cuttings prior to insertion. Some cultivars are easier to propagate than others. Soft-wood cuttings are reasonably easy to root at the height of the growing season. Hard-wood cuttings, complete with a small heel from where they have been torn from the sides of larger stems, are slow to root but less likely to be lost at the close of the growing year.

Where encliandras are grown in the garden or prove especially difficult to propagate, they can be layered in the same way as other shrubby herbaceous plants. Thin wire pegs help to hold branches at ground level. Sometimes it is easier to strip all leaves and immature branchlets from more mature growth. This can then be laid out with plastic covers until shoots are well established.

Garden compost heaps often provide the best rooting conditions for layering branches of fuchsias. It was the practice in years gone by, when old stems failed to produce cutting material as fast as was wished, to spray them with tepid water several times a day to encourage the appearance of new shoots that would otherwise not have sprouted. When time allows, this idea is still worth adopting occasionally. The exceptions are for those fuchsias with hairy leaves. Foremost among these are some of the species like *F. hartwegii*, *F. boliviana* var. *luxurians* and *F. fulgens*. It is wise to ensure that leaves do not sit on the compost surface, that growth is active, that stems are full of sap, and to treat them with fungicide before insertion. *F. fulgens* and its variants are slow to come into growth after any rest period. The older a plant becomes, the later it is to start into regrowth. One way to avoid problems with the propagation of hairy-leafed fuchsias is to cut back stock in the late summer so that cuttings can be taken from new growth before the onset of the shortest days.

With some fuchsias, it is important to pay special attention to light. Variegated, yellow and ornamental foliage fuchsias are notoriously difficult to propagate under conditions of very poor light and losses will be greatest then. Higher light levels increase success because of the reduced chlorophyll content in the plants' leaves. The best shoots to take for cutting material, in an effort to increase success rates from ornamental foliage types, are those from the most upright branches. Those hanging below the horizontal level will rarely thrive, and if they do, then not quickly. In some cases it might be worthwhile tying branches into a higher position with canes to encourage the production of more vigorous shoots.

The Future

Commercial growers, needing large numbers of plants in a short time from certain high-value subjects such as rhododendrons, frequently use micropropagation techniques. Minute portions of plant tissue are grown in petri dishes under sterile, and ideal, conditions. The low cash value of fuchsias makes the outlay of large sums on such items as special growing cabinets uneconomic. The lack of any significant viral problem in the genus also makes the use of such techniques unnecessary, if not undesirable.

With the steady dwindling of the world's fossil fuel reserves – for example, oil – greenhouse economics will come under increasing scrutiny. Moves are already afoot to use double-glazing on commercial glass houses. A few such greenhouses for amateurs are currently on sale, although demand for them is still limited by their cost. Variable-density glass is now commonly used for such things as sunglasses and it seems likely that, in years to come, glass with special properties will be produced on a wide scale for greenhouse work. It might be that this would reduce light levels to an acceptable range on very bright, hot, days. Perhaps science will allow the enhancement of certain wavelengths to which plants are most responsive, other bands being reduced or eliminated in the process. The glass would act in much the same way as photographic filters do today, i.e. infra red.

Mobile screens are now common within commercial greenhouses. They are made from a variety of different materials that allow considerable savings to be made on heating bills during the night, when demands are most likely to be high. They act by reducing the physical area to be heated and by slowing the loss of heat upwards into the top of the greenhouse. Some of these screens can be placed to one side of the plants when not in use, but they can also help to reduce the full heat of the day's sun on cuttings and adult plants alike by giving shade. You can expect to see a greater use of such screens for fuchsia growing in the years to come.

Cuttings can now be taken in rooting sleeves. These are most commonly made from plastic and can be useful for producing many cuttings within a very small area. At the moment, they have no advantages for fuchsias and are mainly used for ripe-wood cuttings of other perennials.

Plants such as chrysanthemums are frequently treated with chemical inhibitors that reduce the size of marketable plants to a more acceptable level. Chemicals can also be used to create more bushy growth. At the moment, when fuchsias are treated with such products, they can be kept in small pots for longer before being sold. Customers will eventually find their purchases bursting into vigorous growth again (about 12 weeks later). The following fuchsias respond to treatment with B-9 (see Glossary): 'Carmel Blue', 'Dollar Princess', 'Annabel', 'Beacon', 'Beacon Rosa', 'Pink Spangles' (also called 'Mieke

Meursing'), 'Winston Churchill', 'Bealings', 'Snowcap' and 'Display'. Not all fuchsias respond equally to treatment with such chemicals.

It is likely that fuchsias will be among the last ornamental plants to be affected by modern gene transference methods. The search for special colours, unusual features and pest- or disease-resistance is unlikely to be undertaken on a commercial scale without a significant financial incentive. Because cutting material is so easy to propagate, registering special changes is difficult to regulate, even if there are commercial reasons for doing so. Nevertheless, these methods will no doubt arrive on the fuchsia-growing scene eventually.

In summary, we have examined the methods employed by professionals and by amateurs in their fuchsia propagation. We have looked at suitable composts, the production of mother plants and the place of light, heat and humidity in relation to success ratios. Different propagating methods have been dealt with, as have ways of increasing even the most difficult stock. We have had a glimpse of the future. When all has been said and read, however, there is no substitute for experience, or for a scientific approach that is able to incorporate technical advances in fuchsia growing.

Creating Better Bushes

Fuchsias, like other plants, rarely grow into perfectly shaped bushes on their own. There are various ways of improving on natural shapes. The first of these is to remove developing growth. Nipping, stopping and pinching are all terms used for the process of removing the growing points from fuchsias as they develop. There are several reasons why this might be worthwhile, most notably, in commercial terms, so that extra material is available for cuttings. From the point of view of the amateur gardener or competitor, other reasons are more likely, as we will see in a moment.

Removal of the growing point is most obviously advantageous for cuttings. Each growing point starts as a single shoot with leaves and immature side-growth buds. If the central growing point ('lead shoot') is removed immediately above a pair of leaves, two new branches are encouraged to grow. Increasing the number of side shoots ('laterals') makes for denser, bushier and generally more attractive

plants. Fuchsias grown out-of-doors will normally produce side shoots more freely than will those grown under glass. This is because air moves the branches. Japanese experiments have shown that the same results can be achieved by gently moving the branches of cuttings (with a fine brush) by hand, two or three times a day.

Nipping is the method most commonly employed by competitors to encourage the production of laterals. Commercially, chemicals are often used to encourage the production of laterals' growth. The increased number of branches brings a bonus in the quantity of flowers that can be carried. This is an obvious advantage when a large flush of bloom is required on a particular date, for an exhibition or competitive show. Pot-grown plants are likely to be more stable when fully flowered if their growth is shorter and bushier. Nipping ensures that this happens.

If the process of nipping continues without respite, growing fuchsias will not flower. Nipping should cease about eight weeks before flowers are required, but there is a wide variation in the flowering times of different cultivars. Seasonal changes from one year to another will also play an important part in the timing of show plants in flower. At the height of the growing season, fuchsias such as 'Dollar Princess' and 'Orwell' will usually come into bloom about seven weeks after their final nip. Other cultivars like 'Peppermint Stick' and 'Sweet Leilani' may take as many as thirteen weeks and then come only slowly to their peak. As a rule, singles and small semi-double fuchsias need about eight weeks before they will flower. Larger doubles usually require from ten to twelve weeks. Terminal flowering, or *triphylla*, fuchsias are best left for fourteen weeks if exhibition plants are required.

By removing the growing point of a developing cutting, it is possible to create an open centre to the plant. This encourages air movement when the foliage and stems are still very sappy and most likely to be affected by botritis. Leverage on any branch is reduced if nipping is carried out early in a plant's life. If stopping occurs after a branch has become leggy, the weight of its blooms can be considerable and, in the case of a cultivar such as 'Lye's Unique', this can result in breakages among the immature branches. Extra support can be gained by allowing the lower branches to

Fig. 5 Forming a show-quality bush:

    *a: The tip is removed from a rooted cutting, just above its
        second pair of leaves.*

    b: New shoots appearing from the remaining leaf axils.

    c: The four growing shoots.

    d: The advanced, bushy plant (reduced in scale).

rest on the pot edges or on the ground if fuchsias are planted out-of-doors. A well-shaped plant is easier to prune as it ages; strength is gained by the balance and symmetry created in its formative stages. Such advantages are not usually applicable to commercial practice, where clearly they would be uneconomic. They are, however, relevant in the search for excellence pursued by keen competitors and enthusiastic amateur horticulturists.

The practice and advantages of shaping small fuchsias in their early stages can be most clearly seen if you make experiments on cultivars like 'Blue Waves' or 'Pixie'. Take one such fuchsia cutting, allow it to root well, and nip out the growing point just above the first pair of leaves. Within a short time, new side shoots appear and these in turn are removed above the first pair of leaves. A third and final stop is carried out above the next leaves that develop, so that eight branches form the basic framework in an open and spreading way. The same advice is often given on pruning roses. Cut away growth so that an open, cup- (or tulip-) shaped centre is created. Health and strength are increased in this way and bloom numbers are multiplied. For show plants, it is possible to continue with this programme of nipping, but for normal gardening purposes, even when plants are kept for several years, it is unnecessary.

Some fuchsias have especially short internodes and bushier growth than others do. The two examples just mentioned have reasonably long internodes and it is easy to practise nipping and shaping on them. Others like 'Countess of Aberdeen' and 'Nellie Nuttall' have much shorter internodes and do not respond well to nipping at every leaf joint. In such cases it is best to nip by measurement rather than by the number of leaves along each branch: about every 5.8 cm (2 in) would be advisable. It is worthwhile nipping in such a way that leaves face different angles. If the first set of leaves has been left facing north and south, the next stop should leave the topmost leaves facing east and west.

Early nipping will promote bushy growth with a multiplicity of branches. At the height of the growing season, fuchsias can grow (at their optimum speed) at a rate of more than 3.14 cm (1.25 in) a week. In the case of a show plant that is not nipped for the twelve weeks before display, branches should extend by at least 35.8

cm (14 in). Plants of over a metre in diameter can be produced in pots of about 15 cm (6 in) in width. There may be more than five hundred branches and over one thousand flowers on a perfect exhibition cultivar such as 'Pixie'. Some of the best modern cultivars, like 'Nellie Nuttall', which carry more than two flowers in each leaf axil (multiflowering), can achieve these same flower totals on plants with fewer branches and smaller frames.

Branch angles play an important part in creating the final shape of each fuchsia. Some cultivars, like 'Linda Goulding', have an angle of branching of about 25 degrees from the vertical. This results in stiffly upright plants that are most useful for bedding into the open ground, where their habit of growth keeps both foliage and flowers cleanly above soil level. Fuchsias in this group, which are generally either singles or semi-doubles, often have as many as four flowers to a leaf joint, held near the periphery of the plant where they are clearly visible. 'Lindisfarne' has a branch angle of around 35 degrees. Fuchsias like this are frequently used to create quarter standards. They will often make perfectly shaped exhibition bush plants, and usually carry large numbers of branches. Flowers on fuchsias in this group are usually numerous and clearly visible. 'Blue Waves' has branches that are carried at an angle of about 45 degrees. This is perfect for plants that are to be grown as full standards. Many fuchsias with similar branch angles will have large double flowers produced at the rate of one or two in each leaf axil. 'Pixie' has branches at a similar angle, but this is an exception to the rule; many of the older fuchsia cultivars produce branches at this angle, but it is less common among modern cultivars.

Some fuchsias like 'Autumnale' and 'Jack Acland' produce their branches and leaves at or near to the horizontal, and their sideways branching can be extensive. These are the fuchsias most suitable for use in hanging pots, full round baskets and half- or wall baskets. Fuchsias like these need to be displayed at or near eye level if their full beauty in flower is to be appreciated. The lower the angle of the branches, the higher the display position should be in order to set the subject off to its maximum advantage. Fuchsias like 'Cascade' and 'Thunderbird' are more truly cascading in their habit of growth. They often carry multiple branches that hang at their outer extremities with large numbers of flowers. These need to be lifted higher than fuchsias with a more horizontal habit, and they rarely flower across the entire top of a plant. This makes them very difficult to use for competitions, but does not detract from their beauty in garden displays, where they often lend themselves best to wall baskets on board fences.

Branches often appear from below ground level on exhibition pot-grown fuchsias. These can spoil the symmetry of a plant, although they are advantageous when bush fuchsias grow out-of-doors. Such branches tend to be very upright in habit and much stronger than surrounding branches. Warmth and water will often restore growth from below ground level, albeit at a slow rate, for fuchsias that have been caught by frost.

If fuchsias have been pinched to create an open centre, they can be pruned to just above the eight-branch level. Before this, it is often wise to trim back half the top growth and to strip away the leaves. Final pruning is then carried out as the fuchsias start into regrowth with increases in daylight and warmth. Standard fuchsias are treated as if they were bushes on stems, and pruned back accordingly. Sometimes there is doubt about whether branches have died: there is a simple way to tell if the wood is still alive. Rub a thumbnail across the bark so that the state of the wood below the surface is visible. If the wood is green, this offers the promise of regeneration.

One interesting aspect to look out for if you keep fuchsias from year to year is that internodal length steadily decreases, in pot-grown plants especially, with each succeeding season. If plants have very short internodes, this progressive shortening can be a drawback. Where, however, a fuchsia is too long in the joint to begin with, it can be an advantage to keep plants for longer periods, in order to show more attractive features on the display bench. Cultivars such as 'Phyllis', 'Mrs W. P. Wood' and 'Checkerboard' look better if they are shown in this way, as second-year plants.

Another, less-common approach to shortening internodal length is second stopping. Courage is required: take growing points away, wait until new ones appear, and then remove these as well. The process does not work equally well with all fuchsias, but as most of those with long internodes are vigorous anyway, they are likely to respond without much difficulty. If second

stopping is carried out successfully, four new stronger and shorter shoots will appear from each joint. This type of nipping is best carried out early in a plant's life, in order to build a strong framework and dense habit. Cultivars such as 'Celia Smedley' and 'Beacon', both upright in habit, are the best plants to experiment on before trying the technique on other cultivars.

Sometimes fuchsias grow too tall and weak for their own good. This is called etiolation and it is commonly associated with low light levels. Stems elongate unnaturally, become pale and weak and turn towards the direction of maximum light. This can be a positive disadvantage if symmetrical show plants are wanted. Lean-to greenhouses and conservatories may cause difficulties of this sort. High temperatures and high nitrogen levels in the feeding programme will exaggerate the difficulties, too. Lowering the temperature and the air humidity can therefore be beneficial. Higher-than-normal potassium feeding can also be used to help to reduce internodal lengths. There are some advantages associated with etiolation if the condition is not extreme. Shoots become juicier and are less likely to flower, which helps in propagating difficult subjects. Taking the tips from such branches can boost cutting production at the height of the flowering season.

Low light levels are not always the result of poor greenhouse siting. They will naturally be affected by the time of year. Greenhouse shading can also cause problems, especially if it has been put in place during a particularly sunny period that is then followed by an extended spell of dull, cold weather. Perfect conditions can only be guaranteed if growers respond flexibly to changes in the environment.

Excessive heat within the greenhouse during the darkest days of the year also encourages etiolation. Recent experimental work has shown that this problem will not arise as long as night-time temperatures are maintained at above daytime ones. Removing excessive daytime heat is likely to prove even more difficult and costly than providing adequate and stable heating levels. As we have already seen, nitrogen can be used deliberately to elongate internodes, but this is only advisable when atmospheric and soil moisture levels are low. Some fuchsias have naturally sappy growth that can be stiffened and shortened by reducing nitrogen, heat and moisture levels. At the same time, additional potassium fertilizer can be administered and light levels maximized. 'Little Ouse', 'Marcus Graham' and 'Pink Marshmallow' are among those cultivars that can benefit from alterations to an otherwise normal fuchsia-growing routine.

Shortened growth has its advantages if it is not carried to excess. It is most likely to occur naturally among small, single-flowering fuchsias. Internodal length decreases; leaf size is similarly affected; growth can slow to the point where new side shoots cease to appear. Some fuchsias, like 'Nellie Nuttall', 'Look East' and 'Estelle Marie', appear to stunt more easily than others do. This leads to a loss of cutting material and can mean that branches cease to grow and bloom. Some fuchsias tend towards extremes in their natural habit. 'Eleanor Leytham' is notoriously difficult to start into regrowth.

Too much heat and light from the sun can cause more unwanted problems than stunting. An increase in shade, air moisture levels and high nitrogen feeds will only partially compensate during prolonged hot spells. Some of those fuchsias that stunt most easily, like 'Nellie Nuttall', seem to suffer from a depletion in trace elements at such times. Calcium depletion may well occur. Weak doses of chelated trace elements may be given if the plants do not thrive.

Some fuchsias have special characteristics that can be used to advantage when the plants are being shaped. Terminal-flowering, *triphylla* fuchsias often produce their leaves alternately on the stems, rather than opposite each other. This means that if nipping is undertaken at every joint, only one shoot will appear. Even when this sort of fuchsia produces leaves in pairs, nipping at every joint is rarely beneficial. In the majority of cases, terminal-flowering fuchsias are best given longer intervals between stops. The bulk of them will tolerate being pinched at about 10–15-cm (4–6-in) intervals and still break into new growth without difficulty.

Several of the terminal-flowering fuchsias have slightly hairy leaves and seem to tolerate, and in some cases benefit from, having all top growth cut away so that new shoots are encouraged to come from below soil level when the new season gets under way. The fuchsia called 'Thalia' in the United Kingdom and USA (and 'Koralle' in Germany) gives excellent results and in huge tubs can grow to be a very large plant, given the chance. Such plants are not frost-tolerant but will accept hotter and drier conditions better than many more conventional fuchsias. Old plants are generally slower to resume growth at the start of each season; it pays to propagate and grow again from cuttings so that maximum vigour can be maintained. When it comes to producing stock, terminal-flowering types are rarely as successful as others are. Larger cuttings usually give better results on the propagating benches. Tips from already-rooted cuttings often provide the best material for propagation.

Fuchsias from the *encliandra* section do not benefit much from nipping in a slow and deliberate manner, but they respond well to being clipped with scissors or small shears. This maintains a dense habit and neat shape. These fuchsias can be trained to a variety of shapes and will gain from being tied in and selectively stopped.

Many of the lesser-grown species do not respond well to stopping. For this reason, it is sometimes very difficult to take cuttings from and to shape older plants. Of course, some species like *F. denticulata* and *F. procumbens* will root and sprout comparatively easily. Others, especially some of those with felty or hairy leaves, do better at times of active growth – for example, *F. hartwegii* and *F. boliviana* var. *luxurians*. Others of the wild fuchsias die if cuttings are removed from young and immature plants; *F. magdalenae* is one such species. It is wise to see that difficult subjects are very well established before any attempt is made to cut them back. Alternatively, a plant may be sacrificed in order to produce several cuttings that can be grown on as older plants. The shaping of such subjects is best carried out using canes and ties to keep them well balanced. Once wood has hardened, the canes and ties can be removed to give a natural appearance.

There are other ways of shaping fuchsias to keep them upright and looking natural. Wires are often used to train immature growth into desired shapes. Plastic-covered wire is the best. It should be thick enough to prevent it cutting into the branches as they move. Wires need not be attached to canes if other branches can be used as supports. Coarse nylon yarn and green twine are alternatives to wire and these have a helpful flexibility. If canes are used, as they are sometimes for show purposes or to prevent wind damage, they should be as unobtrusive as possible. It is usually sufficient to place one split cane near the centre of a pot as a young plant matures. This will help to stabilize it in its developmental stages. Later, it is likely that several canes will be placed around the perimeter of the pot and a series of ties strung round them to hold the branches into more upright positions. With show plants, these ties and canes are usually removed just prior to staging and judging. Canes used should not detract from the fuchsia or attract attention to themselves, but should enhance the plant's beauty. Fuchsias with very large flowers, such as 'Royal Velvet', can benefit from the discreet use of canes. The larger the flower, the heavier it is likely to be; extra support is sometimes necessary if the flowers are to be seen to advantage, which they need to be in garden displays.

Pot fuchsias, growing or standing out of doors, are likely to be blown over by high winds. Double potting is one way of preventing such a problem. Different parts of the garden will be differently affected by prevailing winds. It is sometimes possible to reduce the likelihood of problems by moving plants to sheltered spots. Ladders and ladder-racks are sometimes used to give additional stability to double-potted show plants. The ladder is laid flat, usually raised a short distance above the ground on bricks, and the pots stand between the rungs. Short ladders can also be used to prevent movement when plants are transported to shows by lorry or van.

There is a popular misconception that turning plants a quarter-turn every day (or week) will help to produce perfectly symmetrical pot fuchsias. This is rarely true. You need only to look at trees and shrubs growing out-of-doors to see they are not all affected in this way; or they would all be leaning towards the light! Perfectly shaped plants are usually grown from symmetrically shaped cuttings or seedlings. They are then given plenty of space around them so that there is no competition for available light. If too many fuchsias are grown within a restricted space, such as a lean-to greenhouse or garden frame, growth will be adversely affected. Rotating plants is a poor compensation for providing them with adequate space and light.

Proportion and style are difficult qualities to explain, although most people know when one plant looks better than another does. Little plants in large pots are often seen in classes for beginners at fuchsia shows. Large plants in tiny pots are less common but no more attractive. In addition, ties and stakes can make growth look artificial if applied carelessly. Pot-grown fuchsias should look as if they have been dug from one garden and are ready to be replanted into another. Fuchsias look best when they are symmetrical, healthy, floriferous (at the appropriate time), bushy and natural in appearance.

Shaping fuchsias is an interesting pastime. They will generally give very good results with the minimum of experience and care. Superb show-quality plants in pots are not as easily produced, and there is always something new for the enthusiastic exhibitor to discover. Daily, hourly or even immediate care helps the plants to reach the true heights of perfection. Because fuchsias are so amenable and rewarding, life for the enthusiast is never boring and dull. It is a good idea to keep detailed notebooks that can be used for reference. There are so many things that can be done throughout the year and so many fascinating lessons to learn.

CHAPTER 5

Bedding Fuchsias

Fuchsias have been used in summer bedding schemes for about a century. In major urban parks, they fill a valuable role. Some plants like 'Koralle', 'Gartenmeister Bonstedt' and 'Tom West' are notable for their long-lived flowers and for their attractive foliage. Many specimens are grown as standards (see Chapter 6), and used as dot plants to add height as well as beauty to overall designs. Such bedding schemes are changed seasonally, and winter alternates with summer, dividing the gardening year into two. The trend has spread worldwide.

In order to maximize this seasonal use of fuchsias for summer bedding purposes, they are pot-grown in greenhouses and planted out as well-established specimens, often on the verge of blooming. At the end of summer and before the first frosts, they are raised and placed again into pots, before being brought into greenhouses for the coldest and darkest months. Alternatively, fuchsias can be discarded at this time so that new ones can be produced from cuttings in the following spring; this has the advantage of requiring less winter space and heat, so reducing costs.

Formal summer bedding is most commonly seen in public parks and island beds. Fuchsias can be displayed similarly around living accommodation. Island beds often form the centrepiece of car-turning circles. Side borders still benefit from dot plants placed judiciously among more permanent greenery. Fuchsias, being so versatile, really come into their own if a little imagination is used in their planting.

Soil preparation plays a large part in the successful outcome of such schemes. Ground is normally forked in order to remove pernicious weeds. Humus is added to provide nutrients and to give a friable crumbly structure to the soil. Drainage needs to be good, but humus helps to provide moisture even when there is little rainfall; it also reduces the need for irrigation systems. Surface hoeing and forking needs to be kept to a minimum once planting has been completed, as fuchsia roots can so easily be damaged. Many growers will make use of weed-suppressant mats, which allow rain to permeate downwards, and cover the whole area with chipped bark once planting is complete.

Fuchsias dislike really dry conditions. They are best watered well upon planting, and periodically thereafter. Liquid feed can be provided via a diluter if a watering system is used. Watering is best carried out late in the day in order to reduce evaporation and leaf burn during sunny spells.

The selection of fuchsias made in this chapter is from plants that have upright habits. Having said this, it is true to say that many fuchsias are suited to a variety of purposes and that such a selection must, to some extent, rely on the element of personal choice. Leo B. Boullemier (1991) in *The Checklist of Species, Hybrids and Cultivars of the Genus Fuchsia* carries the most comprehensive description of known fuchsias. However, many of these have been superseded by better introductions.

People have tried to measure and compute the differences between fuchsias but, in practice, great variations can be caused by even small changes in their environment. Some of the reasons for these changes have been discussed elsewhere in this book. Colour is highly variable, as well as size, but to the experienced eye there are still qualities that mark out all great introductions. Foremost among these qualities is a lack of obvious faults.

The plants' blooms need to be visible, of high quality and numerous. Flowers should be displayed at the end of each branch and should not be hidden by other branches and leaves. Multiflowering – that is, more than one bloom produced in each leaf axil – is also a great asset: it helps to provide more flowers over a longer period. Blooms should be attractive in their combination of shape and colour. They should also be different from or better than other fuchsias in cultivation.

These selected fuchsias have been arranged in alphabetical order, and have been listed with the year of their introduction and the name of their raiser. Most fuchsia growers find that specific hybridists produce the kinds of plants they wish to grow, and concentrate on obtaining all their stock. Older cultivars have a more limited colour range and their shapes are less varied. Flowers are described as single, semi-double or double and brief descriptions are given of their tubes, sepals and corollas. The most suitable purpose for each plant is suggested. Lastly, stopping dates have been given: this information is not cast in stone but provides a general guide based upon my personal knowledge, gained in East Anglia and around the world.

'Aalt Groothuis' (Beije 1997) Single. Both the tubes and the flyaway sepals are white. The violet corollas are saucer-shaped. Blooms are held near the periphery of the plant. Leaves are plain green. Growth is upright and strong. Ideal for planting as half standards to be used as dot plants in the border. Nine weeks.

'Alde' (Gouldings Fuchsias 1988) Single of the intermediate sort. Sturdy tubes and sepals are pale orange. The corollas have pleated, apricot-coloured petals. Multiflowering is normal. Branches are upright and slightly arching. It makes a good bush in a pot. Nine weeks.

'Alison Woods' (Gouldings Fuchsias 2001) Double. The tubes are reddened and waxy. The spreading sepals are flesh pink with green tips. Corollas are dense rosettes of lavender and pastel-pink petals. Growth is strongly upright and it makes good half-standards or tub plants. Eleven weeks.

'Annabel' (Ryle 1977) Double. The white of the tubes and sepals is touched with pink but the corollas are creamy white. Leaves have a yellow tinge and the habit of 'Annabel' is upright and elegant. 'Annabel' makes attractive bushes and standards to show levels. Ten weeks.

'Bealings' (Gouldings Fuchsias 1983) Double. This fuchsia has white tubes and sepals with corollas that are bright violet before they mature to pink. It is multiflowered, upright and freely self-branching. 'Bealings' is arguably the top British show double. Eleven weeks.

'Becky' (Gouldings Fuchsias 1994) Single. 'Becky' has short tubes and upswept sepals that are a dark and glossy red. Its bell-shaped corollas are dark aubergine maturing to red. Show-quality growth is upright, bushy and amenable. Needs some protection. Ten weeks.

'Beryl Shaffery' (Shaffery 1997) Single. Its tubes and sepals are very pale pink. Upward- and outward-pointing corollas are saucer-shaped, pink with a hint of magenta. 'Beryl Shaffery' has a sturdily upright and self-branching habit. Ideal as a bush planted in the summer border. Nine weeks.

'Blue Waves' (Waltz 1954) Double. Rose tubes and sepals are here combined with campanula-violet petals that have pink flashes on them. Growth is strong and bushy. This is a versatile and showy fuchsia that makes good standards or large garden bushes. Eleven weeks.

'Border Queen' (Ryle 1974) Single. Tubes and sepals are rhodamine pink, but the corollas are amethyst violet. Bushy and self-branching growth helps to provide superb bushes and standards. This fuchsia has an enviable reputation throughout the United Kingdom. Twelve weeks.

'Canny Bob' (Hewitson 1998) Single. The tubes and sepals of these upward- and outward-pointing blooms are white. Corollas are salmon orange. Multiflowering is normal. Growth is stiffly upright, but side shoots are produced freely. 'Canny Bob' looks well in the border or in tubs. Ten weeks.

'Carnoustie' (Gouldings Fuchsias 1986) Double. Both sepals and tubes are pink. Corollas are a frilly mixture of mauves and pinks. Leaves are lime green and side shoots are abundant. This fuchsia looks well when grown in pots for conservatory displays. Twelve weeks.

'Caspar Hauser' (Springer 1987) Double. Scarlet tubes and sepals adjoin turkey-red corollas that have their outer petals splashed with brighter red tones. This is a multiflowered fuchsia and its growth is upright, strong and self-branching. It is useful for show work. Eleven weeks.

'Celia Smedley' (Bellamy 1970) Single. The sepals and tubes are neyron rose and the corollas are bright currant red. Growth is exceptionally strong and upright. 'Celia Smedley' is popular with beginners to showing and will make very large standards easily. Nine weeks.

'Checkerboard' (Walker & Jones 1948) Single. Each thin tube is red. The recurving sepals are white and they contrast with the dark red of the corollas. Growth is upright, robust and graceful. This fuchsia grows well as a standard and as a bush in large garden tubs. Nine weeks.

'Christine Shaffery' (Shaffery 1993) Double. This fuchsia has ivory-white tubes and sepals. Its petals carry mottled shades of lavender, lilac and pink. A bushy and upright habit of growth helps this multiflowered fuchsia to make excellent show plants comparable to 'Bealings'. Ten weeks.

'Continental' (Gouldings Fuchsias 1985) Semi-double or double. Both the sepals and tubes are white. The petals are pink with rose-coloured picotee edges. 'Continental' is peripheral and multiflowering. Its upright habit and unusual flowers suit it to garden displays. Ten weeks.

'Delta's Bride' (Vreeke/Westeinde 1992) Single with pale pink tubes and sepals. The large saucer-shaped corollas are slightly paler in colour. Blooms are held near the branch ends on growth that is sturdily upright. Best used in sheltered positions with high-fertility soils. Nine weeks.

'Delta's Drop' (Vreeke/Westeinde 1992) This single fuchsia has cherry-red, glossy tubes and sepals. Its petals are spoonbill-shaped; they are mauve when young, but turn red when mature. Branches are stiffly upright and, although growth is self-branching, early nipping improves things more. Nine weeks.

'Delta's Groom' (Vreeke/Westeinde 1993) Single. Its tubes and flyaway sepals are dark aubergine red. The corollas look like square bells and they are even darker in colour. 'Delta's Groom' is vigorously self-branching in habit. Its branches and flowers are resilient and weather-resistant. Ten weeks.

'Earl of Beaconsfield' (Laing 1878) Single of the intermediate type. Its tubes are long and, like the shorter sepals, orange. The corollas are brighter orange. This fuchsia has a strong and versatile habit and is well suited to summer conservatory displays. Ten weeks.

'Earre Barré' (De Graaff 1989) Single. The tubes and upswept sepals are dark, and glossy red; aubergine-stained. The flared sepals of the corollas are white with veins darkly stained red/aubergine. Growth is upright and amenable. It makes an attractive dot plant as a standard. Eight weeks.

'Emily Austin' (Bielby/Oxtoby 1990) Single. Tubes and sepals are small and pale pink. The little corollas are peach-coloured and large numbers of blooms are peripherally displayed. Growth is self-branching and upright. 'Emily Austin' makes superb show plants. Nine weeks.

'Estelle Marie' (Newton 1973) Single. The tubes and sepals are white and the corollas are violet. Blooms are held upwards and outwards in vast numbers. Growth is short and stiffly upright. This fuchsia is perfect for summer bedding and for window-box planting. Eight weeks.

'Excalibur' (Gouldings Fuchsias 1983) Single or semi-double. Petaloids are contained within the outer ring of petals; these, like the sepals and tubes, are rose pink. Blooming is profuse and peripheral. Growth is stiffly upright, self-branching and suitable for summer bedding displays. Eleven weeks.

'Finn' (Gouldings Fuchsias 1988) Single. Tubes are ivory and the gently upswept sepals are white. The corollas are an unusual shade of rusty red. This multiflowered fuchsia has a strongly upright and bushy habit that helps it to grow as a bi-coloured show stalwart. Ten weeks.

'Flying Scotsman' (Gouldings Fuchsias 1985) Double. Tubes are short, thick and reddened. The sepals are pink and recurved. Petals have a rosy red background with white marbling. Growth is strongly upright and is ideally suited to growing full standards or tub plants. Eleven weeks.

'Fuchsiade '88' (De Graaff 1988) Single. Aubergine is the colour of these corollas, sepals and tubes as well. Blooms are petite, peripheral and numerous. 'Fuchsiade '88' has stiffly upright growth that lends itself to tub planting or to the production of pillars. Nine weeks.

'Galadriel' (De Graaff 1982) Single. These tubes and sepals are white. The small, cup-shaped corollas are orange. Multiple blooms are held near the ends of the branches on stiffly upright growth. 'Galadriel' is particularly suitable for use in bedding schemes. Nine weeks.

'Gay Parasol' (Stubbs 1979) Double. Both the tubes and sepals are white, shading to pink. The rosette-shaped corollas are burgundy red. The many flowers are prominently displayed. Growth is upright and sturdy. Attractive pot plants are easily grown. Ten weeks.

'Gleneagles' (Gouldings Fuchsias 1986) Single. The tubes and sepals are flesh pink. Corollas are violet to mauve. Blooms are held peripherally, pointing upwards and outwards; multiflowered. Young leaves are bright yellow. Growth is stiffly upright. Does not like excessive heat. Eight weeks.

'Grace Durham' (Gouldings Fuchsias 1984) Single. While the sepals are pink and recurved, the tubes are red and the petals of the bell-shaped corollas violet. 'Grace Durham' is multiflowered and is a self-branching show type. Good bush plants may be formed. Nine weeks.

'Graf Christian' (Strumper 1993) Double. Tubes and the swept-back sepals are ivory white; the latter, when mature, are tinged with pink. Corollas are a marbled mixture of pink and mauve; petals have picotee edges. Growth is sturdily upright and ideal for creating large standards. Eleven weeks.

'Graf Spee' (Gouldings Fuchsias 1989) Double. The tubes and the sturdy upturned sepals are white. The corollas are large, irregular, and rosy red. This peripheral and multiflowering fuchsia has a sturdy and upright habit suitable for showing in pots. Ten weeks.

'Gruss aus dem Bodethal' (Sattler/Bethga 1893) Single. The tubes and sepals are a glossy, almost waxy, red. Corollas are very dark violet; almost black. Growth is shrubby and upright. 'Gruss aus dem Bodethal' is best grown in pots and is a great 'oldie'. Ten weeks.

'Gwen Dodge' (Dyos 1988) Single. White is the colour of both tubes and sepals. Corollas have white centres and lilac-blue outer petal zones. Flowers are upward-pointing with asymmetrical outlines; multiflowered. Growth stiffly upright. Looks well in the summer flower border. Nine weeks.

'Hathor' (Springer 1985) Single. Tubes and sepals are pink, but the saucer-shaped corollas are much darker and outward-pointing. Growth is sturdy and upright. 'Hathor' makes a showy garden plant in tubs or in moist and fertile garden borders situated in semi-shade. Nine weeks.

'Heidi Ann' (Smith 1969) Double. Cherry-red tubes and sepals are joined to corollas with lilac petals that have rose-pink veining. This stiffly upright, short-jointed and many-branched fuchsia is very free-flowering. It is always popular for showing and bedding although of diminutive stature. Nine weeks.

'Hessett Festival' (Gouldings Fuchsias 1985) Double. These very large blooms have white tubes and long, white, recurving sepals. The corollas have lavender petals with paler mottling. Growth is self-branching, upright, amenable and strong. Large pots are best. Thirteen weeks.

'Hidden Treasure' (De Graaff 1997) Single. Longer-than-average orange tubes. The sepals are orange and these usually adhere to each other, forming little lantern-like blooms. Corollas are orange. Multiflowered. Growth is upright and versatile. Ideal in mixed tubs. Eight weeks.

'Hinnerike' (Bögemann 1987) Single. This fuchsia has exceptionally bright orange tubes, sepals and corollas. Blooms are small, but branches are strong and require early nipping. This fuchsia does best when grown in large patio containers with other plants. Ten weeks.

'Isle of Mull' (Tolley 1978) Single. The tubes are reddened, but the appealingly upturned sepals are pink. Its petals are magenta-hued. Growth is arching but stiff, and requires early nipping to obtain the best results from plants used for garden bedding displays. Ten weeks.

'Jennifer Haslam' (Gouldings Fuchsias 1994) Single. This fuchsia has short tubes and flyaway sepals; both are rosy red. The saucer-shaped corollas are flecked with shades of pink and plum. Multiflowered. Growth is firm, self-branching and upright. Versatile and amenable. Ten weeks.

'Joan Young' (Gouldings Fuchsias 1994) Single. 'Joan Young' has short red tubes and fully recurved red sepals. The bell-shaped corollas are speckled with different shades of pink. Multiflowered. Its upright growth is trouble-free and bushy. Best suited to garden displays. Ten weeks.

'Kernan Robson' (Tiret 1958) Double. The sepals are fully recurving and red, but the tubes are pink. Fully pleated and large corollas are a smoky red. Growth is upright and strong, but is helped by some stopping. This fuchsia does best in conservatory displays. Twelve weeks.

'Lancelot' (Gouldings Fuchsias 1983) Single. The tubes and sepals are rosy red, but the bowl-shaped corollas are white with pink veins. 'Lancelot' has strongly upright and amenable growth and, with nipping, will make excellent standards or show-quality bushes. Nine weeks.

'Lindisfarne' (Ryle 1974) Single or semi-double. White or pink tubes and sepals are here combined with bright violet, or mauve, corollas. Growth is upright and bushy. 'Lindisfarne' makes outstanding pot plants as well as show bushes or quarter standards. Nine weeks.

'Little Ouse' (Gouldings Fuchsias 1988) Very large double. Both the sepals and the tubes are pale pink. Corollas are powdery blue with some pink mottling. A vigorous and self-branching habit helps to make very large plants with masses of bloom for garden displays. Twelve weeks.

'Look East' (Heavens 1987) Single of the pansy-flowered sort. Tubes and sepals are white, but petals are mauve with white insertions. There are large numbers of outward-pointing flowers on stiffly upright and short-jointed bushes. Suitable for display purposes. Nine weeks.

'Lumière' (Van der Post 1988) Single. The tubes and sepals are pink and the corollas are white with fully flared, saucer shapes. This fuchsia has an upright and vigorous habit that requires early nipping and it will make an excellent garden bedding subject. Nine weeks.

'Lye's Unique' (Lye 1886) Single. Tubes are long and, like the sepals, white. The pleated petals of each corolla are salmon orange. Growth is stiffly upright and long-jointed. 'Lye's Unique' is a classic of its type and is most suitable for mixed bedding or container plantings. Nine weeks.

'Marcus Graham' (Stubbs 1985) Double. The tubes and sepals of 'Marcus Graham' are pale salmon or pink. Its large corollas are a delicate shade of salmon. Growth is strong and especially suitable for large standards or showy garden bushes planted in big tubs. Twelve weeks.

'Martin's Umbrella' (Beije 2001) Single. The tubes and fully recurved sepals are bright eye-catching orange/red. Its petals form large orange/red bells. Growth is strong and upright. It makes a splendid half-standard in the garden where its flowers attract immediate attention. Nine weeks.

'Mieke Meursing' (Hopwood 1968) Single or semi-double. The tubes and sepals are red, but the corollas are pink with red veins. Multiflowering is normal. Bushy, free-branching and upright plants can be used to create perfectly shaped show bushes. Ten weeks.

'Nancy Lou' (Stubbs 1971) Double. Fully recurving sepals and tubes are pale pink. Petals are a creamy white. These flowers are of classical beauty. The strong and upright habit helps to create garden standards or large bushes in tubs with little difficulty. Eleven weeks.

'**Natalie Jones**' (Gouldings Fuchsias 1989) Single. The white tubes and sepals often have a subtle hint of pink. Bell-shaped corollas are pink. Multiflowering and peripheral blooming are the norm. An upright and amenable habit lends itself to conservatory displays. Ten weeks.

'**Nellie Nuttall**' (Roe 1977) Single or occasionally semi-double. Both the tubes and sepals are bright and shiny red, but the petals are white with pink veins. Growth is densely bushy and upright. Extra nitrogen and trace elements help in producing show bushes. Eleven weeks.

'**Nettala**' (Francesca 1973) Single. Tubes and spreading sepals are waxy-textured and red. Petals are spoonbill in shape; bright red. Growth is upright and sparsely branched. 'Nettala' is particularly heat- and drought-tolerant and provides a different and interesting summer border point. Nine weeks.

'**Nickis Findling**' (Ermel 1985) Single. Sepals and tubes are orange with a hint of rose. The corollas are a brighter orange. Flowers are held upwards near the plant's periphery. Growth, on this summer bedding gem, is upright, bushy and tolerant of hot and dry conditions. Eleven weeks.

'**Nimue**' (Gouldings Fuchsias 1983) Single. On this fuchsia the tubes and sepals are flesh pink, but the petals are lavender with a bluer edging. The many-branched, upright growth makes superb show bushes if some protection against the weather is afforded. Nine weeks.

'**Norfolk Ivor**' (Gouldings Fuchsias 1984) Semi-double or fully double. Short ivory-coloured tubes join sepals that are white with a hint of pink. Corollas are lavender blue to pink. Growth is upright, strong and amenable; 'Norfolk Ivor' will form a very good large standard. Eleven weeks.

'**Orwell**' (Gouldings Fuchsias 1988) Double. Short, pale tangerine tubes and sepals are here combined with the much darker, fully ruffled petals of the corollas. This multiflowering, early-blooming fuchsia has upright growth and makes good show plants. Eight weeks.

'**Peter Bielby**' (Bielby 1987) Double. The tubes, and the flyaway sepals, are scarlet. The irregularly shaped corollas are a paler red, with salmon splashes on the outer petals. Growth is very strong and ideally suited to the creation of standards or large garden bushes. Twelve weeks.

'**Pink Fantasia**' (Webb 1989) Single. These tubes and sepals are bright pink or red. Corollas have almost fluorescent mauve or violet petals. Heavily multiflowered plants carry upward-pointing blooms. This one is ideal for summer bedding displays. Ten weeks.

'**Plumb-bob**' (Gouldings Fuchsias 1992) Large double. The tubes and sepals are ivory white with a hint of pink on them. Corollas are red with mauve overtones to their petals. Foliage is green and growth strongly upright. Makes large standards and bushy garden plants. Twelve weeks.

'**Robbie**' (Lamb 1984) Single with flyaway white tubes and sepals. The corollas are medium-sized, cornet-shaped, and pale pink with darker pink veining. Growth, which is upright and strong, is enhanced by early nipping. Makes a good bush or half-standard in the mixed border. Ten weeks.

'**Robert J. Pierce**' (Gouldings Fuchsias 2001) Single. The tubes are short and creamy white. Mature sepals, sweeping upwards, are white tinged with red. Corollas are russet red and saucer-shaped. Growth is upright and sturdy. It makes a lovely quarter standard. Ten weeks.

'**Rose Fantasia**' (Wilkinson 1993) Single. Tubes, sepals and corollas are baby pink. The flowers are held upwards and outwards on the periphery of each branch. Growth is stiffly and acutely upright; amenable to nipping. Very drought- and heat-tolerant. One for the summer border. Nine weeks.

'**Royal and Ancient**' (Gouldings Fuchsias 1986) Single. Petals, sepals and tubes are pink. The large, bell-shaped corollas have wavy edges. Growth is upright and elegant. It is also helped by early nipping. Show-quality standards and bushes can be grown. Ten weeks.

'**Royal Velvet**' (Waltz 1962) Double. The tubes and sepals are crimson, but the corollas are purple with some red veins. The long-jointed growth is strong and upright. Good full standards and large garden display plants are easy to grow. Often underrated. Twelve weeks.

'**Scarborough Rosette**' (Unknown) Double. Flesh-pink tubes and sepals are found here with violet, rosette-shaped corollas. Blooms are held near the plant's periphery on bushy but stiffly upright growth. Raised, this fuchsia is ideal for indoor displays. Eleven weeks.

'**Shelford**' (Roe 1986) Single. Both the tubes, and the sepals that open to the horizontal position, are flesh pink, but the corollas are white with pink veins. A pale, classical beauty. Growth is upright and self-branching. Good show bushes may be grown. Nine weeks.

'**Sir Alfred Ramsey**' (Gouldings Fuchsias 1984) Single. While the tubes and sepals are rose pink, the bell-shaped corollas are violet-coloured. Leaves have a yellow cast. Growth is bushy, strong and amenable. Show bushes are relatively easy to grow. Ten weeks.

'**Snowcap**' (Henderson 1880) Semi-double. The sepals and tubes are scarlet, but the corollas are white with red veins. Growth is upright and bushy. One of the most famous fuchsias used for competitions, this may be grown as a top-quality bush or half standard. Ten weeks.

'**Steeretje**' (Weeda 1987) Single. The tubes are of medium length, pink in colour with just a hint of aubergine. The slightly pendant sepals are similarly coloured. The corollas are very pale aubergine. Growth is stiffly upright. 'Steeretje' is a gem for the conservatory. Ten weeks.

'**Tennessee Waltz**' (Walker & Jones 1951) Double. These tubes and recurving sepals are rose madder. The petals are a mixture of lilac, lavender and rose. This popular fuchsia has upright, bushy and hardy growth. It makes a good half-standard and bush pot plant. Twelve weeks.

'**Thamar**' (Springer 1987) Single, with small pansy-eyed blooms held upwards and outwards. Tubes and sepals are white. Petals are pale blue with white insertions. Growth is upright and bushy. It makes a good show plant in medium or large pots. Ten weeks.

'**Tom Knights**' (Gouldings Fuchsias 1983) Single. White tubes and sepals are found here with lavender-blue corollas. Multiflowering and peripheral-blooming, like its sports 'Sportsknight' and 'Knight Errant', this stiffly upright fuchsia grows well in large pots. Nine weeks.

'**Walz Jubelteen**' (Waldenmaier 1990) Single with many upward- and outward-pointing flowers. Its tubes and horizontal sepals are flesh pink. The corollas are salmon pink. Growth is sturdily upright. 'Walz Jubelteen' is versatile, eye-catching and popular. Ten weeks.

'**William Grant**' (Gouldings Fuchsias 1999) Semi-double or double. Both the tubes and the flyaway sepals are pink. The petals of each corolla are dark aubergine maturing to ruby red. Growth is strong and amenable. Ideal as a container plant or as a garden standard. Eleven weeks.

CHAPTER 6
Standards and Other Shapes

Large ornamental plants are not easy to grow, or to house once grown. Perhaps because of this, their impact upon viewers can be enormous. Most people will have seen standards, half-standards and quarter-standards, but fewer will be familiar with mini-standards, bonsai and topiary made with fuchsias. Pillars, pyramids, cones, fans and espaliers are also far from common and are usually associated in people's minds with large plants and enormous gardens.

This size can be awe-inspiring on occasions, but most of us could not provide facilities for such monsters. W. P. Wood's book *A Fuchsia Survey*, first published in 1950, contains illustrations of some early efforts. He shows James Lye with some of his pillars, and his son-in-law George Bright with some of his exhibition fuchsias similarly grown (pages 44–5). In the same volume, Wood shows some of the massive standards of 'Marinka' that were reputed to have been about fifty years old (opposite page 61). Moving such plants to shows must have been almost as daunting a task as growing them.

Gardeners often visit shows and exhibitions so that they can keep up to date with new ideas. The best of these are then adapted to suit individual needs; time, space, money and inclination are the limiting factors. There is a great deal of interest to be gained from trying to do something that is unusual and demanding. Considerable prestige accrues when outstanding attempts are shown to other growers. However, just as much interest can be generated by growing some of these ornamental shapes on a smaller and less demanding scale.

Standards

Standards, as a form of plant training, are well known to most general gardeners, who will have seen roses or other plants grown in a similar way. Quarter-standards are usually recognized by fuchsia enthusiasts as suitable for the show

bench and the greenhouse benches where their flowers may be raised nearly to eye level. They stand between 30.5 cm and 45.5 cm (12–18 in) high. Half-standards are rather taller, at between 45.5 cm and 75 cm (18–30 in), while full standards are from 75 cm to 105.8 cm (30–42 in) in height.

Heights such as these are fixed for show purposes and exact measurements may vary from one location to another. Where competition is the aim, it is essential to find out the sizes required while the stem length is still adaptable: this is before the head, like a bush but on its own long stalk, is formed. Standards for garden display can be of any size (within reason). Given adequate facilities and time, stems of over 2 m (78.5 in) in length may be formed, thus creating giant specimens. One of the limiting factors in the search for size is the damage that may be caused by wind. Problems will be most acute with fuchsias that have thin or brittle growth. 'Lye's Unique' is one of those fuchsias that has a tendency to drop branches from newly formed standards under the weight of its blooms.

Fuchsias, unlike many other plants, do not need to be grafted onto other stocks. They can be run up on a vertical lead shoot, nipped out at the desired height and formed into a bush on a stalk; lower shoots are removed steadily. Of course, this process usually takes some time and it is tempting to take less trouble in shaping the head of a standard than you would with a bush fuchsia. The resultant shape may then have leggy branches that can exert considerable leverage when they come into flower. It is better to stop early shoots at every second or third joint in order to make the centre of the head compact and therefore less liable to wind damage.

Standard stems need to be vertical and straight if they are to carry the optimum amount of nutrients. Misshapen stems always seem to look worse as they age. Of course, some cultivars like 'Celia Smedley' make ideal stems with little help, while others, such as 'Cascade', struggle under the care of even the best growers. Split canes are normally placed next to the stems when they form and are still quite short. Later, ordinary canes can be used to replace them; these should be picked carefully for their height and appearance, because the fewer times that canes need to be replaced, the less root disturbance occurs. Some of the modern, plastic-covered metal stakes are preferable because they do not rot where air and soil meet, as their cane counterparts do. An essential part of staking standards as they form is to run the support well into the bushy head. This will help to prevent the wind from snapping the top growth off just when it is becoming most attractive.

Ties should be treated as disposable rather than as permanent features of standards. In the early stages, it is probably best to use a coarse nylon yarn to hold the standard stem against its support stake. It is usual to fasten ties at about 7.5 cm (3 in) intervals: there is no hard-and-fast distance, and it is better to use too many ties at first and to remove some of them later. Plastic-covered wire is often used to replace the temporary wool ties. Toggle ties made from plastic may also be used, but the type of tie used is less important than that it should be unobtrusive in appearance and effective in its support. As stems age and lengthen, they also expand in girth. If no attention is given to this matter, stem constriction will occur and this might reduce food supplies to the standard head or even cut the stem in two; or weaken it so that wind can wreak havoc. Wide ties are less likely to cut into a stem than those that are narrow: the latter offer little useful support.

The majority of fuchsia growers remove side shoots from the stems of standard whips when they are still small and therefore less likely to cause permanent scarring. Of course, this does not apply once the desired height is achieved, and bushy growth is being promoted at the top. When side shoots are removed from leaf axils, it is common practice, and wise, to keep the leaves themselves on the stem to help the plant to grow. They are usually taken off once the standard head has formed a substantial bush on top of the stem. There are advantages in leaving side shoots in place for longer periods, too. These relate to the greater increase that can occur in stem girth. A thicker stem will then be

Fig. 6 Fuchsia standards.

able to feed and support the head much more efficiently and attractively. It is probably wise to shorten the side shoots to about three leaf joints, when this method is employed, so as to avoid adversely affecting the formation of the lead shoot. Later, side shoots can be removed, a few at a time, using a very sharp blade and cutting upwards: pulling them off downwards tears heels from the main stem and leaves unsightly scars.

Fuchsias growing as standards should be given optimum conditions and discouraged from flowering until their heads are quite large. High-nitrogen fertilizers will help to promote foliage and growth at the expense of ripening and flowering. The longer that stems can be kept green and unripe, the faster their girth will increase. This in turn speeds up the heads' growth. Leaves will normally be much larger on whips, or standards, at the formative stage, than they would be on an ordinary plant.

There are occasions when the stem's upright growth needs to be encouraged and promoted, and a simple technique can be employed to achieve this. A black or dark tube with each end open is fastened to the cane with tape so that the fuchsia's apical tip is enclosed and forced upwards towards the light. The position of the tube is altered so that the whip never grows clear of its top. Ties are placed lower on the stem in the normal way.

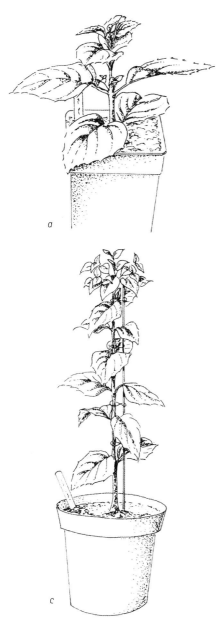

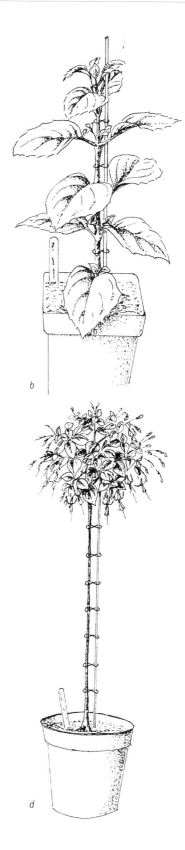

Fig. 7 Forming a standard:

    a: A normal cutting with its tip intact.

    b: A split cane is placed next to the elongating stem and
       the first ties are positioned.

    c: The tip is removed once the plant reaches the desired
       height. The lower side shoots are removed and a bush
       forms on the stem.

    d: The finished standard. Leaves and shoots have been
       removed from the stem, up to the level of the head.
       Ties are clearly not restricting the stem's growth. The
       standard looks neat and well-balanced.

Shoots sometimes appear from below ground level and compete for nutrients with the existing stem of a standard. It is wise to cut these away cleanly with a sharp knife, well below soil level. If they are severed at the soil surface, they will persist and often become even stronger. Also, pulling them away rarely achieves permanent freedom from regrowth. Such shoots, if left, will ultimately spoil standard fuchsias, making them less attractive and more like bushes.

Breezes are one of the worst enemies of standards. It is essential, therefore, when plants are put out-of-doors, that they are anticipated. Fuchsia standards are usually taken from their pots and planted in the ground during the longest days of the year. Extra stakes can then be driven at an angle towards the prevailing winds and tied to the fuchsias' vertical supports. Potted standards can also be placed out-of-doors, but these are obviously much harder to protect from wind damage.

Fuchsia standards need protection from frosts if they are to survive from year to year. This is usually afforded by heated greenhouses, but unheated glass or sheds may also be used for overwintering. It is quite a good idea to wrap standard stems with pipe lagging before placing polystyrene chips around the root ball and wrapping the partially pruned top in a paper sack. Pruning in the autumn usually consists of cutting growth halfway back before defoliating completely. The latter helps to remove overwintering pests and diseases. When days lengthen and growth restarts, further pruning can be carried out to remove dead or crossing branches. Because most fuchsias have fibrous roots, they should never be allowed to dry out entirely; even in the middle of their rest period, some moisture will be needed if fatalities are to be avoided.

Repotting is usually carried out once growth restarts in the spring. It is often best to remove as much old soil or compost as possible before the standard is replaced in a smaller pot. In areas where vine weevils are a serious problem, the roots can be washed free of soil before repotting takes place. Soil-borne pests can also be combated by the strategic use of such products as pesticides and nematodes.

Fuchsia standards were often used in Victorian and Edwardian times as dot plants in formal bedding schemes. Although local authorities in Great Britain undertake fewer of these schemes than they used to, their popularity in other countries in this respect has not declined. Private gardeners also make great use of them to provide extra height and size among their other plants. With the rise in patio and yard gardening, resulting from a decline in the average size of modern gardens, container planting has also become very popular. Short standards find a welcome in such places and add impact, as well as giving a long flowering season. Fuchsia standards planted in tubs should be removed over winter, as if they had been planted in the garden.

Standards grown for competition are almost the same as those produced for garden display, except that the length of clear stem, from soil level to the lowest branch, is likely to be stipulated. Sometimes the size of pot is similarly defined or restricted. Size alone is unlikely to win prizes. Quarter- or table standards are best displayed on benching so that their blooms can be seen at, or near, eye level. Half- or full standards may stand on the floor, although the latter might be improved by raising them a short way above the ground. The one major problem with showing large standards is that of transporting them to show halls. If this can be achieved without damage, they are much more impressive than most other show plants and will often win 'Best in Show', even for beginners.

Espaliers

Espaliers are two-dimensional structures that have a front and a back, but little side view. A central stem or spine is run vertically up a wall and side shoots are trained horizontally from it. To help in creating this shape, it is usual to make a framework of canes or wires so that the branches can be tied into position before their wood ripens. Nipping is often carried out so that only sideways-pointing shoots are retained; those growing forwards and backwards are rubbed out.

Branches are tied to the supports with coarse nylon yarn, as with standards. Later, stronger and more permanent ties, often made from plastic-covered wire, replace them. Branches will increase in girth as plants age and ties will need to be replaced before they constrict the stems. Branch angle affects vigour, and it is sometimes advisable to allow branches to grow upward for a time before they are bent down and fixed horizontally onto the framework. In an effort to encourage side shoots and evenly-distributed flowers, some growers tilt their plants backwards at an angle of about sixty degrees while they are being formed, so that side shoots are promoted more evenly across the complete framework. Large pots, stood vertically, often do not have enough weight to prevent their plants from falling over, and it might be wise to fasten big specimens against a wall in order to avoid damage.

Fans

Fan-trained fuchsias have come back into fashion thanks to the efforts made by fuchsia enthusiasts like Frank Snelling, in England. His exhibition plants have travelled widely to public displays. With Frank and his wife in attendance, many keen growers will have been able to learn about the techniques required to form and sustain such monsters. Branches on fans radiate from the base like the tail feathers of a peacock, unlike espaliers that have a vertical stem from which horizontal branches are trained like ladder rungs off a central stave. Ideally, both types of growth should give a semi-circular shape with a flat base. Fans, like espaliers, are two-dimensional.

The basic framework on which the fan's branches are tied is best made from plastic-covered metal piping, which will not rot. Cross-supports may be of wire with the exception of one firm support used to maintain the spread and shape. Shoots that appear from below ground level can be incorporated within the spread of the fan, unlike those that needed to be removed from standards. Side shoots are trained into the extra spaces as the branches rise and spread. Slow and steady growth is to be encouraged in order to avoid flowers appearing only on the outer limits of the branches. Fans need to be grown facing the available light and to be inspected periodically from behind to ensure cleanliness and shapeliness.

Mini-standards

Mini-standards are most often seen as a miniaturization of the standard form and, in fact, all of the ornamental shapes may be grown in scaled-down form so that they can be displayed on benches or within much smaller confines than their larger brethren. Clear stems

may range on these mini-standards from 15 cm to about 30 cm (6–12 in) according to individual competition rules. For show purposes (in the United Kingdom), classes requiring miniaturization usually have a pot size restriction of about 12.5 cm (5 in). Mini-standards are also fun to produce.

Encliandras like *F. obconica* make excellent subjects to learn on, because their natural habit is smaller and neater than that of many other fuchsias. As a rule, those fuchsias with smaller flowers, internodes and leaves are likely to make the best subjects for mini-standards.

One of the key elements in growing standards is that of proportion between the various parts. Large pots with small plants look as unsightly as those that appear top-heavy. Competitions frequently have classes for mini-standards. This is not to say that such plants cannot be displayed in many of the other competitive classes at the majority of venues. Novelty value, combined with extra height, will often give them a competitive advantage over shrubby fuchsias with larger flowers. At home, in the conservatory, they can look outstanding and attract much interest.

Bonsai

Root restriction is just one of the ways in which the keen grower seeks to limit the growth of bonsai plants. Fuchsias do not have a long history of being grown in bonsai form, but then Japan and its neighbours have short histories of fuchsia cultivation. Bonsai is a classical art form in which recognized, stylized shapes are created. It is steadily gaining popularity among fuchsia growers. There is also a gradual realization that this is not just a matter of miniaturizing or stunting fuchsia growth. Among those shapes which may be created are the following:

Bunjingi or literati – Trunks are grown at a slight incline, or upright, with branches only at the top.

Chokkan or formal upright – These have strong vertical trunks with branches arranged pyramidally and uniformly, except to the front.

Fukinagashi or windswept – Trunks are tilted at an angle with branches growing in one direction as if windswept.

Han-Kengai or semi-cascade – Growth is jutting as from a cliff, and not cascading downwards as from rocks.

Hokidachi or broom – An upright trunk carries fan-shaped branches like a besom.

Ishitsuki or rock clinging – The miniature tree grows above and on a rock with its roots clinging to it and reaching down into the soil.

Kengai or cascade – Trunks and branches hang over the edge of a pot that has been lifted for display purposes.

Moyogi or curved informal – The trunk winds in ever-diminishing curves towards its top.

Shakan or slanting – This style is like Fukinagashi (windswept), but the branches grow in any direction. Roots are exposed in the direction of incline.

Fig. 8 An established bonsai fuchsia.

Bonsai fuchsias are trained by using pliable wire to create the desired outline for the trunk and main branches. Scissors may be used to restrict the growth to the desired shape, and root pruning can be carried out once the main outline of the trunk and branches has been formed. Fuchsias may be grown out-of-doors for much of the year (even in the United Kingdom) but, unprotected, bonsai fuchsias are liable to be killed or damaged by hard frosts. Containers, too, must be frost-resistant if damage is not to occur accidentally when winter sets in. A wide range of suitable pans and pots is now available for serious bonsai fuchsia enthusiasts.

Watering should be undertaken with care and, because fuchsia roots are fibrous, plants should never be allowed to dry out completely. Dilute and evenly balanced fertilizer can be used occasionally to maintain the health of bonsai specimens. Attention must also be given to the control of pests and diseases, but there are no special factors that apply solely to bonsai fuchsias.

Topiary

Within Western civilization, topiary has played a greater part than bonsai, but it has been confined in the main to evergreen subjects growing permanently out-of-doors. There is no reason why ornamental shapes should not be created from plants like fuchsias, even grown in pots and tubs. The main restriction is one of available space during windy or cold spells. Miniaturization may be brought to this art-form, too. Stems and branches may be wired into the desired form. A framework may also be provided so that growth can be trained against it and held in place. Side shoots that are unwanted may be nipped out in the normal way to leave only those which contribute directly to the finished structure.

Shapes beloved of stately gardens are chess pieces, peacocks, bears and many other animals and birds. Simpler shapes include hoops, or circles, and globes. Limits to the number of possibilities are most often created by the gardener's mind rather than by the fuchsia's limitations. As with so many other ornamental shapes, encliandras are probably the best fuchsias to experiment with and frequently give the most satisfying results, in even the most experienced hands.

Pillars

Fuchsia pillars have usually been grown by one of two methods. The first requires that a single vertical stem is trained to the appropriate height. The second method uses two stems, the first used to form the lower half of the structure only, and the second to create only the top half. Side shoots are nipped to give a shape that resembles a large tube. Single stems are difficult to make evenly circular from bottom to top, but are slightly easier to manage overall. Double stems are used to create bottom and top halves separately. It is possible to make such pillars from two independent fuchsias planted next to each other, and to attach them to a central stake for

Fig. 9 Fuchsias in a garden setting. Standard fuchsias in urns; bushy plants overhang the wall, softening its outline to create a restful atmosphere.

TABLE OF THE BEST CULTIVARS

M	Mini-standards		E	Espaliers
$^1/_4$	Quarter-standards		F	Fans
$^1/_2$	Half-standards		B	Bonsai
FUL	Full standards		T	Topiary
XL	Extra Large Standards		P	Pillars
			PC	Pyramids and cones

NAME	M	$^1/_4$	$^1/_2$	FUL	XL	E	F	B	T	P	PC
Alice Hoffman	X	X						X			
Arabella Improved		X	X			X	X		X	X	X
Beacon Rosa			X	X				X			X
Celia Smedley			X	X	X						
Ernie Bromley				X				X		X	X
Eva Twaites	X					X	X	X	X	X	X
Fuchsiade '88						X	X	X	X	X	X
Fuksie Foetsie						X	X	X	X	X	
Grace Durham		X	X					X		X	
Hawkshead							X	X	X	X	
Jack Stanway			X	X			X	X		X	X
Lindisfarne		X	X	X				X		X	X
Mood Indigo						X	X		X		
Nellie Nuttall	X	X						X			
Obcylin						X	X	X	X		
Orwell	X	X						X		X	
Phyllis						X	X			X	X
Pink Rain						X	X		X	X	
Pumila	X	X	X					X			
Radings Karin	X					X	X	X	X	X	
Richard John		X	X			X		X		X	X
Shelford			X	X				X		X	X
Sir Alfred Ramsey			X	X	X					X	
Snowcap		X	X	X			X				
Waveney Sunrise				X	X		X				

support. Staking and tying for pillars are no different to the methods described for standards. The fact that James Lye and his son-in-law grew enormous pillars does not mean that today's grower has to do the same. Much smaller pillars may be grown and are equally attractive, if not so impressive. Pillars are three-dimensional structures and, like standards, are best displayed where they can be viewed from every direction. Wind is their major enemy, but they are less susceptible to damage than standards when placed in the garden as summer features.

A different sort of pillar may be made using lengths of pipe with holes cut in the sides. Plastic downpipes with a diameter of about 15 cm (6 in) are usually cut to about ten times this width and eventually fastened, in flower, against a wall or fence. The bottom of the pipe is stopped with plastic or marine ply. Plants are inserted through the holes in the side, into compost that has been firmed into position. The pillar is watered through the top of the pipe. It is sometimes thought wise to place a length of hosepipe down the centre; its lower end is stopped and small holes made along it allow water to seep freely into the surrounding compost. Plants like 'Daisy Bell' are suitable for such pillars.

Cones and Pyramids

Cones are rather similar to pillars except that they are wider at their bases and are gently tapered to their tops. Pyramids are cones with even wider bases. Their apices are as near to a point as it is possible to grow and the angle of their sides is tapered evenly from the base to the top. Pillars, cones and pyramids are all three-dimensional structures that appear symmetrical from all sides; all are suitable for growing in pots or tubs. The main stems of cones and pyramids are tied to a central stake and side shoots are nipped to create bushy growth and a symmetrical form. A slow and steady build-up to each framework is helped by regular turning of greenhouse plants, especially if they are in lean-to structures, and by a programme of balanced feeds. The wider base associated with cones and pyramids often creates difficulties with space, and may make large specimens difficult to handle and to move. However, miniaturization is possible with these shapes, too.

CHAPTER 7
Fuchsias in Conservatories and Greenhouses

During the early days of fuchsia culture, it was assumed, wrongly, that they were exotics, that stove-house conditions were required to keep them over winter and to grow them to their full potential. In the early days of the British Fuchsia Society, when poverty was rife and war was just around the corner, every effort was made to prove that fuchsias had a future as hardy garden perennials. Nowadays, we know that fuchsias are both versatile and tolerant but that maximum results can be obtained by providing optimum conditions at all times.

One of the key factors in greenhouse management is to obtain as much light as possible during the darker months. Glazing-bar width is a significant feature that affects the availability of light reaching plants grown under glass. Modern aluminium greenhouses are likely to have the smallest glazing bars and therefore the highest light levels. Fuchsias are sensitive to light intensity when they grow, as all plants with chlorophyll must be, but their flowering is affected most by the length of day.

The ideal greenhouses for fuchsias have a door at each end to allow ventilation during warm spells, as well as access. Sliding doors are probably more popular than those on hinges, as they can be adjusted easily to avoid undue draughts and do not run the risk of slamming in the wind. Summer temperatures can rise to unbearable levels, especially if the floor is concrete, and this will also make it very difficult to maintain humid conditions.

While acknowledging that adequate ventilation is essential, it is also true to say that draughts can damage plants situated near side windows. A wide range of automatic vents can be fitted to roof windows, so that they open as temperatures rise above predetermined levels and close when colder conditions prevail. They work by changing pressure within a cylinder and may have one arm or two. It is essential that they are robust enough to prevent wind getting under the bottom and forcing the window to open suddenly.

A number of books suggest that greenhouses in the United Kingdom are best sited so that they run lengthways from north to south. In practice, for fuchsia growing, there appears to be little benefit in this and they are often situated from east to west. Other factors, such as heavy shade from trees and buildings, appear to be much more significant, for good or bad, in greenhouse siting anywhere in the world.

Sherman (1981) writes of cold spots in the greenhouse and relates them to humidity levels. Cold spots most obviously occur next to glass and where air movement is restricted in heated greenhouses. Draughts are much less obvious and can arise from loose-fitting windows, structural defects and gaps around doors. Some fuchsias, such as 'Pixie' and 'Marinka', show leaf reddening when they are affected by cold and draughts. These fuchsias are useful as marker plants around the greenhouse so that problem areas can be pinpointed and dealt with.

One way of combating draughts is to fix polythene sheeting to the inside of the greenhouse. Most types of sheeting consist of three layers, and are used not only to reduce incoming light but also to save on heating bills. The best polythene to use is that treated to withstand the sun's rays (ultraviolet-light resistant, or UVL). In commercial greenhouses, bubble plastic is used on a much wider scale than ordinary plastic sheeting and it, too, is available in UVL-resistant form. It is relatively easy to fix the sheeting to the inside of greenhouses as, for aluminium glasshouses, there are clips to speed and simplify the job. Joints can be sealed using special tape produced for the purpose. Fixing in place 2.54 cm (1 in) or 5.8 cm (2 in) polystyrene boards can help insulation around the base of the greenhouse.

Mobile screens can reduce heating costs at night, when they will not affect available light levels, and are also useful during the days when excessive heat is a problem and light levels are at their greatest. Mobile screens act by reducing the physical area to be heated and by slowing the loss of heat upwards into the top of the greenhouse. They are usually situated a short distance above the fuchsias and can be made from a variety of different substances. The cost of such products needs to be considered against any savings in money and plant damage that they can make in their lifetime.

Colours can play a part in greenhouse temperatures. Dark peat beds can absorb warmth during daylight hours in the winter and, acting like storage heaters, will release this heat slowly during the night. Many fuchsia growers have made use of greenhouse whitening, painted on the inside or outside of the glass, during the longest and hottest days. Green net shading seems to be most effective when fastened to the outside of greenhouses, with a space left between it and the glass. It is difficult, however, to erect and to remove. Wind can cause problems with it, too.

Benches are generally covered to protect them from the large amounts of water used on growing fuchsias. Polythene sheeting should be thick enough to accept some wear without frequent punctures. Sharp sand or gravel are often placed on top of this, and they can be wetted during hot weather, thus raising air humidity around the fuchsia foliage. Specially manufactured capillary mats can also be used to help raise air and plant moisture levels, and in order to reduce watering.

Humidity within the fuchsia greenhouse is relative to temperature. Warm air has a greater moisture-carrying capacity than its colder counterpart. Sherman (1981) explains the phenomenon succinctly. One cubic metre of air with a temperature of 10°C (50°F) has a relative humidity level of 50 per cent; when its temperature is reduced to 0°C (32°F), its relative humidity rises to 94 per cent, or nearly fully saturated. Evaporation soon ceases, even from the plants, and condensation forms. As temperatures rise in this same greenhouse, relative humidity drops and evaporation from the fuchsia leaves increases. Increased evaporation leads to greater heat transference. Keen gardeners or commercial growers can study the practical implications of these facts once they have acquired a humidity gauge. It will be found that the majority of fuchsias prefer temperatures around 13°C (55°F) with a relative humidity of around 56 per cent. There are, however, exceptions to this rule, like

F. triphylla and some of its hybrids that prefer warmer temperatures and lower humidity levels. This also seems to be the case for a few other species, such as F. lycioides and F. magdalenae.

As with humidity, temperatures are always relative. Attention should be paid to temperatures, and it is therefore important to buy an accurate thermometer and site it carefully within glasshouses. If it is to register effectively, it is best sited at, or just above, plant level and where sunlight cannot rest on it. Most fuchsia growers have little idea what the temperature in their greenhouse is at the hottest part of the day and even less about the lowest levels at the nadir of the night. It is best to buy a maximum and minimum thermometer that will register the extremes of temperature and can be reset every day to supply fresh readings. They give a useful guide to trends in temperature. The information they provide cannot be acted upon immediately, but the data can then be used to plan the supply of heat and shade, for example.

Though the majority of fuchsias prefer temperatures of around 13°C (55°F), the optimum temperature for cuttings and triphyllas is slightly higher at 18°C (64°F). Thermostatic control is essential to the effective use of resources and to minimize costs. Electric thermostats, easily obtained, are ideal to control and operate almost any type of heating system of any size running on just about any fuel. They eliminate waste by ensuring that heat is generated only when needed. For this reason, it is usually wise to site a greenhouse near to your home, so that electricity can be supplied with the minimum of cost and effort.

Undersoil heating is probably the most effective for fuchsia growing. Warmth is thus greatest where it is needed most, at root level. This warmth rises around the leaves and helps to evaporate moisture from the foliage, maximizing growth rates. Tubular heaters, like the hot water pipe systems of old, work mainly by convection. Cables and hot sheets also provide this rising warmth, as do bed systems like those used for propagating, which act rather like storage heaters.

Fuchsias prefer a relatively dry atmosphere during the darkest and coldest months. They also prefer moving air, best supplied by electric fans; these should be placed so that they do not blow air directly across the fuchsia foliage. In the case of amateurs' greenhouses, small fan units are best placed below the greenhouse bench, to one side of the door and angled so that air is deflected off the glasshouse walls. Careful siting and the deliberate production of turbulence can help to prevent cold microclimates developing within an otherwise controlled environment. In commercial terms, oil burners attached to fans, which circulate dry air from polythene pipes situated at ground level, give ideal results. These units can be adapted to the use of gas with similar results. Small paraffin burners giving heat by convection raise humidity levels too much to be suitable for fuchsias: they tend to shorten internodal growth and to reduce leaf size.

There is little point in heating a greenhouse efficiently if the heat is to be drained from its outer surface by cold winds. This is the 'wind-chill factor' and is of great horticultural importance. Lining the inside of the glass can help to preserve heat but, out-of-doors, windbreaks are helpful. Solid windbreaks, like fences and walls, will provide some protection, but the best windbreaks make no attempt to stop wind. Instead, they concentrate on reducing its force to an acceptable level. Their object is to filter and slow its onward rush.

Horticulturists and farmers have used live windbreaks for many years. The best windbreak plant for commercial nurseries that concentrate on fuchsias is the hornbeam. It is relatively quick-growing, almost free from pests and diseases, easy to clip and deciduous. Such hedges can be clipped to just above the eaves of greenhouses next to them. Wind will then be forced to rise with the angle of the roof. Artificial windbreaks can be expensive to install and will require regular maintenance to keep them in good order. The subject of windbreaks has been dealt with by the Ministry of Agriculture, Fisheries and Food (1985) in their publication *Windbreaks for Horticulture.*

In many nurseries, as well as in amateurs' gardens, shade houses are erected to protect fuchsias from excessive heat and light. In the United Kingdom, which has an unpredictable climate, these can be a mixed blessing. Fuchsias grow best when they are given dappled but clear light, and long days. It may be that houses constructed from shade netting are of value only for limited periods, and that expenditure on them is of doubtful value. Most shade houses have about 40 per cent netting, as too much can cause etiolation among the plants. Ideally, netting should be easily removed (rolled or slid to one side) if prolonged spells of dark, cold or wet weather persist.

Conservatories are rarely ideal for fuchsias, or any other plant. Those sited on the south of houses in England are likely to be too hot for much of the year. North-facing ones are likely to provide inadequate light during the winter months. East-facing structures are likely to pick up the heat of early morning sun; this can burn the leaves where guttation has occurred during the night. West-facing conservatories are usually best, although they are often too hot to be perfect.

A number of other factors are important when growing fuchsias in conservatories. Firstly, they are designed for people rather than plants. Their ventilation is usually inadequate for plants and their atmospheres much too dry. Shading can be difficult to erect and manipulate if plants are present. Blinds are easier to install than shade netting if conservatories are constructed from aluminium rather than timber. Conservatories are more like lean-to greenhouses; their light is directional rather than multi-directional. Temperatures will almost certainly rise to unacceptably high levels during the summer months; few fuchsias are able to cope with temperatures above 27°C (81°F) over protracted periods. Lastly, the type of flooring and heating present can prove important if humidity levels are to be raised in bright, hot weather.

Central-heating controls may not provide the precise winter heat required in a conservatory: it is often best to use a fan heater in order to circulate the air and to obtain the correct temperature. Electrical safety is one of the key features where plants are being watered and cared for. Special equipment is easily purchased in order to provide safe and efficient growing conditions. Air-conditioning units are easily available. They can be used during hot summer spells to reduce conservatory temperatures to more acceptable levels for the fuchsias without the need to open windows. This last point can be of great importance when fuchsias are left for several days unattended and when household security is of paramount importance.

Fuchsias can be placed in large tubs or pots on the conservatory floor. Staging, either a simple bench or tiered benching, can be erected to bring them to a more acceptable level if they are in smaller pots. Hanging containers can be placed on the house wall as long as its temperatures do not become extreme. Ideally, fuchsias should be placed out-of-doors during warm and settled weather: the conservatory will become their base at night and during inclement weather.

Special care is required to control diseases and pests in conservatories. Spraying, or smoking with chemicals, is to be avoided if at all possible. Pot fuchsias can be dipped to apply fungicides, using protective gloves. Natural predators are the best means of controlling pests like whitefly and red spider mite. This subject is dealt with in more detail in Chapter 15 of this book.

Four categories of fuchsias lend themselves to being grown in conservatories and greenhouses. Each has a special niche to fill. Encliandras, with their fine, fern-like foliage and predominance of winter blooms, are easy to manage in small pots. Paniculates lend themselves to being grown in much larger pots and often provide statuesque specimens that can be placed on the floor. Triphyllas are more heat-tolerant and exotic-looking than many other summer-flowering fuchsias. Finally, a number of other fuchsias, especially those with upward- and outward-pointing blooms, are also relatively heat and drought-tolerant. The following is a short list of recommended cultivars in each of these categories. Full details of these are not given here as they appear elsewhere in their appropriate chapters in this book.

Encliandras: 'Bryan Breary', 'Eva Twaites', 'Fuksie Foetsie', 'Katinka', 'Obcylin', 'Prove Thyself'.
Paniculates: 'Dymph Werker van Groenland', 'Grietje', 'Martin's Inspiration', 'Ton Goedman', 'Trientje'.
Triphyllas: 'Adinda', 'Bessie Kimberley', 'Boy Mark', 'Brighton Belle', 'Insulinde', 'Leverkusen', 'Monica Dare', 'Timothy Titus'.
Others (heat-resistant): 'Anjo', 'Big Slim', 'Mary Fairclo', 'Nettala', 'Pink Fantasia', 'Rose Fantasia', 'Walz Jubelteen'.

This chapter has concentrated on showing ways in which fuchsia growers can control environments, like those in conservatories and greenhouses, more effectively. By encouraging a careful examination of all the factors affecting plant growth, we can see how cost and performance levels might be improved. An intensive study of some of the more difficult fuchsias will show that their special needs have to be understood properly before they can be met efficiently.

> **Note:** Temperature conversion methods are as follows:
>
> Fahrenheit to Celsius (Centigrade), °F = (°C × 1.8) + 32.
>
> Celsius (Centigrade) to Fahrenheit, °C = (°F − 32) ÷ 1.8.

CHAPTER 8
Baskets and Containers

An assessment of the fuchsia market shows that sales have increased steadily over many years, and in many parts of the world, relative to other plants. It seems also that the percentage of fuchsias used in baskets has risen steeply in relation to those used for other purposes. These changes have not come about by accident and it is the purpose of this chapter to examine some of the benefits derived from displaying fuchsias in hanging containers.

The first and most obvious reason why fuchsias look so good in baskets and wall containers is that their blooms hang by pedicels from the branches. Plants whose flowers droop in this way may seem to be at a disadvantage when used for summer bedding or for permanent planting in the garden, but many plants, including fuchsias, do not do themselves justice until they are seen above eye-level.

As world population levels have risen, so, in consequence, has the size of the average dwelling house increased and the accompanying garden declined. With this trend, the garden has become more an extension to the house than a place for growing vegetables and taking relaxing walks. Patios and yards may be covered with pergolas, and plants may be containerized because the latter are seen as a disposable and renewable resource. A greater element of fashion and display has entered our gardening world.

One trend in gardening that is not often discussed is that of highlighting small areas for maximum impact. The idea that every part of a large garden should be decorated equally well, or badly, has taken a long time to die. With the concept of highlights comes the realization that eyesores such as manhole covers need not necessarily be hidden. It becomes obvious that, if enough impact is created elsewhere, people's eyes can be drawn towards more attractive features such as hanging baskets.

Fuchsias have exceptionally long flowering seasons in comparison to most other garden plants. With greenhouse care, and a catholic choice of cultivars, flowers may be obtained for the full twelve months of every year. Hanging containers can be used in the modern conservatory as well as outside in the garden. They may also be moved at will to avoid excessive heat and wind, or to create an element of change and variety. If a basket is damaged, does not live up to expectations, or is otherwise unwanted, a new one can be used to replace it. This is a positive advantage to those who have one half of their garden in deep shade and the other half in intense sun; plants may be exchanged periodically between the two different environments to the benefit of them all.

Basket shapes are important. Fully round baskets are at a major disadvantage when they stand on a greenhouse bench or on the ground because of their instability. It is frequently difficult to grow fuchsias in the smallest ones, because they are prone to dry out too fast. Those that are about 30 cm (12 in) or more in diameter provide the best results. Baskets with flat bases make better sense; they are easier to handle, but they usually require more compost to fill them. For the average amateur fuchsia grower, they are easier to line and to make attractive when in flower, but for the commercial grower who has large numbers of them made up for sale, there may be a significant increase in costs.

Half-round, or wall baskets are equally popular with the gardening public. Those with rounded bases are more difficult to stand upright than their flat-based counterparts and are frequently too small to do justice to the fuchsias growing in them, while the flat-based baskets are usually easier to manage. They, too, are much easier to line attractively than their rounded counterparts. Watering can make baskets and half baskets much too heavy to handle, for diameters exceeding 38 cm (15 in); the strain on brackets and wall fixings needs consideration.

Galvanized wire baskets have been used for many years and are generally less attractive than their plastic, or plastic-covered, alternatives.

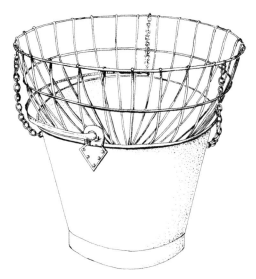

Fig. 10 Preparing a fully round basket for planting. The basket is placed in the top of a bucket to stabilize it.

They look best lined with moss. Plastic-covered wire helps to prevent rusting and prolongs the life of baskets. Hanging containers need not be round. Square ones are often made from wooden splines wired together at each corner and around the bottom. Spaces between the battens give the appearance of split rail fences and add a rustic look to the finished article.

The majority of hanging baskets are suspended by chains. Each year before planting, attention should be given to their condition. Doubtful ones are best replaced. The three or four chains attached to most baskets are fastened at the top with a large ring. There are advantages in attaching a swivel to this so that the basket can be rotated. Spent seed pods, discoloured leaves and diseases or pests can be dealt with much more easily if the basket can be turned once it has been hung. Many fuchsia growers attach a split cane to each chain, so that tripods of canes prevent the chains from collapsing on to the plants when the baskets are lowered from their hooks. Wires can be attached around the chains so that they support branches, and the centres of baskets may be built up until they are hidden by foliage and flowers.

Where moss is unobtainable or undesirable, alternatives will be needed to line all except the solid baskets. Sometimes linings are made from pressed fibre and sold commercially to fit certain sizes of basket. Alternatively, try netting such as

that used for sprout bags or greenhouse shading. This can be cheap as well as unobtrusive. The majority of baskets will also benefit from having a plastic lining placed inside the outer one. This needs to be perforated to avoid waterlogging of the compost, but is useful in reducing unnecessary water loss from the side of the basket.

Baskets and wall baskets can be very heavy if filled with soil-based composts. Soil-less types are more common, but the weight of flowers and water can be surprisingly high even with these. As a rule it is best to use heavier composts in containers at, or near, ground level. Lighter ones come into their own for hanging baskets. When fully rounded baskets are being made up, the chains are best laid to one side. The lining can then be placed in position prior to filling with moist compost. Overfilling should be avoided, in order to provide room for the plants and for subsequent watering. Bushy fuchsias may be removed from their pots and placed around the periphery of the basket at intervals of 10 cm (4 in) to 15 cm (6 in). Some growers place a further fuchsia in the basket's centre, but the disadvantage of this is that it reduces air movement across the young foliage just when it is most prone to fungal diseases. Once a basket has been filled, and any surplus lining material has been trimmed away, it can be hung in position on its swivel. (The ways in which bushy growth can be promoted have been discussed in Chapter 4.) Nipping need not cease when fuchsias are removed from their pots and planted into baskets. Further stopping will help to produce a better shape, more branches and extra flowers.

Sometimes, it is helpful if branches are left to elongate before they are tied into position to fill gaps, and then nipped to promote side shoots. Pegs and canes can be used in the early stages to give a perfect outline to the main branches. These artificial supports can be removed once the stems have matured and stiffened. Stopping dates are given in this book with each cultivar that is listed, and these apply as much to basket fuchsias as to pot-grown ones. They become most important when bearing show dates in mind, with their need for a large flush of bloom.

During the summer months, it can be quite difficult to water baskets with a can without causing damage to the foliage. The majority of growers will find it easier to let fully formed baskets soak up liquid feed by placing them in a bucket for about ten minutes. Feeling the weight of a basket gives a useful guide as to when water is needed and, in the hands of the more experienced gardener, is better than feeling the compost surface.

An idea that could be of considerable help to the elderly or disabled gardener is that of fixing a line and pulley to baskets, so that they can be lowered and soaked before being drained and hung in position again. Retaining lines must be robust enough to take the weight involved without fraying or breaking. They are fastened to the top of each basket and over a pulley before being held to one side by a retaining hook. Lines continue almost to ground level where they are looped over further retaining hooks. To avoid baskets damaging themselves as they rotate in the wind, it is wise to attach a wire or cord to each one. This can then be fastened to the wall nearby and only detached when watering takes place.

Cold nights, and the onset of frosts, will persuade fuchsia enthusiasts that it is time to remove hanging baskets from the garden. When they have been pruned halfway back and have been defoliated, they can be brought under cover for frost protection. If they are to be retained and grown on for a further year, basket fuchsias must have their roots kept slightly moist so that they can remain alive but dormant.

The drawback with overwintered plants is that pests and diseases may be overwintered on them and in their soil. Even vine weevil, unable as it is to fly, seems able to attack basket fuchsias. To avoid such problems, many gardeners empty their baskets each year and replant with fresh material at the start of a new season.

The first and most important point to note when training basket fuchsias for competition is that there is no quick way to obtain the best results. Large baskets will often take much more than a year to build a sturdy framework capable of holding the immense weight of bloom required. The process can be helped somewhat by wiring split canes to the support wires and by ringing through the chains at several levels with wire, as already discussed. Some of the branches may be tied to these supports and then allowed to produce side shoots. The aim is to make the basket look as if it had in it only one large plant that will hang in flower sufficiently well to hide the basket when viewed from one side. Obviously, some fuchsias are more suitable than

Fig. 11 A fully round basket planted up. Note that the centre of the basket is left open to prevent botritis in the young, sappy growth.

others for this purpose. In view of the fact that in some shows full baskets are staged on stands rather than hung from a suitable rack, it is important to see that the centre of a basket will not collapse when it is not hung.

Another idea worth developing is to protect the rim of the basket so that branches in flower, which rest or rub on it, will not spoil or break. Sometimes the top of the basket is wrapped with thick tape or covered with small-bore black pipe lagging. A thick layer of moss is often used for the same purpose. Large baskets are awkward to carry and to transport to shows. It sometimes requires two people to carry them, hung from a pole. Inside a van they can be placed in large bowls filled with wet sand or hung from support wires.

Extra-large baskets can be raised over a period of three years and these will make splendid examples for exhibition. In the first year a 20-cm (approx. 8-in) hanging pot is planted with three fuchsias around its periphery, nipped and grown on to flower. At the end of the season the fuchsias are pruned back as if they were bush plants, so that they have a strong and healthy framework without any overlapping branches. These plants are started into regrowth at the beginning of the next season and are placed, without breaking the root ball, into the centre of a 30.5-cm (12-in) hanging basket. The season is also used for the process of tying-in and stopping so that a strong framework of branches is built up in a symmetrical way. At the end of this second year the plants are pruned, but more lightly than before. In its third year the basket is again brought back into growth before being placed at the centre of a 38-cm (15-in) basket. Feeding and nipping are continued in order to build up the size of the total structure. All nipping ceases in time for flowers to be produced in great abundance on the show date. The same basket can then be used for a further two or three years before its quality starts to decline. Care over cleanliness and the regular use of pesticides will help to keep problems at bay.

I suggest the following as the 'Top Ten' fuchsias for basket work and exhibition (in alphabetical order):

'Arabella Improved'
'Ernie Bromley'
'Jack Acland'
'Jack Stanway'
'Lena'
'Marinka'
'Richard John'
'Seventh Heaven'
'Susan Green'
'Sylvia Barker'

There was a time when plastic in the garden was frowned on by many gardeners, but not any more. Hanging pots have made a tremendous impact on the fuchsia-growing scene and on gardening in general. Most of them come complete with a press-on saucer that can be detached in the early stages to prevent overwatering; its usefulness increases later in the life of the plants. The best-known of the two commonly used sizes is the 20-cm (approx. 8-in) hanging pot. A smaller version suits some of those fuchsias that grow less strongly or that require less root space, such as the encliandras and other miniatures. These hanging pots measure 15 cm (6 in) in diameter. Plastic clip-on hangers are used with these, instead of chains, which have the advantage that they maintain their pyramidal shape when taken from the hooks on which they are usually hung.

There is no need to use a special compost; most growers find soil-less products are the best. This is especially so if they are of an open and oxygen-rich texture. The centre of the pot is filled with compost and dished to prevent water running off too easily. Cuttings or small plants are placed at the edge of each hanging pot. Some people place these, one behind each hanger, while others put them midway between them. There seems to be little difference between the two methods, even from the point of view of competitions. It helps if the plants are placed high in the fresh compost at first, as this reduces losses due to fungal infections.

Early in the life of a hanging pot it is easy to overwater. Moist compost should be used to fill the pot before planting. Some growers dip the base of the pot into a bucket of water so that some moisture is absorbed via its holes and this is a good way to deal with large and well-grown hanging pots in order to avoid damage to the foliage and flowers. Stopping may be carried out as if the hanging pot were a single bushy fuchsia with an open centre. The tendency to let branches grow leggy and then to nip them should be avoided: it is better to nip well at first and then to let the outer branches look longer and more natural. Liquid feeding may be carried out, a little and often, as the compost dries out. The removal of dying flowers and seedpods will help to preserve fuchsias in active growth.

Among the interesting innovations that have appeared in recent years is the proprietary hanging product 'Pocket Garden', made from twin-walled polycarbonate which has been UVL- (ultraviolet light-) protected. It looks like a flat-backed hanging pipe with a triangular front rather than a half-round one. Little fold-in flaps provide spaces for planting fuchsias and help to keep the compost in place. Watering is usually carried out via the 'Pocket Garden's' open top. These containers are rather more difficult to water and maintain than hanging pots, but their unusual appearance makes up for this. They are also much more robust and long-lasting than their appearance would suggest.

Pergolas and covered walks used to be very popular and have become so again; the difference is in the plants that are used to deck them. Formerly, climbing plants like roses and clematis would have vied for space with subjects like wisteria and laburnum in such a setting. These may still be used, but they are likely to be supplemented with hanging pots and baskets of flowering plants like fuchsias. With such structures it is not essential that all the fuchsias are in baskets. Sometimes, pot-hangers fastened to the upright posts can hold fuchsias in flower, giving an effect similar to that of pillars.

Fig. 12 Pergola. Half-barrels can provide an ideal home for shrubby fuchsias. Hanging baskets provide extra height and interest to lighten otherwise bare surroundings.

It is common, and probably desirable, to use only one cultivar when planting hanging pots and baskets for show purposes. This creates a positive impact and appears less fussy than a haphazard mixture of blooms. Sometimes, by careful selection, two different fuchsias may be combined to great effect – for example 'Pink Marshmallow' and 'Haute Cuisine'. The former is a pale and fluffy pink while the latter is dark aubergine; both are doubles. Another idea that has steadily gained ground, especially when fuchsias are grown for garden displays rather than for competition, is to plant encliandras among the other fuchsias. They take the place of lobelia, which often looks drab late in the flowering season, and provide a filmy fern-like background that never overpowers the main subject in a basket.

Tubs and containers are now used extensively to add impact to garden displays. They are especially useful for patio layouts and come in a wide range of materials, sizes, shapes, styles and prices. Some of the smallest ones are not really ideal because they dry out too quickly. Large tubs are easier to maintain and fuchsias tend to grow best in them. Stone, stone substitutes, concrete, fibreglass, plastic, earthenware, glazed pottery and wood are all available and frequently seen. Products made from concrete may look harsh: it is sometimes worthwhile painting their exteriors with full-fat milk to encourage lichen to form and mellow their appearance. Wooden tubs need to be treated regularly with preservative. This should be chosen carefully to avoid damage to plants; creosote is lethal when it has just been applied.

Plastic and fibreglass containers tend to become too hot for fuchsias when they are placed in sunny positions. Equally, where frost is likely, they offer little protection unless precautionary steps are taken before planting. The most suitable material to offer some insulation with the minimum of bulk appears to be thin and flexible polystyrene sheeting. Another approach is to place fuchsias into a large pot, which is then placed within an outer tub. The space between the two is filled with polystyrene chips or vermiculite. As well as insulating the plants, this allows them to be removed each autumn, in their pots, and replaced by others like pansies, ivies and bulbs that provide an interest throughout the darker days.

Large tubs planted with bushy plants often seem to lack sufficient height at their centre. Small standard fuchsias can create a dot-plant effect and improve things considerably. Fan fuchsias can be used instead, if tubs are placed next to garden walls or fences. When they are in hot positions, it might be necessary to leave a space behind them, in order to reduce any reflected heat and so avoid damaging the fuchsias severely. One of the beauties of fuchsias, when compared with the majority of other plants used in containers, is that they may be chosen to cover the edges of tubs in a gentle and unobtrusive way. There is none of that harshness associated with many summer bedding subjects. Even when fuchsias are used with other plants, they tend to give displays a more restful and satisfying appearance.

Fuchsias grown in bottles can look attractive and unusual. Small-flowered types like 'La Campanella' or 'Zulu Queen' tend to do best when planted in such oddities. It is possible to buy bottle cutters, which will provide holes through which to place the compost and cuttings. The bottles are usually watered through their necks. In order to prevent the bottle from falling when it is hung up, it may be best to fold the wire in half, leaving a loop above the bottle neck. Run the two ends down inside the bottle to emerge from the holes made at the bottom for the

Fig. 13 A fuchsia growing in a hanging bottle. Careful preparation and assiduous after-care ensure attractive garden features.

fuchsia plants. The ends can be turned to avoid the wire pulling out. Sturdy wire is required to hold the weight. Fuchsias in bottles should be treated in the same way as any other pot- or container-grown plant. Liquid feeds and regular early stopping will help to make them more attractive. Dark glass is desirable to prevent green algae forming in the compost around the roots.

Plastic pipes are the ones most often used for creating pillars. It is usually best to plant the fuchsias and grow them for several weeks in a horizontal position before they are raised vertically. They could equally be kept supported in a horizontal position by gutter brackets. Watering is best done via a funnel through the top when vertical, or through smaller holes in the side when horizontal.

Ornamental chimneys make ideal containers

Fig. 14 An interesting container with its fuchsia.

and they are still available in a wide variety of shapes and sizes. Because of the limitations on their bore (tall but narrow), it is usual to place them out of the direct wind and sun, and to use only one strong-growing cultivar in each. Another novelty item to fill with fuchsias, which has gained popularity in recent years, is the ornamental chamber pot or bedpan. Many of these carry elaborate designs: there are unlikely to be many gardens using identical pots. Colanders can also be turned into interesting plant holders. They look best if they are painted attractively before being planted up. They can be treated like hanging baskets, with more holes drilled near their top rims and chains attached from which to hang them. There are bound to be yet other quirky containers which will add novelty to garden displays.

Window-boxes were all the rage in Victorian and Edwardian times. Today they are all too often underused and undervalued. Wooden troughs are easily made and maintained. They will last for many years if drainage holes are drilled in their bases, and they are treated regularly with a preservative (one that is harmless to plants). Fibreglass, plastic, concrete and other substances are used as commercial alternatives. Even plastic growbags may be used if there is adequate space for them.

Older houses frequently have wide windowsills that will support troughs without difficulty. If you use one for this purpose, it is wise to place small wooden splines under the window-boxes to allow the troughs to drain. Soil-less composts can sometimes prove too light to keep plants stable. Stones can be placed in the bottom of the boxes before filling them with a soil-based compost.

Because wind can be so troublesome around the edges of buildings, it may be necessary to fix such troughs with hooks and wires, to prevent accidents. Troughs have one major advantage, however: they can be seen from inside the house as well as from outside. If windowsills are too narrow, or non-existent, strong brackets may be fastened firmly to the wall just below the window where they will provide more-than-adequate substitutes.

As we have seen, hanging containers provide excellent settings for fuchsias, both for garden displays and for exhibition. Floor-standing fuchsias can enhance tubs and many other containers. Their graceful pendant flowering habit adds beauty to the most unlikely settings. A vivid imagination, combined with a practical application, can provide stunning effects with fuchsias using the most meagre of resources.

Methods of growing and displaying fuchsias in baskets have been dealt with. The rest of this chapter is devoted to a list of those fuchsias that are best suited for hanging containers, where their blooms are shown to advantage. I have made a selection from the best of those which are currently available: these are the fuchsias which give the widest possible colour range and which provide the most flowers for the least effort. Spreading or pendant fuchsias must have many of those features that are essential in other successful fuchsias.

Fig. 15 A classic container. An example of the many large ornamental containers ideally suited to growing and displaying fuchsias.

The most significant growth factors in basket fuchsias are a self-branching habit and a robustness that allows them to cope with a wide range of weather. It is also essential that the internodes are not too long and that growth is not brittle. Features such as frost-resistance are not considered important but heat- and wind-tolerance are vital to a basket fuchsia's success in the garden.

'Abigail' (Springer 1988) Single. The tubes and spreading sepals are pale pink. Corollas are saucer-shaped and pansy-eyed; white and violet. Growth is spreading but self-branching. 'Abigail' is best grown and displayed in hanging pots in sheltered positions where the colours are brightest. Ten weeks.

'Alison Ruth Griffin' (Gouldings Fuchsias 2000) Double. Tubes and sepals are pale pink; the latter spread and twist horizontally. Corollas are pastel ɔink; four spreading clusters surround the central pendant petals. Growth is strong and self-branching; best in large baskets. Eleven weeks.

'Anne Strudwick' (Gouldings Fuchsias 1998) Double. This cultivar's tubes are short and, like the arching sepals, pale salmon in colour. Corollas are marbled in shades of dark and light salmon. Growth is spreading and amenable; best displayed in sheltered areas of the garden in wall baskets. Eleven weeks.

'Ann Roots' (Gouldings Fuchsias 1991) Single. Its spreading sepals and shorter tubes are cream-coloured with red stripes. Big, bell-shaped corollas have wavy edges and are pale lavender in hue. Spreading and elegant branches make this fuchsia suitable for large baskets. Ten weeks.

'Applause' (Stubbs 1978) Double. Tubes and flyaway sepals are coloured flesh pink. Its full corollas are salmon pink. Growth is spreading, sturdy and suitable for large baskets or tubs. The full beauty of its colours develops when protection is given against wind and sun. Eleven weeks.

'Arabella Improved' (Lye 1871) Single; typical of the Lye type. Short sepals and longer tubes are creamy white. They contrast well with the rosy red of the petals. 'Arabella Improved' has vigorous, bushy and arching branches that suit it for large, fully round baskets. Nine weeks.

'Audrey Booth' (Gouldings Fuchsias 1995) Double. 'Audrey Booth' has pale pink tubes and sepals. The corollas are a darker shade of pink and are substantial in size and texture. Branches are strong and arching. Most suitable for garden display in large fully round or half-baskets. Twelve weeks.

'Barry M. Cox' (Gouldings Fuchsias 1994) Single. This fuchsia has white tubes and fully recurving white sepals. Its corollas are bright red. This floriferous plant has extremely strong growth; robust and pendant. It is easily shaped for shows, doing especially well in wall baskets. Nine weeks.

'Bella Rozella' (Garrett 1989) Double. The tubes and fully recurved sepals are pale pink. Each corolla has magenta-coloured petals. Buds are lanceolate. Its habit is spreading, and the weight of blooms lowers the branches even further. 'Bella Rozella' looks best in hanging baskets. Ten weeks.

'Ben Jiggins' (Gouldings Fuchsias 2000) Double. Tubes are short and rosy red. Sepals are horizontal with upturned (steer-horn) tips; also rosy red. The corollas are substantial; their petals are lilac with rosy red marbling. Growth is strong, self-branching and looks best in large baskets. Twelve weeks.

'Betty Jean' (Gouldings Fuchsias 1998) Double. The tubes are white, as are the horizontally flared sepals when mature. Its double corollas are lavender blue with pink marbling. Multiflowered. Growth is evenly self-branching and spreading. It is at its best in large baskets. Eleven weeks.

'Bicentennial' (Paskesen 1976) Double. 'Bicentennial' has white tubes and sepals that mature to orange. Its corollas are magenta and orange. The leaves have a slight orange cast. Growth is arching and responds best to warm and sheltered positions. Mixed planting suits this one. Ten weeks.

'Big Charles' (Moerman 1988) Double. Long, very thin, tubes and shorter arched sepals are white with a hint of pink. 'Big Charles' has corollas that are fully ruffled with mauve and pink petals. Growth is spreading or pendant in flower and most suitable for hanging pots. Twelve weeks.

PLATE I 'Misty Morn'

F. 'Tricolor'
Alison M. Jones

PLATE II 'Tricolor'

PLATE III 'Northern Pride'

F. 'Maori Pipes'
Alison P. Jones

PLATE IV 'Maori Pipes'

F. 'Constable
Country'
Alison M. Jones

PLATE V 'Constable Country'

F. 'Plumb-bob'
Alison M. Jones

PLATE VI 'Plumb-bob'

PLATE VII 'Gerharda's Aubergine'

F. 'Lancelot'
Alison M. Jones

PLATE VIII 'Lancelot'

PLATE IX 'Edwin J. Goulding'

PLATE X 'Linda Goulding'

PLATE XI 'Miep Aalhuizen'

PLATE XII *F. procumbens*

1 *F. cylindracea* ♂   2 *F. cylindracea* ♀

3 *F. thymifolia* subsp. *thymifolia*

4 *F. dependens*

5 *F. gehrigeri*

6 *F. magdalenae*

7 *F. pallescens*

8 *F. sanctae-rosae*

9 *F. scabriuscula*

10 *F. steyermarkii*

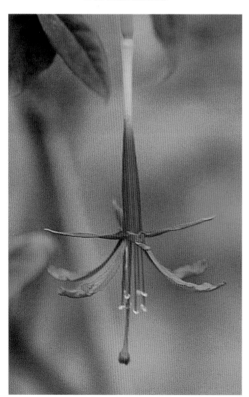

11 *F. venusta*

12 *F. apetala*

13 *F. insignis*

14 *F. juntasensis*

15 *F. pilaloensis*

16 *F. tilletiana*

17 *F. jimenezii*

18 *F. lycioides*

19 *F. excorticata*

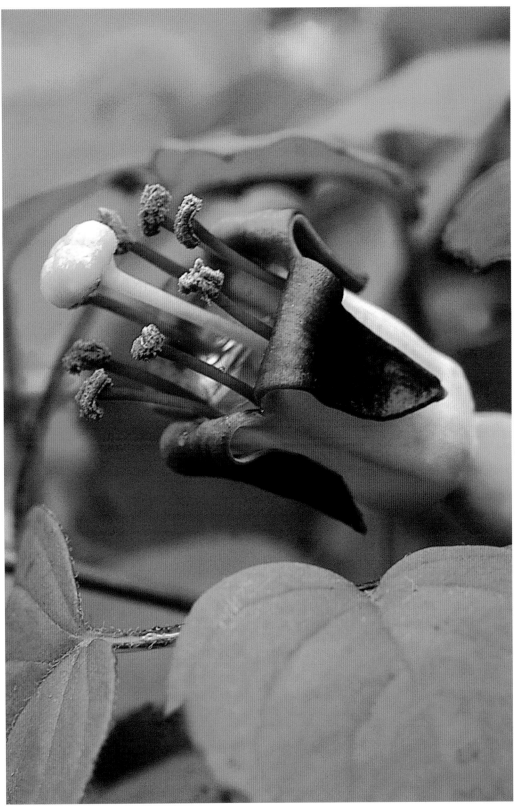

20 *F. procumbens*

21 'Ben Jammin'

22 'Conspicua'

23 'Forfar's Pride'

24 'Hawkshead'

25 'Hobo'

27 'Mauve Beauty'

26 'Jack Stanway'

28 'Graf Witte'

29 'Pixie'

30 'White Pixie'

31 'Alton Water'

32 'Adinda'

33 'Brian Kimberley'

'Blush of Dawn' (Martin 1962) Double. Sepals and tubes are white, but the corollas are lavender blue before maturing to pale pink. This spreading fuchsia is not the strongest-growing one, but it is always popular. It is probably at its best grown in hanging pots. Do not overwater. Twelve weeks.

'Brian A. McDonald' (Gouldings Fuchsias 1996) Double. 'Brian A. McDonald' has light tangerine tubes and fully recurving sepals. The corolla centres are a rich salmon hue; outer petals are marbled with tangerine. Growth is spreading or pendant but self-branching. It is ideal in wall baskets. Eleven weeks.

'Brian Stannard' (Gouldings Fuchsias 1988) Single. Both tubes and recurving sepals are flesh pink in colour. Corollas form lavender-hued bells. 'Brian Stannard' is heavily multiflowered, has strong and short-jointed growth with plenty of side shoots. It looks best in hanging pots. Nine weeks.

'Brookwood Joy' (Gilbert 1983) Double. Creamy pink tubes and sepals top large corollas that have lavender and pink streaks in their petals. Growth is vigorous, self-branching, robust and spreading. This fuchsia looks best in large baskets displayed at eye level. Thirteen weeks.

'Byron Rees' (Gouldings Fuchsias 1998) Substantial double. The tubes are ivory white. Its sepals are coloured pale salmon. 'Byron Rees' has darker salmon corollas with orange marbling. It is multiflowered. Growth is strong and arching; ideal for large tubs and baskets. Twelve weeks.

'Captain Al Sutton' (Gouldings Fuchsias 1999) Semi-double. The tubes and fully recurved sepals are bright red. Corollas are rosy red; each petal has a white insertion. This basket fuchsia has a strong and spreading habit. It looks best when grown in wall or fully round baskets. Ten weeks.

'Cecile' (Whitfield 1981) Double. The tubes and sepals are pale pink; the latter are tipped with green. Densely petalled corollas are a subtle shade of lilac. Growth is strong, self-branching and short-jointed. 'Cecile' grows well in full baskets and shady positions but is very versatile. Twelve weeks.

'Cheers' (Stubbs 1979) Double. Its tubes and sepals are coral pink, the latter being slightly darker on their undersurfaces. The blooms are large and showy. A strong, spreading habit enables this hybrid to show itself to best effect in full baskets in sheltered gardens. Twelve weeks.

'Colin Chambers' (Gouldings Fuchsias 1995) This is a large and heavy double. Its tubes and recurving sepals are red. Corollas are dusky red with paler marbling. Growth is strong and versatile. This fuchsia looks best in large tubs and half baskets when it is grown in light shade. Twelve weeks.

'Daisy Bell' (Unknown 1977) Single. Both the tubes and sepals are red with a hint of green. The corollas are carmine-coloured. The flowers are long, thin and numerous. Leaves have a golden glint and the habit is pendulous and strongly self-branching. This is one for hanging pots. Nine weeks.

'Dark Eyes' (Erickson 1958) Double. Red tubes and sepals combine in these flowers with large, dark-violet corollas. Growth is strong, self-branching and spreading. This versatile fuchsia is equally suitable for hanging pots, wall baskets and fully round baskets. Twelve weeks.

'Dawn Carless' (Carless 1993) Large double. The tubes and sepals are pink. Corollas are marbled shades of pink and lavender. Side shoots are produced freely and the branches are spreading, or pendant in bloom. It is best grown in hanging pots in shady positions in the garden. Eleven weeks.

'De Groot's Moonlight' (De Groot 1996) Single. The tubes are long and aubergine-coloured. Spreading sepals are similarly hued. The corollas are a much darker aubergine. Growth is spreading to pendant. 'De Groot's Moonlight' looks best in a hanging pot on a pergola. Ten weeks.

'Devonshire Dumpling' (Hilton 1981) Large double. The tubes and sepals are plain white, but the frilly white corollas are touched with pink. Growth is strong and spreading, with plentiful side shoots. 'Devonshire Dumpling' grows well in fully rounded baskets and sheltered positions. Twelve weeks.

'Eira Goulding' (Gouldings Fuchsias 1996) Double or semi-double. Tubes are ivory-white. The recurving sepals are pale pink. Corollas open lavender blue but mature to magenta. This floriferous fuchsia has arching branches. It is versatile enough to grow well in garden tubs and window-boxes. Ten weeks.

'Fancy Pants' (Reedstrom 1961) Double. Red tubes and sepals are combined with the puff-ball appearance of the dusky violet petals in the corollas. Leaves are pale green; growth is spreading and strong. Here is a fuchsia that does well in hanging pots and wall baskets. Twelve weeks.

'Fiona' (Clark 1958) Single. Tubes and flyaway sepals are white on these blooms. The large bells of the corollas open as lavender blue and gradually alter to mauve. Strong and arching growth withstands heat well and large baskets or half baskets can be grown without difficulty. Eleven weeks.

'Gerharda's Aubergine' (De Graaff 1989) Single. This is one of the darkest of its type, having aubergine tubes, sepals and petals. All mature to beetroot red. The strong and spreading branches make it suitable for hanging pots or baskets. Foliage is at its best in cool conditions. Ten weeks.

'Gipping' (Gouldings Fuchsias 1988) Single. Its large bell-shaped corollas are a delicate shade of pink, like its tubes and green-tipped sepals. Lemon-coloured leaves grow on plentiful and spreading branches. This fuchsia does best in full baskets in sheltered garden positions. Ten weeks.

'Golden Anniversary' (Stubbs 1980) Double. Sturdy sepals and tubes are white, but the corollas open violet at first before maturing into ruby red. Young leaves are lettuce green and the habit of growth is spreading. Here is a candidate for hanging pots as well as full baskets. Twelve weeks.

'Golden Swingtime' (Unknown 1981) Double. Both the tubes and sepals are waxy red. The petals of the corollas are white with red veins. Growth is strong and spreading. This foliage sport from 'Swingtime' is popular and tough. It is perfect for garden displays. Eleven weeks.

'Gwendoline' (Gouldings Fuchsias 1996) Double or occasionally semi-double. The tubes and spreading sepals are light pink. Corollas have pale lavender centres with ruffled pink outer petals. Its habit is spreading. This fuchsia is best grown in wall baskets in sheltered positions. Eleven weeks.

'Gwen Wallis' (Gouldings Fuchsias 1997) Double. Its tubes and flyaway sepals are white, although the latter are tinged with a little pink. Corollas a subtle shade of lilac. Growth is self-branching and spreading. It makes a good basket or hanging pot plant in the garden display. Twelve weeks.

'Haute Cuisine' (De Graaff 1988) Double. The sepals and tubes are dark red, but the corollas on these large blooms are a dark aubergine colour. Growth is strong and spreading, but it prefers cool and shady positions where it does well in large, fully round baskets. Twelve weeks.

'Hermiena' (Lavieren 1987) Single. The white tubes and sepals are touched with pink. Petals start as dark violet before maturing to rich plum. 'Hermiena' is multiflowering and self-branching. Its spreading growth looks well in window-boxes, tubs and mixed baskets. Nine weeks.

'Irene L. Peartree' (Peartree 1993) Double. This sport from the famous fuchsia 'Swingtime' has pink tubes. Its sepals are pink with green tips. The corollas are pink, too. Growth is robustly strong and spreading. It is at its best in very large baskets in garden displays. Twelve weeks.

'Irving Alexander' (De Boer 2001) Double. The tubes are long, thin and white. Sepals are long, thin and white, with red tips. Corollas are short and dense; marbled pink and lavender. Multiflowered. Growth strong and spreading. It is ideal for wall- or full garden baskets. Ten weeks.

'Jack Rowlands' (Gouldings Fuchsias 1998) Double. The tubes are ivory white. Its swept-back sepals are flesh pink. Each corolla opens lavender blue before maturing to pale salmon; slightly marbled. Growth is strong and spreading. It is ideal for baskets and other hanging containers. Twelve weeks.

'John Boy' (Gouldings Fuchsias 1996) Double or semi-double. The tubes and recurved sepals are bright pink. Its corollas are violet-centred with violet and pink marbled outer petals. It has a spreading and self-branching habit, which is ideal for baskets grown in sheltered garden positions. Ten weeks.

'Joy Bielby' (Bielby 1982) Double. The tubes are white with red streaks and the white sepals have a pink overlay. Corollas, too, are white with rose-pink flushing. Self-branching but lax growth helps 'Joy Bielby' to produce half- or fully round baskets of high quality. Twelve weeks.

'Kathy's Sparkler' (Stubbs 1983) Dense double. Tubes are ivory white. The spreading sepals are pink with green tips. The petals are flecked and marbled in shades of lavender and pink. This fuchsia has a spreading habit that is best suited to hanging pots and window-boxes. Twelve weeks.

'Kelly Stableford' (Gouldings Fuchsias 2000) Double. It has white tubes. The sepals are white outside but are pale pink on their undersides when fully recurved. Corollas start as lilac blue and turn to rosy pink. Growth is strongly self-branching. It looks best in mixed basket plantings. Eleven weeks.

'Kit Oxtoby' (Bielby/Oxtoby 1990) Double. The tubes and sepals are creamy white. Corollas are pink. Its growth is spreading and strong and this is helped by early nipping. Fully round baskets can be displayed on garden pergolas where they can be seen at eye level. Twelve weeks.

'Lavender Ann' (Gouldings Fuchsias 1999) Double. The tubes and flyaway sepals are rosy pink in colour. Corollas are marbled in shades of violet, mauve and pink. Growth is strong, spreading and self-branching. It is best grown in wall baskets and hanging pots, in bright light. Twelve weeks.

'Lena' (Bunny 1862) Double or semi-double. Flesh-pink tubes and sepals are found with petals that change from purple to plum as they age. A spreading, hardy, versatile and many-branched habit has helped this fuchsia to its position as one of the best for growing in baskets. Nine weeks.

'Letts Delight' (Gouldings Fuchsias 1986) Double. Each tube and fully recurving sepal is rose pink. The many-pleated corollas are lavender at first before turning to pink later. Multiflowering is the norm. This self-branching fuchsia is best suited to wall baskets and hanging pots. Twelve weeks.

'Love in Bloom' (Stubbs 1977) Double. The tubes and recurved sepals are rosy red. Corollas are firmly textured, and petals are variably marbled in violet and pink. The robust growth is self-branching. It makes large and attractive baskets and wall baskets for garden display. Twelve weeks.

'Malibu Mist' (Stubbs 1985) Large double. Sturdy tubes and sepals are white, sometimes flushed with pink. Corollas are lavender with a satin sheen. Foliage is matt green and the habit is spreading. This fuchsia needs protection from the weather's excesses. It does well in baskets. Twelve weeks.

'Mancunian' (Gouldings Fuchsias 1985) Double of the parrot-beak type. The tubes change from white to red, but the long recurving sepals remain white. The overlapping petals are white with pink veins. Growth is vigorous, pendant and self-branching. This one is a full basket gem. Twelve weeks.

'Mantilla' (Reiter 1948) Single of the intermediate type. The long tubes and short drooping sepals are bright carmine red like the short corollas. Growth is pendant but strong. 'Mantilla' grows best when situated in warm and bright positions and when placed in large wall baskets. Ten weeks.

'Martin's Double Delicate' (Beije 1999) Double or semi-double. The short tubes and fully recurved sepals are pale pink. Petals in the corollas are mauve with darker lace-edges. Growth is spreading. This fuchsia does best in hanging baskets sheltered from wind and sun. Eleven weeks.

'Mary Shead' (Gouldings Fuchsias 2001) Double. The tubes are pale white with green stripes. Mature pink sepals sweep upwards and outwards. The large, fully developed corollas are marbled pink and pale lilac. Its habit is strongly spreading. At its best in fully round baskets. Twelve weeks.

'Montevideo' (Gouldings Fuchsias 1989) Double. Buds hang like baubles. Tubes are flesh pink. Sepals are slightly darker, arched and with green tips. Densely petalled corollas are salmon-coloured. It has a spreading habit and is most suitable for conservatory displays. Thirteen weeks.

'Mood Indigo' (De Graaff 1987) Double. The tubes and recurving sepals are white. Tightly overlapping petals change from dark purple to red with some marbling present. Growth is strong, pendulous and many-branched. This fuchsia can be used for baskets and for fans. Twelve weeks.

'Orange King' (Wright 1975) Double. Pale pink sepals and tubes top the orange corollas that are full of petals mottled in salmon and orange. Growth is spreading and robust. 'Orange King' is helped by protecting it from full sun and wind. Wall baskets are ideal for it. Eleven weeks.

'Patricia Joan Yates' (Gouldings Fuchsias 1998) Double. Its sturdy tubes are ivory white. The flared sepals are pale salmon. Corollas are marbled in shades of pink and salmon. Growth is spreading and strong. It is especially suitable for fully round baskets and wall baskets. Eleven weeks.

'Peachy' (Stubbs 1992) Double. The tubes and spreading sepals are pale peach in colour. Its corollas are marbled in shades of pale peach and salmon. Growth is spreading and strong. It grows and flowers best when placed in hanging pots and sheltered from the wind. Twelve weeks.

'Pink Marshmallow' (Stubbs 1971) Very large double. The sepals and tubes are pink, but the petals are white with pink veins. Growth is spreading then pendulous, and is vigorous with plentiful side shoots. This fuchsia does well in full baskets in sheltered garden spots. Twelve weeks.

'Pink Rain' (De Graaff 1987) Single. The moderately long and thin tubes are pink. Sepals and petals are baby pink. There are lots of side shoots on vigorous but pendulous growth. 'Pink Rain' is extremely robust, but is at its best in hanging pots or grown as a fan or pillar. Nine weeks.

'Pinto de Blue' (Antonelli 1995) Double. The tubes are white, as are the swept-back sepals which are tinged with pink. Its corollas are dark violet at first, maturing eventually to a warm pink. Growth is self-branching and spreading. It is ideally grown and displayed in fully round baskets. Eleven weeks.

'Popely Pride' (Gouldings Fuchsias 1997) Double. Tubes are ivory white. The pale pink sepals are swept back like steers' horns on maturity. Corollas are a subtle mixture of mauve and magenta. Its habit is amenable and adaptable. It grows best in large, fully round baskets. Twelve weeks.

'Ralph's Delight' (Gouldings Fuchsias 1997) Double. Its tubes are clear ivory white. The sepals arch like bird wings; they are white with pink reverses. Densely petalled corollas open dark plum in colour before ripening to rich magenta. This is a strong and adaptable basket type. Twelve weeks.

'Ratatouille' (De Graaff 1988) Double. The colour of the sepals and tubes is ivory white, but the corollas are pale aubergine. Branches are strong and spread almost horizontally; they have plentiful side shoots. 'Ratatouille' looks well in hanging pots, full and half-baskets. Eleven weeks.

'Rodeo' (Stannard 1993) Single. These tubes are long and triphylla-like. The short sepals and petals, like the tubes, are dark aubergine. Growth is spreading or pendant with multiple side shoots. Here is an excellent addition to the ranks of fuchsias for hanging pots. Twelve weeks.

'Rohees New Millennium' (Roes-Heesakkers 1999) Double. Tubes and sepals glossy red with a hint of aubergine. Corollas are dark aubergine and rounded in outline. Its habit of growth is spreading and strong; early nipping is helpful. This fuchsia makes an excellent fully round basket. Twelve weeks.

'Ron Chambers Love' (Gouldings Fuchsias 1997) Densely petalled double. The white tubes are of medium length. Its arching sepals are pink to orange. Corollas are multi-layered, and are marbled in orange and magenta. The spreading and self-branching habit looks best in wall baskets. Twelve weeks.

'Ruby Wedding' (Forward 1990) Double. The tubes, sepals and many petals of the corollas are rich ruby red in colour. Growth is strong and spreading. It is versatile enough to look at home in any sort of hanging container and has above-average heat and wind resistance. Twelve weeks.

'Seventh Heaven' (Stubbs 1981) Double. This fuchsia has white tubes and flyaway sepals that slowly turn to red. Its corollas are flame red. Growth is strong, arching and versatile. Early nipping helps to produce wall- or hanging baskets and window-box plants. Twelve weeks.

'Squadron Leader' (Gouldings Fuchsias 1986) Double. Each tube and sepal is white, but the frilly petals are a very pale shade of pink. This is a multiflowering, peripheral and early-blooming fuchsia. It looks well in hanging baskets and in large tubs given some protection. Ten weeks.

'Suffolk Punch' (Gouldings Fuchsias 2000) Heavily pleated double. The tubes are rosy red. The flyaway sepals are similarly coloured. Corollas are rather darker matt red. Growth is self-branching, strong and versatile. This fuchsia looks best in very large, fully round baskets or tubs. Twelve weeks.

'Sylvia Barker' (Barker 1973) Single. White sepals and tubes combine with corollas of smoky red on this heavily multiflowered fuchsia. Its branches are produced freely and spread readily. Top-quality show baskets can be grown, but sepals tend to droop in dull and cool conditions. Nine weeks.

'Tom Coulson' (Gouldings Fuchsias 1999) Double. The tubes are short and red-lined. Pink sepals are swept up at their tips. Corollas are dark salmon orange with pink marbling. Growth is spreading and strong. This fuchsia is at its best in wall- or fully round garden baskets. Twelve weeks.

'Veenlust' (Jansink 1995) Double. The tubes and recurved sepals are white. Corollas are scarlet with some white flecks on the outer petals; strikingly bright. Growth is spreading. 'Veenlust' is at its best when planted in large mixed baskets and garden tubs; its colours are radiant. Eleven weeks.

'Vincent van Gogh' (Van de Post 1984) Single of the intermediate type. The tubes are long, thin and pink. The sepals are short, pink and green-tipped. Corollas are baby pink. Growth is spreading and benefits from some early nipping and protection from the weather. Best in baskets. Eleven weeks.

'Wally Yendell' (Gouldings Fuchsias 1998) Substantial double. Its tubes and horizontally held sepals are ivory white. The many-pleated petals of the corollas are clover pink. Growth is strong and spreading. This fuchsia does best in garden wall-baskets displayed at eye level. Twelve weeks.

'Walsingham' (Clitheroe 1979) Double. These sepals and tubes are white, but the petals are pale lilac with wavy edges. 'Walsingham' is multiflowering and has self-branching, arching growth. This early bloomer is best seen in hanging pots raised to head height. Nine weeks.

'Walz Harp' (Waldenmaier 1988) Single. Long, pale orange tubes are joined to shorter sepals of the same colour. The corollas are a darker orange. Spreading, almost pendant branches are helped by early nipping. 'Walz Harp' grows best in hanging pots in sheltered spots. Ten weeks.

'Walz Mandoline' (Waldenmaier 1989) Double. Tubes are moderately long and orange. The shorter sepals are also orange. The tightly pleated corollas are an intensely bright orange when grown in sunny spots. Branches spread and provide eye-catching hanging pots. Eleven weeks.

'Wentworth' (Gouldings Fuchsias 1986) This single is of the intermediate type. Long tubes and shorter sepals are flesh-coloured, but the short petals are bright orange. 'Wentworth' is multiflowering. Pendant growth enables this fuchsia to be seen well in raised hanging pots. Nine weeks.

'Zulu Queen' (De Graaff 1988) Single. These relatively small blooms have aubergine tubes, sepals and petals. They are produced in large numbers and displayed prominently. Growth is arching or spreading. Splendid half-baskets can be produced away from excessive heat. Ten weeks.

Anyone who has been fortunate enough to grow even a small number of the most modern fuchsias, beside some older cultivars, will be amazed at how far they have progressed since the days of the Victorians. Their colour range alone has changed almost beyond recognition since the formation of the British Fuchsia Society in 1938. During my lifetime the proportion of basket types grown by the gardening public in the United Kingdom has risen from less than 30 per cent in 1964 to more than 80 per cent in 2001. American growers have always displayed a high proportion of their fuchsias in hanging containers. The trend in Europe, as elsewhere, is gradually catching up. A quiet revolution in the development of fuchsia hybrids is taking place at an ever-increasing pace and we are fortunate to witness such a dynamic period.

Fig. 16 Ornamental archway: height, depth and a range of interest created in a suburban back garden.

CHAPTER 9
Hardy Fuchsias and Garden Design

The definition of hardiness in fuchsias is not as easy to make as it might seem. W. P. Wood, in *A Fuchsia Survey* (1965 reprint), laid great emphasis on frost-resistance. Tom Thorne, in *Fuchsias For All Purposes* (1964), sought to grade this frost-hardiness on a numerical scale. H1 denoted those which were most tender and needed temperatures above 10°C (50°F). H2 was for fuchsias that could be grown in unheated greenhouses in the United Kingdom. H3 was used for those that were hardy enough to be planted permanently out-of-doors. It is not sufficient to look at the many official trial results to prove this hardiness, for many of the subjects were so robbed of cutting material, or even dug completely from the ground, that the results became worthless. Hardiness is always related to specific places, and those fuchsias that would come through a winter in one locality or country might well fail to do so in a different climate.

If we take our definition of hardiness to mean that a fuchsia planted permanently in the ground out-of-doors will survive several degrees of frost and regrow, that definition lacks something essential. Survival alone is not enough as a measure of hardiness, for many fuchsias will live out-of-doors all the year round. Equally important is the fact that they should flower early enough in the days of longer sunlight to make this effort worthwhile. Hardy fuchsias should have at least three months of flowering if they are to repay their dues in garden space and maintenance costs. Fuchsias must compare favourably with other shrubby plants if they are to be accepted by the wider gardening public, who might have a sentimental attachment to the genus but will also demand results. It is safest to treat the majority of fuchsias as half-hardy and to grow them as such, and to use them principally for summer bedding purposes.

A hundred years ago, hardy fuchsias could often be found near the doorways of cottages and these were frequently much-loved and admired. More impressive are the huge drifts of hardy fuchsias which grace the grounds at Sandringham in Norfolk, where many plants of each cultivar are massed together. Haphazard planting of hardy fuchsias, using one each of several different cultivars, rarely looks effective.

Fuchsias, more than almost any other plant, have the ability to set a garden mood that can be almost other-worldly. Fuchsia colours have a mellowness and a restfulness all their own. Their flowers are produced through the summer and autumn, when colour is often at a premium. Of course, brash bedding plants may be seen in quantities, but their impact is very different. Hardy fuchsias usually grow from between about half a metre to one metre tall (19–39 in). They therefore suit the nearest aspects of large gardens, where they often line garden walks and dot the centres of hardy herbaceous borders. Foliage among the hardiest fuchsias can be both variable and attractive. Colour schemes, which use particular tones across a wide range of different plants, have been popular for many years and fuchsias may be chosen for just such requirements. It only remains to remember that, as a herbaceous and deciduous plant, the fuchsia fills no winter garden slot. As standards, too, they will not succeed where frosts occur.

Hardy fuchsias have a wide soil tolerance. As we have seen, they will grow in acid or alkaline conditions but probably do best when the soil pH is around seven. Texture and content of the growing medium matter greatly to fuchsias. Open, friable soils allow free drainage and high oxygen levels near the roots. When humus is added to these soils, their chemistry can be improved and it is easier for fuchsias to form their fibrous root systems and substantial crowns. A variety of different substances can be incorporated into the soil. Spent mushroom compost, peat, compost bin products, leaf mould, farmyard manure and bracken mould have been used with success. The most

Fig. 17 Cottage doorway with fuchsias.

important factor in permanent fuchsia beds is the removal of pernicious perennial weeds. Where couch grass, ground elder or horse-tail are likely to be a problem, it might be worthwhile to treat them with specific weedkillers well before planting fuchsias. An alternative is to place black plastic sheeting across the surface of the ground to suppress all weeds. This may be left in place for six months or a year before undertaking permanent planting with fuchsias through small slits cut in it. Hand weeding may be used to help in controlling any weeds growing close to a fuchsia. Because they are surface- and fibrous-rooting shrubs, fuchsias should not be hoed around in an effort to remove weeds. Forking, too, should be limited and careful. Bark chippings may be used to cover the black plastic 'mulch', if it has been applied, or they may be used 10 cm (4 in) thick straight onto the soil as a weed suppressant.

Most fuchsias grow best in sheltered positions out of the sun's full glare and away from excessive wind or salt spray. They often thrive where they are in dappled shade like that under apple trees. If hardies are placed under larger trees, care should be taken to see that they have sufficient moisture and light to keep them bushy, strong, healthy and floriferous. Some trees, like sycamores, harbour greenfly, so special attention may have to be paid to pest control on fuchsias out-of-doors.

Sites for permanent planting should be prepared in advance. Soil preparation has already been covered, but the element of design is just as vital to their long-term success. Garden designs are best drafted on paper (or on a computer screen), so that the size and shape of the whole space involved can be seen in perspective. Small groups of a single cultivar, like 'Phyllis', look best when planted in odd numbers, for example five, seven or nine. Larger numbers blend more readily into each other and the exact number planted becomes less obvious. Beds may be planned using a hose to mark the outlines of each section, or lines could be scraped in the soil with a stick. Individual planting stations may be identified in advance with the help of small canes and this ensures the fuchsias look satisfactory from every viewing angle.

Assuming adequate soil preparation, holes should be opened for each shrubby fuchsia. Ideally, plants are taken from pots 10 cm (4 in) or more in diameter, and with well-developed but not tightly constricted root systems. Each fuchsia should be growing strongly, having been fed regularly, and have a moist root ball. Soil for planting into should also be damp, and should be kept so for several weeks afterwards to allow adventitious roots to roam. Fertilizers may be added to the soil when it is prepared, or liquid feeds can be given once plants are in position. Small soil-testing kits are cheap to obtain and will more than repay their cost in helping to ensure planting conditions are as nearly perfect as possible. In gardens where frost is common, extra precautions are best taken prior to planting; fuchsias may be grown on short stems of between 7.5 and 15 cm (3–6 in) and then planted so that their heads, as small standards, are at soil level. Sinking them in this way will help to preserve fibrous roots during severe winters and to encourage the production of shoots from below soil level each year.

The majority of fuchsia books advise that pruning is undertaken in the spring, or as days lengthen. This is not always the best idea. For example, in the East Anglian region of the UK, east winds are common and more fuchsias are lost as a result of wind rock than are killed by frosts. Autumn pruning to within 15 cm (6 in) of the ground will help to keep fuchsia root stocks stable in such conditions. Spring pruning to the same height helps to keep a little more frost away, but at the price of retaining any pests and diseases already attached to the hardy fuchsias for longer periods. In mild winters this can be a disadvantage. Winter mulching with substances like chopped bark will help to allow free drainage while keeping frost from the crown of each plant.

Although fuchsias have a long flowering season by comparison with most other shrubby and herbaceous plants, they do not provide year-round interest as garden hardies. Because of this, it is possible, and probably wise, to use other plants freely to accompany them. The first and most obvious method of extending the flowering season is to plant spring-flowering bulbs under the fuchsias. These will gain some support from the twiggy shoots if the fuchsias are not cut back too hard. Fuchsias, in return, get some frost protection from the bulbs' foliage, especially in the spring when new growth can be caught by sudden drops in night temperature. Brian Mathew, in *The Year-Round Bulb Garden* (1986), describes many suitable subjects for this scheme. Here is a short selection of bulbs and other plants that are well worth considering.

Daffodils and narcissi provide ideal companions for fuchsias, flowering as they do from March to May. Here are my suggestions:

NAME DESCRIPTION

TRUMPET DAFFODILS (Division 1)
'Golden Harvest'	Golden yellow
'Mount Hood'	White

LARGE-CUPPED DAFFODIL (Division 2)
'Carlton'	Pale yellow
'Flower Record'	White perianth and orange cup
'Ice Follies'	Cream perianth and primrose-yellow cup
'Satin Pink'	White perianth and pink cup

DOUBLE-FLOWERED DAFFODIL (Division 4)
'Texas'	Yellow with orange segments

TRIANDRUS DAFFODIL (Division 5)
'Cheerfulness'	Multi-headed, scented, white and yellow
'Thalia'	White; swept-back petals
'Yellow Cheerfulness'	Multi-headed, scented, double yellow

JONQUILLA DAFFODIL (Division 7)
'Sundial'	Multi-headed, scented, yellow

TAZETTA DAFFODIL (Division 8)
'Falconet'	Multi-headed, scented, yellow and orange

PAPILLON DAFFODIL (Division 11)
'Orangery'	White with an orange centre

Other useful bulbs are the early-flowering Triumph, Darwin and Lily-flowered tulips. There is a wide choice of singles and doubles in a multiplicity of colours. All bloom between February and May (in the United Kingdom). Many other tulips are attractive in their own right, but they have stalks that are too short to be grown among hardy fuchsias. Crocuses and *Iris reticulata* also have disadvantages when it comes to size, but may be worth considering if dwarf fuchsias, like *F. procumbens*, are grown on rockeries.

Silver foliage has played a dramatic part in garden schemes for many years. Plants like *Stachys*, *Echinops*, *Yucca*, *Cineraria maritima*, *Achillea*, *Dicentra*, lavender, *Gypsophila*, *Nepeta*, *Elymus* and *Santolina* provide a cool and hazy background to the strong red of pendant fuchsia flowers. The deep scarlet blooms of 'Mary' set before *Cineraria maritima* have to be seen to be believed. 'Margaret' is vigorous enough to look statuesque when interplanted with *Echinops*. The beauty of a dainty *Dicentra* will be enhanced by being close to fuchsias like 'Alice Hoffman' or 'Lady Thumb'. The soft domes of lavender clumps are marvellous foils for the red and white spikes of 'Conspicua', while *Elymus* and 'Phyllis' will complement each other in the hardy border.

A few of the silvery-blue conifers that are not too fast-growing will also lend themselves to beds with fuchsias such as *F. magellanica* var. *macrostema* 'Variegata', which has a silvery-grey colour to its leaves. 'Tom West', planted in groups, can look superb as a hardy plant with silver and grey plants surrounding it. So, too, can *F. magellanica* var. *molinae* 'Sharpitor' with its more bushy habit. Some of the best of the conifers are:

Abies concolor 'Glauca Compacta'
Abies procera 'Glauca Prostrata'
Juniperus squamata 'Blue Star'
Picea subsp. *englemannii glauca* 'Alberta Blue'
Picea pungens 'Koster'
Picea pungens 'Thomsen'
Pinus sylvestris 'Beuvronensis'

There are currently several fuchsias with very attractive yellow tones in their foliage. *F. magellanica* var. *molinae* 'Enstone' has lovely leaves that are a mixture of buttery-yellow and green. 'Genii' has a spiky habit with a golden glow in its foliage. *F. magellanica* var. *macrostemma* 'Aurea' has a vigorous, spreading habit. 'White Pixie' has a yellow glint to go with its smaller stature and red and white blooms.

Golden foliage is plentiful among other hardy garden plants, too. Those conifers with golden foliage include:

Abies nordmanniana 'Golden Spreader'
Chamaecyparis lawsoniana 'Golden Pot'
Chamaecyparis obtusa 'Nana Lutea'
Chamaecyparis pisifera 'Gold Spangle'
Juniperus communis 'Depressa Aurea'
Pinus radiata 'Aurea'

Heathers come into their own in this colour range and can make an excellent complement to fuchsias by extending the flowering season and by providing foliage impact, too. The most versatile heathers are in the *Erica carneas*. The most famous is *Erica carnea* 'Foxhollow', which has lavender-coloured blooms and golden leaves. *Erica carnea* 'Westwood Yellow' is similar but has a tighter habit. Among the *Erica cinereas* is 'Fiddler's Gold'. It is worth examining all the possibilities before planting.

There are many gems of shrubs with strong foliage interest. *Ilex* x *alterclerensis* 'Golden King' will make a slow-growing shrub, or even a small tree if it is grown as a standard. *Elaeagnus pungens* 'Maculata' will also make quite a large shrub. Slightly smaller but equally attractive is *Euonymus japonicus* 'Ovatus Aureus'. Among the

Hostas, mention should be made of *H. fortunei* 'Albopicta', although there are many more which are equally suitable. The climber *Lonicera japonica* 'Aureoreticulata' can form a golden backdrop to the garden border. Many other well-known plants can be combined with fuchsias that have yellow in their leaves to create imaginative garden plantings.

A scheme that is easiest to develop in small town gardens is the clumping of ornamental-leaved vegetables to complement fuchsias and other flowering plants. Lettuces come with fimbriated leaves and red as well as green colouring. Red leaves may also be found among the beetroots; these, like lettuces, are quick to mature and relatively trouble-free. Ornamental cabbages come in a wide range of colours and can look spectacular in a small border. Carrots, too, with their fine and fern-like foliage blend happily with many other plants, including fuchsias. Seed catalogues display many interesting vegetables, such as the purple pea, which can climb around fuchsias in containers hung on the wall or fence. Imagination and a little effort are all that is required to combine much beauty within a very small space.

Another plant, which is set for a big revival of interest, is the ivy, so beloved of the Victorians. It has one major advantage that it shares with the fuchsia, in that it appears to be almost entirely non-allergenic. When people say, "What a pity fuchsias have no scent," it is worth remembering that for many gardeners this might be a price worth paying, as pollen grains (especially those of grass which cause hay fever) can be major allergenic factors. There are a few fuchsias, mentioned in this book (see page 82), which really do have a scent of their own. Leaves, unlike those of so many other plants, are benign to the handler.

There are a number of ways in which permanent plantings of ivies and fuchsias can be made. Ground-cover ivies may be planted so that swathes of their foliage intersperse blocks of fuchsias. There is a wide range of foliage interest among ivies, throughout the year. Among those which are most suitable for this purpose are:

Hedera colchica 'Dentata Variegata'
Hedera colchica 'Sulphur Heart'
Hedera helix 'Brokamp'
Hedera helix 'Glacier'
Hedera helix 'Green Ripple'

Hedera helix 'Ivalace'
Hedera helix 'Parsley Crested'
Hedera helix 'Sagittifolia Variegata'

Ivies may also be used to grow vertically up walls, trees and man-made frames. The following plants produce an attractive effect:

Hedera canariensis 'Gloire de Marengo'
Hedera helix 'Angularis Aurea'
Hedera helix 'Chester'
Hedera helix 'Goldheart'
Hedera helix 'Green Ripple'

Two other ivies that have a place to fill in many gardens are *Hedera helix* 'Erecta', which has candelabra-like branches and a statuesque appearance; and *Hedera helix* 'Spetchley', which has minute leaves and a habit perfectly suitable for rockeries.

The best of the hardy fuchsias are rarely found among the plants beloved of non-specialist gardening journalists: change comes slowly to some areas of horticulture. However, the following selection is of the most attractive and varied fuchsias that have proved themselves capable of withstanding hard frosts, and able to recover and flower early enough in the summer to make planting worthwhile. The list is arranged alphabetically and the approximate size on maturity is given in each case.

'Alice Hoffman' (Klese 1911) Semi-double. Tubes and sepals rose red. Corollas white with red veins. Growth small and compact. Foliage bronzed. Useful for rockery planting; 46 cm (18 in).

'Beacon Rosa' (Bürgi 1972) Single. Tubes, sepals and petals pink with red highlights. Growth upright, bushy and robust. A sport from 'Beacon'. Leaves heavily serrated. Versatile; 76 cm (30 in).

'Ben Jammin' (Carless 1994) Single. Tubes and upper sepal surfaces flesh pink; the latter aubergine underneath. Corollas bright aubergine. Multiflowered. Bushy and short-jointed upright; 76 cm (30 in).

'Blue Waves' (Waltz 1954) Double. Tubes and sepals rose pink. Corollas campanula violet. Growth strong and bushy. Versatile. One for the mixed herbaceous border; 107 cm (42 in).

'Christine Bamford' (Carless 1996) Single. Tubes and sepals pale red with a hint of aubergine. Corollas pink; darker veins. Multiflowered. Upright and self-branching growth. A border gem; 61 cm (24 in).

'Conspicua' (Smith 1863) Single. Tubes and sepals shiny scarlet. Corollas intense white with scarlet veining. Floriferous and showy. Upright, spiky habit. A welcome colour break; 61 cm (24 in).

'Constance' (Berkley Hort. Nurs. 1935) Double. Tubes and sepals flesh pink. Corollas mauve changing to dark plum. Growth upright and long-jointed. One of the best doubles; 76 cm (30 in).

'Display' (Smith 1881) Single. Tubes, sepals and cup-shaped corollas pink. Blooms numerous and jaunty. Short and bushy habit. Leaves glossy. Good for the front of a border; 61 cm (24 in).

'Dollar Princess' (Lemoine 1912) Double. Cherry red tubes and sepals on this fuchsia. Dark purple corollas. A multiflowering hybrid. Bushy and self-branching. Quite hardy and versatile; 61 cm (24 in).

'Ernie Bromley' (Gouldings Fuchsias 1988) Single. Tubes and sepals pink. Violet to mauve corollas. Spreading but self-branching habit. Ornamental foliage. Needs bright light; 76 cm (30 in).

F. magellanica var. macrostema 'Aurea' One of the foliage sports from *macrostema*. Single. Tubes and sepals red. Corollas violet. Growth spreading. Leaves golden; 91 cm (36 in).

F. magellanica var. macrostema 'Variegata' Tubes and sepals red. Violet petals. Strong, spreading growth. Leaves are mixtures of yellow, silvery green and red. Graceful sport; 91 cm (36 in).

F. magellanica var. molinae 'Enstone' Single. Tubes and sepals white. Corollas very pale pink. Bushy spreading habit. Leaves variegated yellow and green. Difficult to start; 61 cm (24 in).

F. magellanica var. molinae 'Sharpitor' Single. The second sport from *F. mag.* var. *molinae*, with identical flowers. Self-branching. Variegated cream and green leaves. Slow starter; 61 cm (24 in).

'Flashlight' (Gadsby 1968) Single. Tubes and green-tipped sepals pink. Corollas pink with a hint of blue. Upright, self-branching and resilient growth. A good foil to brighter-coloured plants; 76 cm (30 in).

'Forfar's Pride' (Gouldings Fuchsias 1999) Double or semi-double. Tubes ivory flushed pink. Hooded sepals pink. Corollas violet with plentiful pink marbling. Growth self-branching upright; 61 cm (24 in).

'Garden News' (Handley 1978) Double. Tubes and sepals pink. Large corollas magenta rose. Growth strong, long-jointed and upright. Best in clumps at the back of the border; 91 cm (36 in).

'Genii' (Reiter 1951) Single. Tubes and sepals cherry red. Corollas dark violet. Growth upright and bushy. Leaves yellow and small. Grow in a sunny spot to enhance colours; 91 cm (36 in).

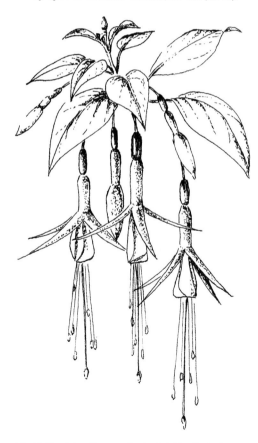

Fig. 18 'Hawkshead', a magellanica hybrid with single flowers.

'Graf Witte' (Lemoine 1899) Single. Bright red tubes and sepals. Corollas violet. Growth bushy. Leaves have a yellow tinge when young. Ancestor of 'Pixie'. Best in the border; 91 cm (36 in).

'Harnser's Flight' (Gouldings Fuchsias 1990) Single. Tubes ivory white. Recurving white, green-tipped sepals. Corollas lavender. Stiffly upright habit. A useful colour change; 107 cm (42 in).

'Hawkshead' (Travis 1962) Single. Tubes, sepals and petals small and white with a hint of green. Pale green foliage. Upright and bushy growth. Useful at the back of the border; 122 cm (48 in).

'Hobo' (Carless 1997) Semi-double. Tubes and swept-back sepals dark red. Whiskery corollas are very dark aubergine. Growth upright, self-branching and spiky. Unusual and adaptable; 61 cm (24 in).

'Hot Coals' (Carless 1994) Single. Tubes and spreading sepals dark blood red. Corollas neatly rolled; dark aubergine to violet. Stiffly upright and short-jointed. Place in front of light colours; 61 cm (24 in).

'Jack Stanway' (Rowell 1985) Single. Pink tubes and sepals. White corollas. Spreading growth. Foliage irregularly variegated cream, green and red. Sport from 'Cloverdale Pearl'; 76 cm (30 in).

'Kath van Hanegem' (Carless 1998) Single. Small dark red tubes and horizontal sepals. Dark aubergine corollas. Heavily flowered. Neat, self-branching rockery type; 30 cm (12 in).

'Lena' (Bunny 1862) Semi-double or double. Tubes and sepals flesh pink. Corollas violet, changing to plum red. Growth spreading and self-branching. Best raised slightly; 76 cm (30 in).

'Margaret' (Wood 1939) Semi-double. Tubes and sepals carmine. Corollas violet with red veins; two-tiered. Growth very strong and bushy. Better than others in its colour range; 122 cm (48 in).

'Mauve Beauty' (Banks 1869) Double. Tubes and sepals bright red. Corollas dusky blue to violet. Growth upright and strong. Leaves have an attractive metallic red glint; 91 cm (36 in).

'Mr A. Huggett' (Unknown) Single. Short tubes and recurving sepals cherry red. Corollas mauve with a magenta flush at the petal edges. Growth stiffly upright and very robust; 76 cm (30 in).

'Phyllis' (Brown 1938) Semi-double. Tubes and sepals waxy-textured; cherry red. Corollas rosy red. Floriferous. Growth long-jointed and sturdy. Strong individual identity. 91 cm (36 in).

'Pixie' (Russell 1960) Single. Tubes and sepals red. Corollas mauve to pink. Growth evenly self-branching. A sport from 'Graf Witte', which in turn sported 'White Pixie'; 91 cm (36 in).

'Prosperity' (Gadsby 1970) Double. Tubes and sepals crimson. Corollas neyron rose. Blooms freely on the ends of its branches. Long-jointed and stiffly upright growth; 122 cm (48 in).

'Pumila' (Young 1947) Single. Tubes and sepals dark red. Petals dark mauve. Growth small and very bushy. Suitable for rockery planting. Useful for small spaces. Versatile; 46 cm (18 in).

'Rose of Denmark' (Banks 1864) Double. Tubes and sepals white flushed with pink. Corollas rosy pink. Peripheral blooming. Upright. Plant in clumps in garden borders; 76 cm (30 in).

'Santa Cruz' (Tiret 1947) Semi-double or double. Tubes and sepals crimson. Corollas rather darker crimson. Leaves large and bronzed. Upright, sturdy and self-branching habit; 91 cm (36 in).

'Tom West' (Meillez 1853) Single. Sport from 'Corallina'. Tubes and sepals red. Corollas violet. Growth spreading. Leaves variegated cream, green and red. Best in sunny spots; 91 cm (36 in).

'Tricolor' (Unknown) Single. The exact origins of this fuchsia are unknown. Tubes and sepals cherry red. Corollas dark violet. Growth bushy and upright. Leaves have green and yellow variegation; 91 cm (36 in).

'White Pixie' (Saunders 1968) Single. Tubes and sepals bright cherry red. Corollas white with red veins. Neat self-branching habit. Leaves rather yellow. Sport from 'Pixie'; 61 cm (24 in).

'Zulu King' (De Graaff 1991) Single. Tubes and pendant sepals very dark red. Corollas dark violet to aubergine. Like *F. mag.* var. *macrostemma* it has wiry and spreading branches; 91 cm (36 in).

Lastly, but by no means least, fuchsias are very well suited to the needs of disabled gardeners. Chapter 6 describes how ornamental shapes can be created with pot-grown plants; encliandras can even be grown on indoor windowsills and they require little space and no special treatment. Among pot plants, fuchsias are the most rewarding in another sense, too: they respond to attention. Many gardeners gain therapeutically from caring for their plants. Nipping, shaping and tying-in provide outlets for creativity. There is always something to do, but little which must be done; obligation gives way to infatuation.

Chapter 8 gives instruction on rigging baskets with a pulley and cord. Elsewhere in the garden, it is possible to grow fuchsias in raised beds, so that their full beauty is nearer to eye level if a wheelchair gardener tends them. Hand weeding is facilitated by making these beds accessible from each side. Black plastic mulch can be used to prevent weeds from growing in the first place. Bark mulch can be used on these raised beds to advantage.

Greenhouses can pose particular problems for gardeners in wheelchairs. It is best to buy a greenhouse that has double sliding doors, and to ensure that the space between the benches is wide enough to accommodate a wheelchair without scraping any knuckles. The benches will need to be placed further apart than normal, and they will also need to be lower so that each pot fuchsia can be reached easily. Shade structures can help to reduce the need to water during hot summer months. Automatic watering systems can be installed, thus simplifying or eliminating many heavy or difficult tasks.

We have seen in this chapter how fuchsias may be planted permanently into gardens as hardies, and examples of especially suitable companion plants have been given. I have also tried to consider the needs of disabled or wheelchair-using fuchsia growers. There is little doubt that the true enthusiast will find a way to achieve many unusual ends, because fuchsias are so adaptable and user-friendly.

CHAPTER 10
Ornamental Foliage

Garden designers have become fascinated by the possibilities offered by plants with ornamental foliage in recent years. Coincidentally, at the same time, the range of fuchsias with attractive leaves has increased markedly. Their flowers, too, are more varied, having fewer washy whites, pallid pinks and mauves than in former years. Such fuchsias do well in bright light and are often selected to enhance gardens already laid out with a range of other plants having a similar foliage interest. Fuchsias have the additional advantage that they are among the few plants suitable for hanging baskets during the summer and autumn months.

Variegation in leaf colour can arise in several ways. Most of these are not mutations, or genetic changes, but consist of chimeral rearrangements. Two or more different tissue types exist next to each other in the leaf. Chimeral rearrangement, or sporting, has produced many beautiful new fuchsias. Stability of these characteristics in sports means that all leaves exhibit the same basic features. Among the notable fuchsias mentioned in this book are 'Alton Water', 'Golden Marinka', 'Red Rover' and 'Tricolor'. They all have green centres to their leaves and these are surrounded by yellow margins. In *F. magellanica* var. *molinae* 'Sharpitor', the margin has become a creamy white. 'Variegated Lottie Hobby' is an example from the encliandra types. Marginally variegated fuchsias do not pass this characteristic on to their progeny raised from seed.

Unstable variegation also appears in fuchsia leaves. Splashing and streaking occur unpredictably. 'Herbé de Jacques' has splashing and 'Tom West' has streaking; both came from 'Corallina' and are identical to it in every other way. In both types of unstable variegation ,segments of depigmented tissue are randomly interspersed between patches of normal green tissue. 'Anjo', *F. fulgens* 'Variegata', 'Jack Stanway' and 'Rosecroft Beauty' are examples from our list. 'Sophie's Surprise', produced by

my late friend Brian Stannard, was the first known example among the triphylla hybrids.

Ornamental foliage is not restricted to variegation. Bronze coloration has existed for many years. 'Autumnale' is one of the most famous basket types, but 'Chameleon', 'Strawberry Delight' and 'Tour Eiffel' are other notable examples. It is likely that this coloration can be traced back through the generations to *F. alpestris*.

Red coloration is allied to bronzing in fuchsia leaves. Triphylla leaves frequently have noticeable red staining on the undersides of their leaves and some, like 'Andenken an Heinrich Henkel', can appear dark red on the upper surfaces of the leaves when they are grown in sunny positions.

Bronzing in fuchsia leaves is just a small step away from yellow. Some fuchsias such as 'Ernie Bromley' and 'Troon' carry a hint of bronze on their otherwise yellow foliage. Other fuchsias have yellow leaves and examples from our list are *F. magellanica* var. *macrostemma* 'Aurea', 'Genii', 'Susan Dianna' and 'Waveney Sunrise'.

The following list of fuchsias has been selected by me from across the categories and includes hardies, basket types, summer bedding ones, encliandras and triphyllas. There is a plant for almost every purpose and there are many other fuchsias that have attractive leaves but which space does not allow us to include here.

'Alton Water' (Ransby 1992) This semi-double or double sport from 'Thames Valley' has pink tubes and sepals, and violet petals. Clearly variegated leaves in yellow and green enhance its spreading growth. It is most attractive when used as an edging for window-boxes. Fourteen weeks.

'Anjo' (Hessen 1991) Single. The tubes and spreading sepals are creamy white, but the corollas are russet red. 'Anjo' is stiffly upright, self-branching, heat- and drought-tolerant. Leaves are a variable mixture of green and yellow. It makes a splendid show in garden tubs. Ten weeks.

'Autumnale' (Unknown) Single. This fuchsia has red tubes and sepals, and violet corollas. Its very long and strong branches have coppery-coloured leaves. Large half- or full baskets look at their best when nipped early and given positions in bright light and away from draughts. Fourteen weeks.

'Celebration' (Gouldings Fuchsias 1988) Double. The tubes and sepals are pale orange, but the petals, which are variable in size, are mottled in various shades of orange. The leaves are lace-edged with yellow, which is enhanced in bright light. This fuchsia does best in baskets. Fourteen weeks.

'Chameleon' (Dowson 1991) Semi-double. The short tubes are red, as are the longer sepals. Corollas have four dark violet central petals; small red and violet petals surround these. Growth is spreading or pendant; leaves have a coppery cast. It looks best in hanging baskets. Fourteen weeks.

'Ernie Bromley' (Gouldings Fuchsias 1988) Single. The tubes and sepals are pink, but the medium-sized corollas are violet or mauve in colour. Growth is spreading, vigorous and self-branching. Its leaves are yellow with a bronze cast. This hardy can also be grown in summer baskets. Nine weeks.

F. fulgens 'Variegata' The variably variegated leaves on *F. fulgens* give it an extra dimension in cultivation which would be militated against in the wild. The leaves are a mixture of white and green. *F. fulgens* is described in the chapter on species fuchsias. It grows well in large tubs. Twelve weeks.

F. magellanica var. *macrostema* 'Aurea' This is one of the foliage sports from *F. mag.* var. *macrostema*. It has single blooms, with red tubes and drooping sepals; corollas are violet. Growth is spreading and the leaves are golden. This hardy also makes excellent baskets. Ten weeks.

F. magellanica var. *macrostema* 'Variegata' Here we have a second foliage sport from *F. mag.* var. *macrostema*. Its flowers are unchanged, being red and violet. The spreading branches carry leaves in shades of yellow, silvery green and red. It, too, is hardy and versatile. Ten weeks.

'Genii' (Reiter 1951) This single has cherry red tubes and sepals. Its corollas have dark violet petals. The small leaves are bright yellow, especially when grown in full sun. The strong contrast between the three primary colours adds impact to 'Genii' planted as a hardy in a garden setting. Nine weeks.

'Golden Marinka' (Weber 1955) Single. This is one of the best-known variegated fuchsias. It has bright red petals, sepals and tubes. The leaves have green centres and yellow margins. Half- and full baskets can be made with very little nipping, but growth is slower than 'Marinka'. Twelve weeks.

'Golden Vergeer' (de Jong 1992) Single. This foliage sport from 'Piet G. Vergeer' has flesh pink tubes. Its sepals are also flesh pink, except for their green tips. The corollas are neyron rose. Growth is upright; leaves are variegated green and yellow. This is an amenable, showy plant. Eleven weeks.

'Goldrezie' (Jetten 1993) Single or semi-double. Its tubes and upturned sepals are white. The corollas are rosy red. Its large leaves have green centres with variable yellow edges. Growth is strong and spreading. 'Goldrezie' is easy to grow and looks best in large wall baskets. Eleven weeks.

'Hampshire Beauty' (D. Clark 1987) Double. Tubes and upward-arching sepals are white. Corollas are multilayered and violet. Leaves are variegated with green and yellow margins. Growth is self-branching and wiry. It looks best in mixed baskets. Fourteen weeks.

'Jack Stanway' (Rowell 1985) Single. This foliage sport from 'Cloverdale Pearl' has pink tubes and sepals with white corollas. Foliage is irregularly variegated with cream, green and red. Its hardy growth is spreading and strong. Full baskets are ideal for it to grow in. Eleven weeks.

'Jean Temple' (Wood 1986) Single. The tubes are rosy red. Sepals, also, are rosy red, with upturned ends. Its corollas are violet to mauve. The habit is spreading and self-branching. Leaves are variably marked with green and yellow. It is best grown in hanging containers. Ten weeks.

'Knight Errant' (Gubler 1985) This sport from 'Tom Knights' has single flowers that point upwards and outwards. Its tubes and sepals are white. The corollas are lavender blue. It is multiflowered. The leaves are variegated green with yellow margins. It looks best in large mixed tubs. Nine weeks.

'Larksfield Skylark' (Sheppard 1991) Single. On this fuchsia the small tubes, sepals and cup-shaped corollas are pale pink. Many side shoots appear on sturdy, upright growth. This variegated sport was found on 'Brenda White' and it is principally a bushy and upright pot type. Ten weeks.

'Red Rover' (Hazard, unknown) Single. The tubes and sepals are bright cherry red. Its trumpet-shaped corollas are violet in colour. The leaves are variegated with green centres and yellow margins. Growth is upright and self-branching. It will make a good half-standard with care. Nine weeks.

'Richard John' (Wye 1998) Single. This is one of two foliage sports found on 'Waveney Gem'. Its tubes and sepals are white, but the corollas are pink with a hint of mauve. Multiflowering is the norm. Growth is spreading and self-branching. Leaves are green and yellow. Nine weeks.

'Rosecroft Beauty' (Eden 1968) Semi-double. This 'Snowcap' sport has red tubes and sepals, and small white corollas. Flowers on this bedding fuchsia are plentiful, and clearly displayed on upright, bushy growth. Slightly distorted leaves show traces of cream, green and red. Twelve weeks.

'Snowdon' (Howarth 1988) Semi-double or double. The tubes are flesh pink, but the spreading sepals are white with a trace of pink: the latter are typically twisted and turned up at the ends. Corollas are white. Growth is upright and bushy. Leaves are lime green to yellow. Ten weeks.

'Sophie's Surprise' (Stannard 1992) Single with *triphylla* parentage. This sport from 'Sophie Claire' has orange tubes, sepals and corollas with outward-pointing flowers. Short and bushy show plants are enhanced by the highly irregular, variegated leaves in yellow, green and red. Twelve weeks.

'Strawberry Delight' (Gadsby 1969) Small double. Both the sepals and the tubes are scarlet. The corollas, however, are white with pink veins. Its basket-type growth is spreading and self-branching. Leaves are a honey to copper colour that is enhanced in bright light. Twelve weeks.

'Sunray' (Rudd, unknown) Single. Tubes and sepals are red, and the corollas are violet. The upright growth is bushy, and the leaves are mixtures of creamy white, green and red. The best clarity of colour is obtained if some protection is offered in the garden against wind. Fourteen weeks.

'Susan Dianna' (Wye 1998) Single. This is the second of two foliage sports found on 'Waveney Gem'. Its tubes and sepals are white, but the corollas are pink with a hint of mauve. Multiflowering is the norm. Growth is spreading and self-branching. The leaves are yellow. Nine weeks.

'Tom West' (Meillez 1853) Single. This fuchsia is a sport from the hardy 'Corallina'. Its tubes and drooping sepals are red. The corollas are violet. Growth is strong, arching at first, then spreading. Leaves are variegated cream, green and red. Best in sunny spots: baskets or hardy. Fourteen weeks.

'Tour Eiffel' (De Graaff 1977) Single. The tubes, sepals and corollas are red with a hint of orange. 'Tour Eiffel' is heavily multiflowered and peripheral blooming. The sturdy and self-branching habit is combined with attractively bronzed leaves. This one is ideal for quarter standards. Ten weeks.

'Tricolor' (Unknown) This single fuchsia was thought to be a sport of *F. magellanica* var. *macrostema*, but there is doubt about its origins. Its tubes and sepals are cherry red. Corollas are dark violet. Growth is bushy and upright. Leaves have green centres and yellow margins. Eleven weeks.

'Troon' (Gouldings Fuchsias 1986) Single. The tubes and flyaway sepals are bright red. Corollas are large pink bells with red veins. Branches are upright and growth is self-branching. Leaves are yellow with a honey-bronze overlay. 'Troon' is best grown in pots or tubs. Eleven weeks.

'Variegated Lottie Hobby' (Unknown) This encliandra sport has single perfect flowers. Tubes and sepals are dark pink, but corollas are rather paler. Growth is bushy and foliage is fern-like: leaves are variably splashed with yellow and green. It looks ideal in mixed tubs. Ten weeks.

'Waveney Sunrise' (Burns 1986) Single. Both the tubes and sepals are very pale pink. The corollas are red. Multiflowering is the norm. Strong and arching branches carry golden yellow leaves with red veins. This one will make very large standards without difficulty. Eleven weeks.

This chapter has given a glimpse of the opportunities to be found in using foliage as an additional and valuable feature when growing fuchsias in the garden. Beauty lies in the merits of each whole plant rather than in its isolated parts. The juxtaposition of mutually complementary plants, flowers and foliage, is an art worth pursuing, an adventure into the unknown.

CHAPTER 11

Special Fuchsias

This chapter covers some categories of fuchsias that have different characteristics to those commonly grown. The five groups are those which are most easily identified and used by fuchsia enthusiasts across the world. They each have special characteristics that make them valuable for particular purposes and special places. Encliandras flower best in the lowest light levels and can be miniaturized without difficulty. Whites produce their most attractive colour in sheltered places, away from full sun and wind. Terminal-flowering (*triphylla*) types are the most heat- and drought-tolerant of the fuchsias: they are ideal as patio plants. Paniculates are not only extremely floriferous and unusual but can be really substantial and statuesque plants. When all definitions fail, there are some fuchsias that I would still not wish to be without and these are grouped together for convenience under our fifth heading, 'Novelties'.

Part one: ENCLIANDRAS

This brief list is of encliandras that are not species and which can be grown by anyone interested in these miniature, axillary-flowering, gems. My own studies on hybridizing these fern-like plants have shown promise, and they are certainly highly fertile and variable when looked at as a group. After all, in the wild, encliandras show every sign of being species in a state of flux. Work elsewhere on hybridizing them has been limited and it is only within the last few years that this field has taken a firm hold on the imagination of fuchsia growers. The key features that still require attention are an increase in size combined with a wider range of colours and shapes. The facts that they have such long flowering seasons and will bloom in low light levels, that they are accustomed to dry conditions and could be used on a much wider scale, are likely to promote their advancement.

Some attempts have been made to cross encliandras with paniculate-flowering fuchsias.

One such attempt was made by Mr B. Breary, who produced 'Edith Hall' by crossing *F. ravenii* with *F. paniculata*. 'Lechlade Tinkerbell' is the earliest to have been produced by crossing paniculate and *encliandra* types. It, together with *F. paniculata*, has a faint trace of perfume on its blooms. 'Neopolitan' has a stronger scent, but the fuchsia with the most obvious perfume is 'Gondoliers'. 'Edith Hall' and 'Lechlade Tinkerbell' are listed for convenience under part four of this chapter.

Please note that within the context of the encliandras, the term 'perfect' denotes those fuchsias that have both male and female parts. Stigmatic flowers also exist and are usually the smallest ones found.

'Coral Baby' (Drapkin 1989) Single and perfect flowers. Tubes, sepals and crinkled petals are coral red. Growth is strongly upright with slightly felty green leaves. 'Coral Baby' is adaptable and attractive. It looks best grown in large tubs or in the summer garden border. Ten weeks.

'Eva Twaites' (Breary 1994) These single, perfect flowers have long pink tubes. The slightly drooping sepals and petals are pink. Flowers are unusual in appearance. Growth is long-jointed but robust. 'Eva Twaites' will make large plants with care and is versatile. Twelve weeks.

'Fuksie Foetsie' (Van de Grijp 1979) Single. These perfect blooms have pale pink tubes, dark pink swept-back sepals and light pink petals. The heavily serrated leaf margins and self-branching but spreading growth makes this an easy and adaptable fuchsia to grow. Twelve weeks.

'Gondoliers' (Gouldings Fuchsias 1987) Single, scented and perfect flowers. The rosy red tubes adjoin white, swept-back sepals with green tips. The petals are pale pink and its blooms are among the largest in this group. Branches are strong and spreading enough for hanging pot use. Twelve weeks.

'**Katinka**' (Goedman 1989) This single has larger than average perfect blooms. Its tubes, sepals and petals are bright scarlet. Growth is shrubby, self-branching and strong. 'Katinka' makes good mini-standards, fans, espaliers and cones. It prefers cool conditions. Eleven weeks.

'**Kleine Sandra**' (Schlikowey 1998) These perfect flowers are single. The tubes, swept-back sepals and the spreading petals start life pink but mature to red. Growth is upright, self-branching and neat. This fuchsia looks best in mixed baskets and large containers. Eleven weeks.

'**Marlies de Keijzer**' (de Keijzer 1999) The pistillate, single flowers are among the smallest in existence. Tubes, sepals and corollas are almost strawberry red. Foliage is gun-metal, or bronze green. Growth is adaptable, shrubby and very strong. It does best in large pots. Twelve weeks.

'**Mendocini Mini**' (Francesca 1975) Single. The perfect flowers have white tubes, partially recurved sepals, and petals; these turn pink as they mature. A lax habit goes well with multiple side shoots; its leaves are pale green. This is a versatile fuchsia. Twelve weeks.

'**Mikado**' (Gouldings Fuchsias 1987) Single. These pistillate flowers are bright orange that darkens to red in full sunshine. Growth is strongly upright and very robust. This miniature fuchsia has the ability to be made into mini-standards or used in mixed tubs and baskets. Eleven weeks.

'**Neopolitan**' (Clark 1984) Single. These perfect blooms appear as three separate colours on the plant, namely white, pink and red. Its flowers are quite large for an *encliandra*. Growth is strong, spreading and rather irregular. This is an interesting and scented fuchsia. Eleven weeks.

'**Obcylin**' (Beije 1999) The best of the encliandras, 'Obcylin' has single perfect blooms. The short tubes and spreading sepals are peach-coloured. Its flared corollas are darker in hue: it is multiflowering. Growth is self-branching and adaptable. It prefers cool growing conditions. Ten weeks.

'**Oosje**' (Van de Grijp 1973) Single. 'Oosje' has pistillate flowers only: their tubes and sepals are red, but the petals change from pale pink to red. Growth is spreading, but bushy and strong. This fuchsia will make a variety of interesting shapes without difficulty. Twelve weeks.

'**Prove Thyself**' (Unknown) These large, perfect, single blooms have ivory white tubes. The spreading sepals are white with green tips. Corollas are pink with a hint of flecking in the colour. Growth is strong, self-branching and spreading. It dislikes being too wet and does best in mixed tubs. Eleven weeks.

'**Radings Gerda**' (Reiman 1984) These blooms are small, single and perfect. Its tubes, sepals and corollas are lavender blue. Growth is stiffly upright and shrubby. This fuchsia is a slow starter, but it makes up for this and is attractively different. It does best in medium-sized pots. Twelve weeks.

'**Radings Inge**' (Reiman 1980) Single. Flowers are perfect and have salmon or pale orange petals, sepals and tubes. Growth is strong, bushy and spreading. 'Radings Inge' is attractive as a show plant or when it is used in tubs or baskets with other plants. Twelve weeks.

'**Radings Karin**' (Reiman 1980) Single. These perfect blooms have tubes that start as dark orange before changing to red, like the tubes and sepals. Growth is sturdy and bushy, and the leaves have undulating edges. It is easy to shape into fans, espaliers and mini-standards. Twelve weeks.

'**Radings Mia**' (Reiman 1986) Single. The pale lilac of the tubes is like that of the sepals and corollas. The very small flowers are pistillate. 'Radings Mia' has spreading but self-branching growth that can be trained into various shapes for the purpose of miniature topiary. Twelve weeks.

The first part of this chapter has taken a brief look into the wonderful, and currently miniature, world of *Encliandra* fuchsias. Within the next few years, I confidently expect a revolution to take place in their development. The colour range, in foliage as well as flower, is expanding inexorably. Double encliandras are a distinct possibility. Multiflowering is on the increase. Exciting times lie ahead.

Part two:
WHITE-FLOWERED FUCHSIAS

White-flowered fuchsias are particularly suitable for gardens that are shady and sheltered from too much heat during the longest days of the year. These plants rarely look at their best when they are exposed to sun and wind. They may be used to give extra height to garden displays if they are used in hanging containers, but are often combined with the silver and white foliage of other plants to create specific colour schemes and unusual atmospheres within small gardens. White, after all, provides a peaceful foil between conflicting colours in so many settings. 'Our Ted', the first white triphylla to be offered for sale to the public, has not been described here but in part three of this chapter. Those fuchsias selected are among the most robust and versatile of the many currently available, being less prone to fungal infections and bloom-marking than before.

'Bobby Shaftoe' (Atkinson 1973) Semi-double. These flowers have white petals, sepals and tubes. They are produced on the ends of rather long branches that require early nipping. The unusual shape of the blooms is worth the effort of producing bush plants for pleasure. Twelve weeks.

'Countess of Aberdeen' (Cocker 1888) Single. Tubes, sepals and petals are all white. Profuse and peripheral blooming is here combined with stiff, short-jointed and upright growth. Protection helps to preserve the flower colour. Pot-grown plants give the best results. Nine weeks.

'Florence Mary Abbott' (Gouldings Fuchsias 1983) Single. Petals, sepals and tubes are white, but the anthers are ruby red. The flowers are held prominently and retain their colour well. Growth is spreading and self-branching; it is best seen in hanging pots. Nine weeks.

'Hawkshead' (Travis 1962) Single. The tubes, sepals and petals are small and white with a hint of green, especially at the sepal tips. It is multiflowered. Leaves are pale green and the growth is stiffly upright and shrubby. 'Hawkshead' is useful in the hardy border. Eight weeks.

'Linda Goulding' (Gouldings Fuchsias 1981) Single. Tubes are short and white and the recurved sepals are white with a hint of pink. Corollas are white with pink veins. Flowers are produced upwards, in quantity, near the branch ends. Pot plants are upright and bushy. Nine weeks.

'Mancunian' (Gouldings Fuchsias 1985) Double of the parrot-beak type. Tubes change from white to red, but the long recurving sepals remain white. Overlapping petals are white with pink veins. Growth is self-branching, vigorous and pendant. This looks best in full baskets. Twelve weeks.

'Patience' (Gouldings Fuchsias 1987) Double with a classical outline. Tubes and upturned sepals are white. The corollas are white with a suggestion of pink. Growth is strongly upright and self-branching. Minimal protection is needed to produce show bushes and standards. Twelve weeks.

'River Plate' (Gouldings Fuchsias 1989) Single. Tubes are white. Sepals are white with pink-flushed tips. Corollas are white and bell-shaped. Flowering is copious. Growth is spreading and lends itself to the production of attractive hanging pots or wall baskets. Ten weeks.

'Roy Walker' (Walker 1975) Double. The tubes and sepals are white, as are the large spreading corollas. The many flowers are held near the branch ends. Flowers are improved if sun and wind are avoided. Attractive show plants or conservatory specimens can be trained. Twelve weeks.

'Snow Goose' (Shaffery 1994) Double with loose, parrot-beak blooms. The short tubes and upswept sepals are ivory white tinged with pink. Petals are white with pink veins. This fuchsia has pale green leaves and is especially self-branching. 'Snow Goose' is best grown in hanging pots. Twelve weeks.

'Torville and Dean' (Pacey 1985) Double with asymmetrical outline. The tubes are usually reddened but the sepals green-tipped; petals are white with a hint of pink. Growth is strong, spreading and self-branching. This versatile plant makes a splendid basket with protection. Ten weeks.

Part three: TRIPHYLLA (TERMINAL-FLOWERING) TYPES

Terminal-flowering, or *triphylla*, fuchsias are now numerous, although for a long time this was not the case. Such fuchsias are particularly suitable for gardens that are warm and sheltered. They are almost always self-cleaning, rarely setting seed on their own, and it only remains for the busy gardener to sweep up spent flowers as they fall. There is still a large element of novelty in gardens that concentrate almost exclusively on these delightful plants. At last, we have fuchsias of this type that will grow happily in hanging containers. All these plants have a long flowering season that tends to improve as the months pass by. As you will see from the following list, I have carried out much original work in this field and most notable among Gouldings Fuchsias' introductions have been 'Our Ted', which was the first white *triphylla* offered for sale to the public, and 'Orient Express', the first bicolour of its type. My late friend Brian Stannard has many fine hybrids to his credit, including the first ornamental-foliage fuchsia with *triphylla* parentage, 'Sophie's Surprise'. Herman de Graaff, who very kindly wrote the foreword to the first edition of this book, has been instrumental in providing aubergine gems such as 'Maori Pipes' and 'Miep Aalhuizen'. Since 1985 there has been an explosion of interest in terminal-flowering fuchsias and a vast increase in their range. The key goal of hybridists is the creation of a group of bright and easily grown bicolours.

'Adinda' (Dijkstra 1995) Single. This terminal-flowering fuchsia has large clusters of salmon-coloured, slender-tubed blooms. These are carried on the multiple upright branches produced. Its leaves are sage green. 'Adinda' makes a moderately large, dense and neat show plant. Ten weeks.

'Bessie Kimberley' (Kimberley 2001) Single. The tubes are long and thin. They, like the short sepals and small petals of the corollas, are scarlet. Flowering is very free. Leaves are blue-green. Growth is of a miniature *triphylla*, upright and free-branching. Ideal for competition. Thirteen weeks.

'Boy Marc' (Stannard 1995) Another single of the *triphylla* type. The long tubes, short sepals and brief corollas are orange. Its flowers are bright and long-lasting. The habit is spreading, with robust and compact branches freely produced. This is an ideal fuchsia to grow in hanging pots. Ten weeks.

'Brian C. Morrison' (Stannard 1993) Single. The substantial orange or reddened tubes are long, but the similarly-coloured sepals are short; their pleated petals are a brighter hue. Growth is strongly upright and self-branching. It makes superb show- and garden-tub plants. Ten weeks.

'Brian Kimberley' (Gouldings Fuchsias 1999) Single of the *triphylla* type. The tubes are long and thinly tapered. Sepals and petals are short. Flowers are orange and exceptionally numerous. Growth is upright and tolerant. This makes a good show-plant in large pots. Eleven weeks.

'Brighton Belle' (Gouldings Fuchsias 1985) Single. The long tubes and short sepals are rosy pink and the corollas are almost salmon. The spreading and self-branching habit helps to produce perfect hanging pots and these are extremely tolerant of hot and dry conditions. Ten weeks.

'Dorrian Brogdale' (Gouldings Fuchsias 1994) Single. These tubes are long, sturdy and pink with a touch of orange. Its short, outswept sepals are similar in colour. So, too, are the parrot-beak corollas: free-flowering. Growth is strong and ideal for hanging positions. Eleven weeks.

'Edwin J. Goulding' (Stannard 1992) Single. Short sepals and long tubes are dark red, but the small petals are a rather brighter red. Continuous and multiple flowering is the norm. Blooms are long-lasting. A free-branching, upright habit provides plants in tubs for garden displays. Twelve weeks.

'Fulpila' (Beije 1998) Single of the *triphylla* sort. The long, thin tubes are pale tangerine. Its shorter sepals are slightly paler and have green tips. Corollas are a darker orange. Its growth is upright and can be helped by early nipping. It makes splendid shallow garden bowls. Eleven weeks.

'Golden Arrow' (Gouldings Fuchsias 1985) Single. Long and very thin orange tubes join green, recurving sepals that carry pronounced spurs at their insertions. The petals are tangerine in colour. Growth is strong but rather spreading, and this suits garden planting. Twelve weeks.

'Grand Duchess' (Stannard 1993) Single. This miniature, terminal-flowering fuchsia has cornet-shaped tubes that, like the very small petals and sepals, are bright orange. Its upright and bushy habit lends itself to reasonably small pots grown for show purposes. Twelve weeks.

'Insulinde' (De Graaff 1991) Single. A faultless terminal-flowering fuchsia, 'Insulinde' has long, orange tubes and short orange petals and sepals. Slightly bronzed and shiny foliage is found with bushy and upright growth. Bedding schemes benefit from its presence. Eleven weeks.

'John Maynard Scales' (Gouldings Fuchsias 1985) Single. This terminal-flowering fuchsia has long orange tubes, short orange sepals and short but brighter orange petals. Its upright growth is exceptionally strong, requires early nipping and is best suited to large tubs. Twelve weeks.

'Koralle' (Bonstedt 1905) Single. On this fuchsia the short petals, small sepals and longer tubes are all salmon orange. The sage green, velvety leaves combine with upright and bushy growth. 'Koralle' does well as a patio plant and as a show bush in medium-sized pots. Eleven weeks.

'Lechlade Apache' (Wright 1984) Single. The brilliant red blooms on 'Lechlade Apache' have long, thin tubes, fully recurved sepals and short petals. This interspecific cross (between two species) has strongly upright and bushy growth that is ideal for big plants in very large tubs. Thirteen weeks.

'Lechlade Potentate' (Wright 1984) Single. The tubes vary from chocolate brown near the seed pods to salmon orange where they join the green-tipped sepals and salmon petals. Growth is strong, upright and adaptable. This fuchsia makes an unusual specimen plant. Twelve weeks.

'Leverkusen' (Rehnelt 1902) Single. It becomes terminal-flowering only gradually. The tubes are moderately long and broad; they, the sepals and the petals are bright scarlet. Growth is spreading, stocky and self-branching. It is perfect for large tubs and is particularly heat-tolerant. Ten weeks.

'Mandy' (Bielby/Oxtoby 1994) Single. Its long, tapered tubes, short sepals and corollas are orange. Flowers are held in axillary whorls near the branch ends. Its habit is bushy and upright. It grows best out of full sun and is at its best in mixed garden borders and containers. Ten weeks.

'Maori Pipes' (De Graaff 1987) Single. This terminal-flowering fuchsia has long tubes that are aubergine, like the short sepals. Its short petals are somewhat brighter. This slow starter has small, leathery leaves and will grow into a large and attractive conservatory tub plant. Twelve weeks.

'Mary' (Bonstedt 1897) Single. 'Mary' is among the brightest of the terminal-flowering types, has long tubes, shorter recurving sepals and small petals; all are scarlet. The narrow leaves are green with a blue cast. This eye-catching fuchsia does best in mixed outdoor tubs. Thirteen weeks.

'Miep Aalhuizen' (De Graaff 1987) Single. Here is another unusual fuchsia that has long, thin tubes; these and the short, recurving sepals and corollas are lavender-hued. Growth is strongly upright but amenable to nipping and capable of making large tub plants. Fourteen weeks.

'Monica Dare' (Gouldings Fuchsias 1999) Another single *triphylla* fuchsia. Its tubes and short, flared sepals are bright orange. The corollas are a brownish-orange. Flowers are peripheral and eye-catching. Growth is sturdily upright and self-branching. It makes an ideal show plant. Twelve weeks.

'Orient Express' (Gouldings Fuchsias 1985) Single. The long tubes are a mixture of pink and white. The short sepals are red-tipped, but the petals are rose pink. These unusual blooms are produced on upright and amenable branches. Attractive show plants can be produced. Eleven weeks.

'Our Ted' (Gouldings Fuchsias 1987) Single. Long tubes, short sepals and brief corollas are all white, although the latter sometimes have a hint of pink. Growth is upright and it dislikes nipping. 'Our Ted' grows best in soil-based composts and warm conditions at all times. Fourteen weeks.

'Pan' (De Graaff 1991) Single. Long pink tubes join short, spreading pink sepals. The corollas are pink. 'Pan' has a strong and arching habit of growth. It is amenable to nipping and tying-in. Good basket plants can be produced, as can plants in mixed garden tubs. Eleven weeks.

'Piper's Vale' (Stannard 1992) A *triphylla* single. It has tubes of moderate length; these are orange. Both the sepals and the corollas are also bright orange. Growth is freely self-branching and spreading. It makes an excellent show plant in hanging pots and baskets. Twelve weeks.

'Rina Felix' (Felix 1984) Single. Here is another unusual fuchsia with long, thin tubes that range from green to red. Its short sepals are green, but the brief petals are beetroot purple. Growth is upright and the leaves are rather leathery. Large pot plants thrive best. Twelve weeks.

'Roos Breytenbach' (Stannard 1993) Single. This, one of the most floriferous of *triphylla* introductions, has long tubes with short petals and sepals: its blooms are crimson. Upright and amenable growth can be helped to produce good show or garden plants in about twelve weeks.

'Small Pipes' (De Graaff 1987) Single. The flowers are smaller than many in this group and are often produced in terminal panicles. Tubes, sepals and petals are pale lilac. The branches are strong and adaptable. Large, bright and floriferous tub plants can be grown. Eleven weeks.

'Thalia' (Bonstedt 1905) Single. This terminal-flowering fuchsia has long, orange tubes and shorter orange sepals and petals. It has velvety green leaves and is one of the most useful terminal-flowering types; regenerates from below soil level. It looks well in large containers and tubs. Twelve weeks.

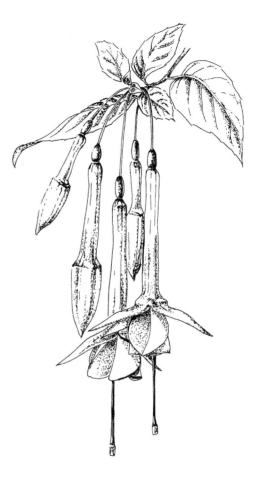

Fig. 19 'Peter Crooks': although not always fully terminal-flowering, this fuchsia exhibits most of the characteristics of the triphylla type.

'Timothy Titus' (Gouldings Fuchsias 1998) Single of the terminal-flowering, or *triphylla* type. The medium to short tubes and the sepals are dusky orange. Its corollas are orange with just a hint of brown. Growth is upright, sturdy and self-branching. It makes a good show plant. Twelve weeks.

Part four: PANICULATES

'Dymph Werker van Groenland' (Beije 2001) A paniculate-flowered small single, this fuchsia has short orange tubes. Its orange sepals open and sweep back; they are green-tipped. Orange petals are slightly longer. Growth is strongly upright: most suitable for large conservatory tubs. Eleven weeks.

'Edith Hall' (Breary 1987) Single. The perfect flowers are held in the leaf axils, or sub-racemes, and are pink maturing to red. The leaves are large and irregular in outline. A strong but spreading habit suits this fuchsia to hanging pots and to edging large garden tubs. Fourteen weeks.

'Grietje' (Bögemann 1984) Single. These perfect *enclandra*-like flowers are bright orange and quite large for their type. They are carried in small clusters on strongly upright plants reminiscent of its other parent *F. paniculata*. It grows best in large pots or conservatory tubs. Ten weeks.

'Lechlade Tinkerbell' (Wright 1983) Single. The tubes, recurved sepals and petals are dark pink and the blooms are perfect. The flowers are held in panicles on the branch ends or on branchlets. Growth is strongly upright and bushy. This fuchsia grows well in large tubs. Twelve weeks.

'Martin's Inspiration' (Beije 2001) A paniculate-flowering single. Its tubes are short, thin and pale orange. The fully recurved sepals are orange with green tips. Corollas are a darker orange becoming almost mauve with age. It is strongly upright and self-branching: perfect as a pyramid. Eleven weeks.

'Panache' (De Graaff 1996) Single. This fuchsia combines the characteristics of *triphylla* and paniculate fuchsias. Sepals and petals are short. They and the longer tubes are tangerine-hued. Flowers are held in multiple racemes. Growth is upright, then spreading when in bloom. Hanging pots. Eleven weeks.

'Ton Goedman' (Beije 2001) Another single with masses of small paniculate flowers. The tubes are rosy pink. The fully recurved sepals are also pink, but with darker tips. Corollas are pink, maturing to red. Its habit is strongly upright and self-branching. It makes excellent pillars. Eleven weeks.

'Trientje' (Bögemann 1992) Single. 'Trientje' is another of those crosses between fuchsias from the *enclandra* and *paniculata* sections. Its perfect flowers are held in small clusters and are dark lilac in colour. Growth is strongly upright: best seen as tub plants in the conservatory. Eleven weeks.

'Wapenveld's Bloei' (Kamphuis 1991) Single of the paniculate type. This hybrid has perfect flowers with rose pink tubes and recurving sepals. Its petals are orange. The habit of growth is strong, forming many side shoots. This fuchsia grows strongly: it looks well in the summer border. Twelve weeks.

Part five: NOVELTIES

When these categories have been defined, there still remain some fuchsias that do not fit neatly into them. Because some of these unusual gems are so outstanding and collectable, it would be a pity if they were to be forgotten. For this reason, they are grouped here as novelties. Perhaps, in years to come, and with the progress of plant breeding, some will come to be seen as the forerunners of new and useful categories of fuchsias.

'Daryn John Woods' (Gouldings Fuchsias 2000) This single fuchsia has long and gently tapered aubergine tubes. Its short sepals and petals are aubergine. Growth is upright, spiky and shrubby. This fuchsia looks best in the garden in large tubs. Fourteen weeks.

'Janneke Brinkman-Salentijn' (Beije 1992) Single. This almost-black fuchsia has no tubes but its spreading sepals and small corollas are very dark aubergine. The flowers are held in the leaf axils on stiffly upright branches that have small leaves. Medium or small pots are best. Twelve weeks.

'Lechlade Marchioness' (Wright 1985) Single. The long tubes are pale orange and the short, hanging sepals are green. Each petal is a very pale orange and the flowers are produced in the leaf axils on bushy, strongly upright plants that do well in conservatory tubs with some support. Fourteen weeks.

'Leonhart von Fuchs' (Strümper 1989) Single. These very long tubes are orange, but the short, spreading sepals are green. Its small petals are a brighter orange. Branches are spreading, especially under the immense numbers of flowers produced on basket plants. Twelve weeks.

'**Little Witch**' (De Graaff 1990) Single. A cross between paniculate and *magellanica* parents, its tubes and sepals are pink, the latter recurved and green-tipped. Corollas are violet. Growth is upright and the leaves small and pale green. It makes attractive mini-standards. Eleven weeks.

'**Martin's Catherina**' (Beije 1992) Single. The short tubes and spreading sepals are waxy-textured and green in colour. Its small corollas are chocolate-hued. Growth is upright and helped by judicious early nipping. 'Martin's Catherina' is very unusual to look at as a pot plant. Ten weeks.

'**Martin's Choice**' (Beije 1999) Single. The tubes are short and they are brick-red coloured. Its sepals are green-tipped and downward-pointing. 'Martin's Choice' has yellow petals. Growth is spreading. This fuchsia makes a multiflowered pot plant. Nine weeks.

'**Spellbinder**' (Gouldings Fuchsias 1996) A single with unusual parentage. Its tubes, recurved sepals and cornet-shaped corollas are dainty and dark red. It carries multiple small clusters of flowers. Plants are strongly upright; helped by early nipping. It makes excellent mini-standards. Nine weeks.

'**Tarra Valley**' (Felix 1987) Single. The short tubes and sepals are green with a waxy texture. Petals are a dark chocolate colour and small. The habit of growth is bushy and its leaves are leathery. This fuchsia will make a large, but rather short pot plant with very little help. Ten weeks.

'**Très Long**' (Van der Post 1990) Single. The immensely long tubes are pale orange. Short sepals are green and pendant. The small petals are pale orange. Growth is strong, but side shoots are slow to develop. 'Très Long' is best grown for conservatory displays. Fourteen weeks.

'**Vuurwerk**' (De Graaff 1988) Single. These flowers are produced in the leaf axillae. They have dark orange tubes, drooping green sepals, and orange petals with a hint of brown in them. The growth is spreading and reasonably bushy. 'Vuurwerk' does best in pots. Twelve weeks.

'**Walz Lucifer**' (Waldenmaier 1991) Single. The tubes are medium to long, and thin. They and the recurving sepals are rosy pink. The petals are bright orange. Blooms are produced in the axillae on very bushy and upright plants. This is best grown as a pot plant. Fourteen weeks.

CHAPTER 12
Exhibiting Fuchsias

Planning, Persistence and Plantsmanship

Three qualities are necessary for a fuchsia competitor to be successful at the highest level. We will call them The Three P's. The first of these is Planning, for there is no possibility of winning consistently at the best shows unless adequate preparation has taken place long before the event. Foremost among the tasks undertaken is a close inspection of previous and current schedules so that all the rules and regulations are understood and nuances of meaning grasped. Ideally, there should be a careful inspection of the venue and it is clearly best if this can be undertaken during previous events. Planning for those that are some distance from home might even necessitate an examination of parking and accommodation in the area. It certainly involves choosing the right plants early enough to maximize their potential in any given pot-size class.

Persistence is the second of the three qualities. This calls for practical attention to the regular care of potential show fuchsias. Water and food should be given at the optimum time, and in the best way for each plant's requirements, so that there are no periods of stress. Perfect show plants can only be produced by persistent attention to detail. Not many growers have dedication to the highest degree. This quality might apply to 'never giving up' but, at all times, it implies seeking ways to make the most of the plants and circumstances to hand.

The third of the three P's is the quality of Plantsmanship. Most growers find this the hardest to understand. Perhaps it is best described as that creative element in a competitor's personality that allows maximum, and often unexpectedly good, results to be obtained from the plants and the ways in which they are staged to advantage. In past years it might have been possible to win major awards by putting fuchsias on the bench in uniform and boring clusters. Greater sophistication is called for nowadays if judges and visitors are to be impressed.

The Best Fuchsias

Top-quality show plants are most easily grown from plants well known for their predictability and high performance. Such plants are often called 'Bankers'. These fuchsias are usually found to have relatively short internodes and to be strong and self-branching. Their natural vigour allows them to be nipped and trained to enhance the finished show plants. Foliage should be attractive in its own right and should complement the colour of the flowers. On inspection, such fuchsias are found to have very few obvious faults.

Beginners to competition showing often place too great an emphasis on the size of the flowers carried by a plant. In practice, many top show fuchsias have semi-double or single blooms that are small but are carried in immense numbers on well-shaped plants. The first characteristics of value are thus earliness and predictability of flowering. These are matched by continuity and quantity of blooming. Older hybrids were often spasmodic in their flowering and few carried more than one bloom in each leaf axil. It is also essential that a fuchsia has flower colours that are attractive and that have a greater impact than others around them.

Staging to Advantage

There are a number of ways in which a show plant's impact can be maximized. The first and most obvious one is by creating the biggest and best fuchsia possible in the pot size given. A good small plant should never beat a good large one if all other things are equal. This does assume, however, that the larger plant does not look gross in proportion to its container.

Fuchsia flowers have their greatest impact when they are seen at eye level. This may be most obviously achieved by growing plants in one of the standard shapes. Even if this extra height is unavailable, it is almost certainly possible either to raise plants on small stands or to lift them on stacks of upturned pots. Such arrangements of course need to be adjustable: more or fewer pots being used to obtain the maximum results.

Drapes can be used to great advantage in providing an appropriate and complementary setting for plants on display. These should not be obtrusive but can often add considerably to an exhibit's overall effect. The yellow leaves of an ornamental-leaved fuchsia such as 'Alton Water' may be enhanced by a black velvet drape, and the subtle shades of 'Jack Stanway' by layers of pale pink or grey chiffon.

The art of staging can be very important to showing. This is partly for its effect on the judge, but also because the more attractive a display of plants, the greater its impact on the visiting public. Most of us have vivid memories of outstanding exhibits that combined the best of plants with the most advantageous staging methods. There follows a brief look at some of the possibilities.

A fuchsia on its own can be raised to give it impact when compared with other plants nearby: the effect might be purely psychological but that, after all, is part of the game. Pairs of plants can be staged side by side or one behind the other. In the latter case it is worthwhile raising the back plant to give it greater interest and to enable it to be seen properly, but with its pot hidden.

Using extra pots at the back, three fuchsias may be staged to give a pyramidal shape, with two plants at the front and bottom; the formation can also be reversed, with two plants at the back. The deliberate use of drapes also allows plants to be staged in a style reminiscent of flower arrangements. Such displays can be given an off-centre emphasis, with plants staged at varying heights. I have experimented with such arrangements over several years at many major shows, and they certainly add interest to an exhibit, giving it an edge over others.

Four plants can be staged with two raised behind and two low at the front. They could also be placed in a diamond formation with a single low plant at the front, two slightly higher flanking fuchsias, and a single plant raised higher still at the back. Five or more fuchsias are given the same imaginative treatment to ensure the exhibit maximizes their advantages and impresses those who come to see the show. The experienced exhibitor always tries to add impact and interest to optimize the effect of the fuchsias, rather than settle for standard practice and mediocrity.

Attention to Detail

Of course, taking such trouble over staging fuchsia exhibits would be a waste of time if other procedures were neglected. The first, and most obvious, thing to do is to remove all dead, discoloured and damaged leaves from the plants. Branches that have died back should also be trimmed away, so that plants that are examined closely by the judge are worthy of inspection and free of fault. Many exhibitors also clean the leaves with small cotton wool or cloth swabs dipped in a dilute mixture of milk and water. This treatment leaves the plant with lustrous foliage, and usually looks more natural than some of the proprietary leaf-shining solutions that are suitable for house-plants.

Canes and ties need to be checked to see that they are secure and unobtrusive. The ideal time to place these in position is early in the life of a plant. Later, great care needs to be taken if branches and flowers are not to be damaged when the ties are inserted. Ideally, there should be no stakes or ties in bush or shrub plants, but this is clearly impossible if standards or other ornamental shapes are exhibited. The shape of a plant can often be improved by tying branches to fill gaps in its structure, in the early stages of development. The pliability of young stems allows this to be done with little difficulty. It is not impossible to alter the position of branches, with care, even on mature show plants. It might also be worthwhile cutting away branches that detract from the plant's symmetry.

The essential ingredient in a competitor's armoury, then, is to make the very most of each individual plant and its characteristics. Additionally, each pot should be cleaned (or changed for an identical one), and it should stand on a saucer to ensure that water marks do not appear on the bench beneath. The plant label should also be clean and legible; many competitors place the label at the front of the plant, where it can be clearly seen, once they have decided on its best aspect. Others remove the label and rely instead on a card that bears the fuchsia's name.

Dead and damaged flowers should be taken away. In most cases, seed pods are also better removed from the exhibition plant if it is to win; the exceptions are species and encliandras.

Flowering Times

Stopping dates can be the most perplexing things to determine. No two years have exactly the same weather and no two gardeners or their gardens provide identical conditions. Nevertheless, a rough guide is essential if success is to be obtained with show plants and, in this book, approximate intervals have been given with named plants. Precise timing is not possible but most fuchsias will stay in bloom, as perfect show plants, for several weeks provided that temperatures are not too high. The most effective way of keeping plants in flower is to keep them growing as strongly as possible, using balanced fertilizers. This is contrary to the expectations of many growers, who concentrate their efforts on supplying proportionately more potassium at flowering time.

Blooming can be most effectively retarded by lowering ambient temperatures without significantly reducing light levels. Raising temperatures will increase flower production and shorten timing, but the range within which this is effective is usually between 10°C (50°F) and 21°C (70°F). One way of achieving more acceptable temperatures is to grow show plants under shade structures out of doors during summer. Air movement, and therefore wind damage, is likely to be greater there than in a greenhouse, and there will also be an increased risk of insect damage to the blooms as they open.

Exhibitors often remove flowers that open prematurely on their plants. It is often best to remove large buds, too, so that the plant does not waste energy on producing unwanted bloom. Extra growth will provide the extra flowers needed. It is sometimes possible, when fuchsias come into flower much too early for the planned show date, to remove the lead shoot from each of the main branches. Obviously, this needs to be done with great care if the side shoots that will be produced are to come into bloom instead.

Bloom Quality

Mature flowers are often bruised by visiting bees. Plants like 'Flirtation Waltz', with its rather fleshy blooms and pastel shades, are among the easiest to mark. Whites and pinks are most likely to show such damage. Doubles are more susceptible than singles and semi-doubles. Some other fuchsias have flowers that have inherent faults. 'Display' is one of these; its sepals show clear splitting where they are joined as blooms mature and open. Monotone and dull-coloured flowers, for example 'Swanley Gem', are unlikely to impress the judge as much as the bright bicoloured flowers of 'Finn'. This area – the selection of the best plants for the job – is one in which some exhibitors excel. Show plants should produce the best results for the least effort over the longest period and with the minimum of faults.

Final Details

Effective exhibitors will ensure that entries are correctly filled in and given to the show secretary before the closing date. It is wise to look carefully at all the possible combinations of plants in order to maximize the returns for the efforts taken. Sometimes an entry placed in a different class, or a plant placed in a different group, will gain an extra point or two and this can be significant when it comes to prizes based on a pointing system. Many top competitors try to stage their fuchsias before the actual show, to consider all the options. This allows the work done on show day to go ahead with speed and confidence.

Before plants are taken to be staged, a 'goody-bag' of equipment should be prepared containing those items that help to present the best possible effect at a show. I have found the following items useful: scissors, twine, thin plastic-covered wire, canes (usually of the split and green sorts), pots, saucers, labels, pens, a schedule, a bucket and watering can, cloths and – finally – the exhibitor's cards. It is very easy to arrive at a show only to find that an essential item has been left behind.

The following selection of fuchsias is taken from the chapters in this book dealing with specific types of growth. It details those plants most likely to produce prize-winning results in each show category. Full details of each fuchsia can be found within the chapters given and are not repeated here.

Bush (Chapter 5):
'Bealings', 'Beryl Shaffery', 'Christine Shaffery', 'Galadriel', 'Grace Durham', 'Graf Spee', 'Joan Young', 'Lindisfarne', 'Nellie Nuttall', 'Nimue', 'Pink Fantasia', 'Rose Fantasia', 'Shelford' and 'Tom Knights'.

Standard (Chapter 5):
'Blue Waves', 'Celia Smedley', 'Checkerboard', 'Flying Scotsman', 'Graf Christian', 'Lancelot', 'Norfolk Ivor' and 'Peter Bielby'.

Basket (Chapter 8):
'Alison Ruth Griffin', 'Arabella Improved', 'Betty Jean', 'Cecile', 'Gwen Wallis', 'Hermiena', 'Lena', 'Pinto de Blue', 'Suffolk Punch' and 'Sylvia Barker'.

Hardy (Chapter 9):
(The contents of this list are governed not so much by quality as by the out-of-date nature of show hardy lists. These will need to be checked before growing and entering in classes for hardies.)

'Beacon Rosa', 'Dollar Princess', 'Genii', 'Graf Witte', 'Margaret', 'Mauve Bauty', 'Pixie' and 'Pumila'.

Ornamental foliage (Chapter 10):
'Alton Water', 'Anjo', 'Golden Vergeer', 'Jack Stanway', 'Knight Errant', 'Larksfield Skylark', 'Red Rover', 'Richard John' and 'Tom West'.

Encliandra (Chapter 11):
'Fuksie Foetsie', 'Katinka', 'Kleine Sandra', 'Marlies de Keijzer' and 'Obcylin'.

White (Chapter 11):
'Florence Mary Abbott', 'Patience', 'Snow Goose' and 'Torville and Dean'.

Triphylla (Chapter 11):
'Adinda', 'Bessie Kimberley', 'Insulinde', 'Koralle', 'Monica Dare', 'Thalia' and 'Timothy Titus'.

Paniculate (Chapter 11):
'Grietje', 'Lechlade Tinkerbell', 'Martin's Inspiration' and 'Wapenveld's Bloei'.

Not all competitions judge individuals' performances. Some are for groups of fuchsia enthusiasts or their clubs. Planning, persistence and plantsmanship are just as essential to success in these events. Outside the world of competition there is a gamut of events to promote fuchsias. Church displays, festivals, stands at general horticultural shows and carnival floats are among those which have been attempted. There are always opportunities for those with imagination and energy to put this versatile flower before a public that is increasingly interested in its potential as the most popular garden flower.

CHAPTER 13
Calendar of Care

The main purpose of this chapter is to provide a quick checklist for busy gardeners. It does not purport to be fully comprehensive, but contains the key elements needed for each of the twelve months of the year. In the United Kingdom the year starts in January, as day length begins to increase, and finishes with the darkest month, December. Of course, these months will vary from one part of the world to another but the general principle based upon day length remains. Such things as frosts will also affect different areas to different degrees, and some compensation will need to be made for places with different climates from that found in the south-east of England.

I suggest that this Calendar of Care is used as the starting point from which to construct your own individual year planner. The year planner itself can be kept from one season to the next and enhanced as experience grows. This will allow for variations relating to different parts of the world, and even microclimates, to be dealt with according to need.

Many gardeners make use of a diary to note when special actions were required or particular conditions prevailed. Although these are unlikely to be the same for any two successive years, such notes do provide a general guide and an aid to memory. Details can be kept about weather conditions, temperatures, light levels, humidity, pest or disease increases and special conditions required for show plants. In later years these notes make for interesting reading – and can prevent the repetition of avoidable mistakes. After all, as any earnest gardener will tell you, one disaster is unfortunate but to have two the same is carelessness.

MONTH ONE

Remove debris from resting plants. Do not let root balls dry out completely but water sparingly. In heated greenhouses spray fuchsias with fungicides to reduce fungal attacks. Wash greenhouse glass to obtain the maximum light available indoors. Do not crowd young plants: this reduces air circulation and light.

MONTH TWO

Handle the plants regularly as this is the best way to learn about their individual needs. Water more frequently and start to feed with half-strength balanced fertilizer. Prune back to actively growing shoots. Ventilate greenhouses on sunny days. Pot-on young plants: pot-back old ones. Nip to shape.

MONTH THREE

Feed and water regularly now. Pay attention to cleanliness inside and outside the greenhouse. Cuttings should be available now and will root readily. Take care not to let fuchsias become too leggy and large. If you are buying-in fuchsias, watch them carefully for any signs of pests or diseases.

MONTH FOUR

Continue feeding with balanced fertilizers. Try to avoid steep rises in temperature under glass on sunny days, by ventilating and shading as required. Take cuttings and shape plants carefully. Pot-on fuchsias, if possible, when they show plenty of active white roots around the edges of their root balls.

MONTH FIVE

Plenty of water, feed and ventilation are needed by actively growing plants. Attention should be paid to the last stopping date for show plants: about 8–12 weeks. Protect plants from pests by a carefully prepared strategy. On hot days increase the air humidity within greenhouses by wetting the floors.

MONTH SIX

Continue all general care as before. Ventilate greenhouses. Fuchsias to be planted out-of-doors should be placed in well-prepared sites and protected from late cold spells occurring at night. Protect plants from pests and diseases. Take cuttings to be grown-on as biennials for showing next year.

MONTH SEVEN

Continue to water and feed frequently. Do not forget to protect plants against visiting pests. Shade fuchsias under glass if temperatures rise very steeply. Dead-head fuchsias to keep them tidy and growing to their full potential. Prepare plants for showing and read show schedules carefully in advance.

MONTH EIGHT

It is very tempting to cease daily care of fuchsias during hot and sultry spells. Feeding, watering and cleanliness are more important as temperatures rise more regularly. Dead-head flowering plants. Make a note of those fuchsias that do well in particular situations, and of new ones to buy.

MONTH NINE

Clean greenhouses (and heaters) so that they are ready to house fuchsias. Start hybridizing as temperatures and day lengths decline. Continue watering but reduce feeding slightly. Take special care to see that plants do not catch pests and diseases before overwintering indoors.

MONTH TEN

Remove plants from the garden if they are to be overwintered under glass. Trim top growth half-way back and stop feeding altogether. Water sparingly. Check that glass is clean and that insulation is effective before providing artificial heat. Dead-head hardy fuchsias out of doors.

MONTH ELEVEN

Trim hardy plants to half their size, clean borders and mulch with, for example, bark to protect against frosts. Take care not to overwater fuchsias kept indoors. Check that heaters are working and make use of maximum/minimum thermometers to ensure optimum conditions are provided whenever possible.

MONTH TWELVE

Take special care of any small fuchsias being overwintered under heated glass. Handle plants frequently and pay special attention to disease-control measures. Light is now at its lowest. Do not be tempted to use too much heat or nitrogen. Order catalogues so new fuchsias can be bought early.

CHAPTER 14

Problem Identification

The purpose of this chapter is to aid diagnosis of those problems that afflict fuchsias. Simple steps can be taken to assess the cause when plants are suffering from an ailment. Establishing the causes of such troubles places us in a strong position to combat them.

This chapter would be not be complete on its own; Chapter 15 addresses the background knowledge and understanding behind this diagnostic chapter. The two chapters are to be used in tandem: reference letters in this chapter relate to the individual sections of the next chapter, listed in alphabetical order by problem within their appropriate sections (see below). Once a provisional diagnosis has been made in this chapter, further details can be sought by following the cross-reference to Chapter 15, 'Pests and Diseases'. Descriptions of each problem are given and corrective measures are described for each.

In order to simplify diagnosis, this chapter channels enquiries into three specific areas:

flowers, foliage and growth. Experience has proved this to be the most effective way of directing one's efforts. Do not read the whole chapter every time you need to consult it. Rather, if something is adversely affecting the foliage, turn directly to the foliage section. Refine your enquiries from a broad diagnosis, bearing in mind that the following are only presented in Chapter 15:

Part One: Pests (and their predators)
Part Two: Diseases
Part Three: Genetic Changes
Part Four: Chemical Controls
Part Five: Other Controls

Besides these possibilities there remains the largest group of signs and symptoms. These 'cultural' problems might present as deficiencies, wayward patterns of growth or slight deviations from what we have been led to expect from our plants. The code designated throughout this chart for cultural problems is U.

FLOWERS:

The first part of this diagnostic chart relates to

the size, colour, presence and viability of the various parts of each bloom.

No blooms	Nipping can be prolonged for too long. Low light levels or excessive nitrogen fertilizer encourage this fault. Varietal quirks and inferior stock may be responsible. U
Enlarged and containing more parts than normal; often joined, like Siamese twins	Gigantism: most common in some cultivars like 'Estelle Marie'. Not caused by pests or diseases. Does not carry abnormal chromosome counts that might be useful in hybridizing. Best removed from show plants. Some fuchsias, like 'Mrs W. Rundle', have lumps and bumps appearing irregularly on their tubes and sepals as a normal characteristic. S
Larger-than-normal flowers	Often found on whips or when few blooms are present. High nitrogen feeds and poor light levels encourage them. U

Smaller blooms than normal	Starvation, hot weather and concentration on high potash feeds will make them more likely. U
Mixtures of flowers and foliage; often green, white and red	Fasciation: more common when day length shortens. Not caused by pests or diseases. Of no value for hybridizing or vegetative propagation. R
Changes in colour, especially when they occur in petals only and result in paler colours in subsequent blooms on one branch only	Sporting or mutation: propagation may retain the new characteristic and result in a new and worthwhile cultivar. T
Very pale colours	Growing in poor light or with excessive nitrogen. Occasionally found at the end of the season as a transient aberration. Least appealing when bright reds are affected. U
Very bright colours	Growing in intense light and wind. Excessive use of potash feeds. Most unsatisfactory when white flowers are affected. Move to sheltered positions. U
Colours different from those expected	Misnaming is common. Sometimes this is as a result of a marketing ploy but more commonly it occurs as a simple mistake. Nurseries often misplace a label from the next fuchsia in their catalogue and it might be worth checking their list to see if this has occurred. Amateurs often label fuchsias with the name of the person from whom they obtained the cultivar and such names will not be found in check lists. U
Sepals brown on their inner surfaces	Caused by early and hot sun, and excessive moisture within maturing buds. Most noticeable on creamy white sepals like those of 'White Joy'. Move such plants to more sheltered positions and do not water in the evenings. U
Sepals brown at their tips	Premature opening of buds by hand may cause this. Ageing results in sepals turning brown first, as does bruising by movement and wind. U
Premature dropping of flowers	Cultural shock will cause this on some cultivars like 'Our Ted', which dislike being moved. Dry indoor atmospheres will also cause bud drop. Humidity trays, filled with wet gravel, help to prevent it. Small, bright-flowered cultivars are least likely to be affected. Poor light levels sometimes cause this. U
Flower dropping	This is a natural ageing process when blooms pass maturity. Some cultivars are naturally slow to shed unsightly and brown flowers. Self-cleaning is a desirable characteristic most likely to be found in triphylla types. U

Holes bored in the flower tubes	Some insects like bees and wasps drill through the hypanthium in order to obtain nectar. In some regions humming-birds are also known to do it. This might be because the tubes are too long for nectar to be reached, or just out of laziness. M
Lack of petals	Apetalous fuchsias occur among the species: examples are *F. tilletiana* and *F. procumbens*. Some hybrids exhibit this usually less-than-desirable feature. Wasps sometimes cut them away from mature flowers. Damage is mainly restricted to a few plants, especially those out of doors. M, U
Lack of anthers	Gynodioecious bloom production is to be found among the *Encliandra* section. Some other species, such as *F. procumbens*, appear to carry this as a variable characteristic. Wasps may remove anthers once they are formed and carrying pollen. M, U
Inability to set seed	There are a number of different reasons for this. Some cultivars never set seed. Others will cross with a limited range of other fuchsias. Refer to Chapter 16 on hybridizing. Wasps sometimes remove styles and stigmas. M, U
Lack of viable pollen	This is natural with some cultivars such as 'Mary'. Other fuchsias may produce no pollen at all; triphyllas are loath to produce pollen except in very warm conditions. Windy, dry and hot weather adversely affect pollen production and viability. U

LEAVES:

The majority of problems relate directly to cultural shortcomings. We have seen how few pests and diseases affect fuchsia flowers. This may be because leaves and young stems carry large amounts of highly nutritious sap. Leaf disorders are easily grouped into the following categories: colour changes (to brown, red or yellow), size, extras (often the excrements of insects), physical damage and defoliation.

Leaves brown at their apices	Burning occurs as a result of moisture, which collects at the apex, being caught by early sunlight. Overnight exudation from the leaf openings, located along the leaf margins, runs to the leaf tips. This area also burns most easily if plants become excessively dry and hot. Spraying in hot weather can also cause this problem. U
Leaves brown overall	Dead leaves may result from chemical sprays, frosts, dead roots, broken branches and from fungal attacks. L, P, Q, U

Rusty or dull red leaves. Young and old leaves lost	Red spider attacks show first as colour changes affecting leaves of all ages. Close inspection of each affected leaf, if necessary with a magnifying glass, will show the little creatures and their fine webs. Rust attacks should be considered. H, Q
Red leaves on normally green cultivars	Redness can be found on cultivars such as 'Marinka' and 'Pixie' when plants have been subjected to a chill or cold draft. The redness does not go away. Marker plants can act as early warning agents to show when cultural conditions are unsatisfactory. U
Leaves red above and with orange pustules on their undersides	Fuchsia rust can often be spotted first by the dull red coloration of the upper leaf surface. Pepper-like grains are apparent on the underside of the leaf. Diseased leaves are best picked off and destroyed. Affected plants should be treated with a fungicide known to be active against this condition. Weeds growing nearby, such as rosebay willow herb, should be removed. All newly purchased plants should be quarantined for a fortnight to ensure freedom from pests and diseases. Q
Old leaves turn yellow and fall	This is a natural ageing process that can be exaggerated by high phosphate and potassium, especially in sunny spells. Increased nitrogen feeding will help to reduce it somewhat. Plants grown on the biennial method with root restrictions are most likely to be affected. U
Yellowing of young leaves	Mutations sometimes occur as variegation and may be seen by observant growers. Some cultivars naturally have yellow foliage without variegation. T
Dark veins and pale interspaces	Deficiencies are first shown as variations in colour between veined and unveined sections of the leaves. Chelated trace elements can be used to correct this problem over a period of three weeks. Trace elements most likely to be required are iron, magnesium and calcium. They must be provided in an assimilable form in order to combat chlorosis. U
Symmetrically rounded sections removed from leaves	This is the work of the leaf-cutting bee. Leaf sections are carried into underground galleries where they appear like cigar stubs and act as egg chambers. Douching the foliage with dilute and smelly liquid (see Part 5 of Chapter 15) will help to reduce visits. K

Irregular patches cut from leaves	Vine weevil adults remove sections from the leaves at night. Torchlight searches may be used to locate them. Specific pesticides can be used to prevent their eggs hatching and growing below soil level. A variety of caterpillars also may be found and removed, or treated with a pesticide. C, L
Leaf hanging limply on its pedicel	A few cultivars like 'Susan Ford' may be found to have a single leaf drooping at any one time, but not the same leaf every day. This is a cultural oddity and not caused by pests or diseases. U
Very large leaves	Standard whips will create much-enlarged leaves. Some, like 'Royal Velvet', may be greatly increased in size when growing conditions are perfect. Some species such as *F. fulgens* naturally have large leaves when compared with most hybrids. High nitrogen feeds, poor light, warmth and high humidity will produce this effect but also create a predisposition to fungal disorders. U
Very small leaves for the cultivar	High-potash feeds reduce leaf size, especially in bright and hot conditions. U
Very small recurved leaves with waxy surfaces and short internodes	Paraffin oil heaters may give off substances that have this effect on fuchsias. Dry moving air, such as that provided by electric fan heaters, gives ideal conditions for fuchsias. U
Leaves produced alternately rather than opposite each other on the branches	When conditions are perfect for strong growth, some cultivars will show this as a normal characteristic, especially when light levels are low. Terminal-flowering or *triphylla* types are most likely to be affected. U
White flakes on the undersides of leaves	Whitefly, their eggs and body casings adhere to the undersides of leaves. Aphicides should be used to remove pests. Debris can be wiped off. O
Grey mould on the upper leaf surface	Aphids drop honeydew as they feed. The resultant black and grey fungus can be washed from the leaves although it is dirty and sticky. Aphicides should be used to remove the pests. F, O
Furry mould especially affecting leaf pedicels, both on plants in propagating beds and on adult plants	*Botritis cinerea* can kill single leaves or run over whole branches and plants. Fungicides should be used to prevent further damage. More light and air should be provided around the foliage. P, U

GROWTH:

Problems affecting fuchsia growth may well not be as clearly visible as those afflicting their flowers and foliage. They are, however, more likely to have serious underlying causes and consequences. In this chapter they are grouped according to whether a part of the plant or the whole plant is affected. This means that the smallest problem appears first and the most serious one, death, is placed last.

Lopsided growth	This is most likely among basket fuchsias such as 'Fiona'. Sometimes leaves on one side are larger than those on the other side. Staking into a vertical position will help marginally. Root growth is also likely to be stronger on one side than on the other. U
Etiolation	Poor light, excessive heat and high nitrogen promote etiolation. U
Spittle around the stems near growing points	Froghoppers can be found hiding under the frothy spittle. They may be killed by hand or with insecticides. Such attacks are usually short-lived and outdoor fuchsias are most likely to be affected. D
Furry grey mould affecting young, immature growth	*Botritis cinerea* runs along branches and leaves. It should be treated with fungicides. Growing conditions will need to be improved. Foliage sprayed daily with water, or careless watering in dull conditions, encourages attacks. P
Not thriving: shoots and roots	Old compost is often acid and unsuitable for fuchsias in pots. A fresh medium with a neutral pH is ideal. Check for vine weevils on overwintered plants. Look under the leaves for pests like red spider mites. On propagating benches, and at the base of larger pots, ants are sometimes a nuisance: proprietary substances can be bought to kill them without harming the plant. Feed a balanced fertilizer, a little and often if plants appear to be starving. Give a tonic of chelated trace elements. Some cultivars are naturally less vigorous than others. Root restriction and overpotting are equally damaging on occasion. Overwatering and overpotting can lead to stagnation and a reduction in 'air-filled porosity' in the compost. Sciarid flies usually affect cuttings or seedlings more commonly than larger, established plants. A, H, I, L, U
Distorted growing points	Greenfly, Western Flower Thrips (WFT), capsid bug, leaf hopper, gall mite and some chemicals can cause this. Insecticides will cure all except the last of these. WFT-infested stock is best destroyed. Directions should be followed on the correct use of chemicals. B, E, F, G, N, U

Blind growing points	Nipping young shoots too early can sometimes damage the nearby side shoots before they start to elongate. *Triphylla* types in flower often cease growing vegetatively. Some sprays will cause this. Slugs may nip the first leaves from seedlings. J, U
Whole plant limp	Limp plants might be dry. Just as often, in very hot weather, they are unable to absorb and transpire sufficient water. Excessive moisture can drown fuchsias in pots. Heat can also burn and kill roots. Double potting or shading, plus raising air humidity, will help to reduce damage. Excessive dosage with fertilizers and insecticides will kill plants occasionally. Consider vine weevil. L, U
Plant rots at base of stem, later constricting and dying	Fungal diseases abound in the plant kingdom. Hygiene is especially necessary for seedlings and cuttings. Re-using compost for the same genus of plants is inadvisable. Fungicides may be used to treat cuttings, their compost and older plants. If much-needed stock is affected and caught early enough, the tops of the plants may be cut off and used again as cuttings. P, U
Defoliation	Red spider and caterpillar attacks have already been mentioned. C, H
Plant falls over without roots	Vine weevil larvae eat the roots of many pot plants like fuchsias. Preventive measures should be taken during the summer (in Great Britain, for example, two months after the longest day) in order to prevent problems later. Notches cut from leaves should be noted and adults combated. Pesticides should be active over several months to kill the grubs when they hatch. Nematodes can be used to combat them. L

Having read this chapter, one might be forgiven for thinking that fuchsias are prone to many pests and diseases. In reality this is not the case at all; for a start, they do not suffer from any known viral disorders, as do most other garden plants. The factors adversely affecting flowers, foliage and growth are both easy to diagnose, using this chart, and interesting in their own right. Inadequate hygiene and poor cultural practice are responsible for the majority of problems. In fact, sloth and ignorance are the fuchsia's main enemies. If you have read the chapter this far, you are not likely to be a gardener guilty of the former characteristic! In the next chapter I have set out guidelines to combat the latter. Then, armed with knowledge and the means of control, we can confidently repeat this ancient dictum as our own: '*Nil desperandum*'.

CHAPTER 15

Pests and Diseases

Most fuchsia growers will be seriously bothered, at one time or another, by problems concerning their plants. Many but not all of these difficulties are associated with cultural conditions. This chapter is concerned with those pests and diseases that may affect fuchsias and how to combat them effectively. Sometimes, as we will see, natural predators can be useful in fighting for the health of our plants, and these are discussed together with any drawbacks. Such predators have no adverse effect on fuchsias but, for a variety of reasons, might fail to be fully effective in protecting them from all harm. Chemical cures are also discussed in this chapter in some detail; increasing restrictions on their availability and range contribute to difficulties where contact or systemic controls are in use.

PART ONE: PESTS

A   ANTS
Ants can sometimes be a problem on propagating benches that are kept too dry, on plants grown in pots at ground level and on fuchsias planted directly in the soil. The problem comes not from any direct attack upon the fuchsias but from the root disturbance caused by underground colonies and from the aphid colonies encouraged for the production of honeydew.

   Ant predation Various products are available to combat ants and few of them have any serious consequences for plants if they are used as directed. None of them rely on predation.

B   CAPSID BUG
Capsid bugs belong to the order *Hemiptera* and the sub-order *Heteroptera*: they have two different types of wing and have stabbing or sucking mouthparts. Their damage is restricted to distortion of immature, or green, fuchsia stems. They are closely associated with leafhoppers. Their wings are folded flat on their bodies when not flying. Over two hundred species of capsid bug exist in the British Isles alone. *Lygacaris pubulinus*, the common green capsid, attacks many different plants, including fuchsias, and is active during the summer months. It mainly affects plants grown out of doors.

   Caspsid bug predation This seems to be commercially non-existent and I have read no literature on natural predation.

C   ELEPHANT HAWK MOTH
The significance of the Elephant Hawk Moth lies mainly in the fact that one of its principal hosts is the willow herb, which is itself the source of so much fuchsia rust. The moths themselves are highly attractive and, although there is some evidence that they may be able to pollinate some of the long-tubed fuchsias and are increasing in numbers again, they do not damage the plants. Their caterpillars, which are dull brown, eat leaves but rarely do significant damage to growing fuchsias.

   Elephant Hawk Moth predation Nothing has been documented on this subject.

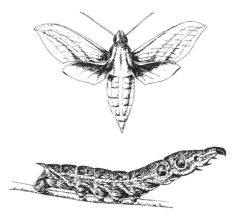

Fig. 20 A hawk moth and its caterpillar: although there are several different hawk moths in the British Isles, they are relatively rare.

D   FROGHOPPER

Froghoppers are true bugs in the order *Hemiptera* and the sub-order *Homoptera*, like leafhoppers. *Philaemus spumarius* can be seen as a small mottled brown bug, some 7.5 mm (0.3 in) in length, leaping from stem to stem and from plant to plant, especially out of doors. Larvae are small and green, hiding themselves from predators in the familiar frothy cuckoo-spit. Damage caused by froghoppers is similar to that found after attacks by other bugs and is usually restricted to plants grown outside.

Froghopper predation This appears to be unknown.

E   GALL MITE

Asculops fuchsiae is a gall-producing mite that attacks fuchsias. These minute creatures may cause reddening and, less often, produce galls (swollen and distorted foliage) affecting the growing points, leaves and petioles. They are somewhat difficult to control, as may be expected with any gall-producing pest. (Perhaps those galls with which most gardeners in the United Kingdom will be familiar are the oak and blackcurrant ones.) Eggs are laid in the plant tissues and as the larvae hatch and begin to grow, galls begin to develop. The larvae continue to feed within the gall chambers until they are ready to bore their way out.

Gall mite predation This is unknown in the wild.

F   GREENFLY

Greenfly come from the superfamily *Aphidoidea* that is within the order *Homoptera*. They are plant-sucking bugs with soft bodies. Their wings, if present, are membranous. They all feed on plant sap and exude large amounts of sugary liquid called honeydew. This substance is used as food by many other insects. Nobody knows for certain why aphids drink such large amounts of sap, unless it is to increase their mineral or vitamin intake. Sap is taken up with the aid of the fluid pressure within plant tissue. Sometimes aphids inject substances into the leaves in order to break their food down into an assimilable form. Many aphids are environmentally specific. They are often found on the undersides of leaves or nestled around young shoots, where they frequently distort and damage the foliage.

Aphids are parthenogenetic; that is, females can go several generations without needing to be fertilized. Females are also viviparous; that is, they can produce live young. Sometimes, eggs hatch before they are laid and young nymphs are born that already carry the next generation inside them. When colonies become too large or food supplies too small, winged forms develop and swarm in the same way as ants and bees. They always overwinter as females in their wingless form. Winged aphids are called *alatae* and wingless ones are called *apterae*. During the early part of the year all the young are females and it is only later in the summer that males are born. Aphid nymphs escape from their eggs by cutting through the embryonic membrane with the sclerotized saws on their heads.

Aphids have two glands at the rear of their backs that are called flexible siphunculi. These exude a caustic solution onto the heads and eyes of small predators that attack them from behind, usually by grabbing one of their back legs. Sometimes, when this happens, aphids are able to kick predators off the leaf surface. This siphuncular fluid has a scent that acts as a warning to other aphids, telling them that predators are nearby, as well as securing the release of some aphids when they are attacked. Aphids that live near the periphery of plants, like those on fuchsias, usually have longer siphunculi than those living in more closed environments, such as root-feeding aphids. Aphids have alternative host plants on which they overwinter, like the spindle tree. During the summer they live on fuchsias and many other plants.

Greenfly predation Cryptic coloration is developed by some aphids in diffuse colonies and used by them as camouflage.

Ant colonies protect other aphids, like black bean aphids, by attacking and removing enemies from their midst.

Parasitic wasps often lay their eggs in aphids' bodies. When these hatch out, the wasp larvae feed on the aphids' tissues before leaving through a hole that they cut in the ectoskeletons. Dead, hollow, usually straw-coloured aphids are often to be found among aphid colonies. Wasps belonging to the family *Braconidae*, of the genus *Aphidius*, commonly attack greenfly in this way. Others, like those from the genus *Praon*, attach their hosts to the leaf surface within fine gossamer cocoons. Chalcid wasps act as natural predators but the predator that is usually produced commercially to combat aphids in greenhouses is the midge *Aphidoletes aphidomyza*.

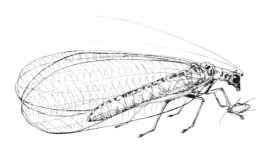

Fig. 21 Adult lacewing with aphid

Fig. 23 Adult ladybird

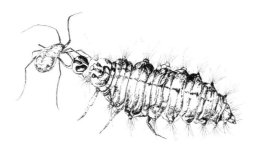

Fig. 22 Lacewing larva and prey

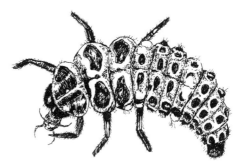

Fig. 24 Ladybird larva

Lacewings are among the natural predators of greenfly. They are often called 'golden eyes' because this is the colour they appear when they reflect the light. They lay their eggs on leaves near aphid colonies. They are attached by stalks of hardened mucus, usually in clusters, and this helps to protect them from other predators. Hatching occurs a little over a week after eggs are laid. Some lacewings, like *Chrysoperla carnea*, are green in colour, while others, such as *Kimminsia subnebulosa*, are brown. They do not fly much. They and their larvae attack aphids. The larvae have large jaws that they use to suck the tissues of other insects. Adult lacewings often lift aphids clear of the leaf surface and then suck the body fluids through their mandibles.

Ladybirds are equally common predators of aphids. Many overwinter naturally in the British Isles but large migrations of European ladybirds often arrive to supplement local numbers. Increases in numbers occur on a cyclical basis every three or four years. Ladybirds come from the genus *Coccinellidae* and their special feature is the spots that they carry on their wing casings.

These vary in number, among the forty or so species of the beetle, from two to twenty-four. The commonest species of this beetle in the British Isles is the seven-spot or *Septempunctata*, or 7-punctata. Beetles of the two-spot are also very plentiful. Wing casings vary in colour from red with black spots to yellow with black spots, but some, with black wing cases, have red or yellow spots. As these colours suggest, ladybirds have few natural enemies of their own because they exude a violently unpleasant, yellow caustic fluid from their leg joints that will deter most predators. Adults and larvae consume large numbers of aphids. Larvae are slate blue in colour, with yellow blotches, and are about 1.27 cm (0.5 in) long.

Hoverflies are the third common predator of greenflies. Superficially, they resemble wasps but have no stings. There are about two hundred and fifty species of hoverflies, *Diptera syrphidae*. The line drawings in this book, which show a range of natural predators, give an example. Hoverflies feed on pollen and nectar and are therefore often seen in large numbers around fuchsias in flower. Males are the more

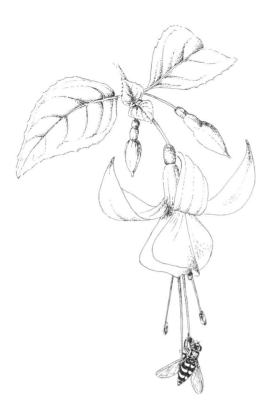

Fig. 25 Hoverfly on a fuchsia, showing the characteristic angle at which these insects sit on flowers.

active and are frequently seen hovering, waiting for females. Hoverfly larvae have no legs or eyes, although they are sensitive to changes in light level, and they hunt by smell, most often at night. They look like slugs and suck fluid from their prey through arrow-shaped mouthparts. Eggs are laid on leaves near aphid colonies and they hatch after a few days: they then go through three transformation stages before they eventually become adults, after about twenty-nine days. When they are not feeding, larvae often shelter in folds or rolled-up leaves, where they can be seen in groups as they rest. Hoverflies are themselves heavily parasitized.

G   LEAFHOPPER

Leafhoppers, or true bugs, are from the order *Hemiptera* and the sub-order *Homoptera*, with wings that are identical to each other and that form angled roof shapes over their abdomens when not in flight. *Cicadella viridis* is the common green leafhopper seen widely across

the British Isles. It is about 7.5 mm (0.3 in) long. Leafhoppers, like capsid bugs, puncture plants with their stylets and suck sap. The damage they do is similarly restricted to distortion of young stems, especially on outdoor plants. In fact, sucking is probably too active a term, for most sap-sucking insects use the positive pressure of sap within a plant's tissues to force liquid out; their rostrums act as capillary tubes when inserted into the plants' tissues.

Leafhopper predation This appears to be undocumented and unknown.

H   RED SPIDER MITE

The two-spotted mite or red spider, *Tetranychus urticae*, is the bane of many horticulturists. It lives on the undersides of leaves and is so minute it is difficult to observe until attacks have reached critical proportions and are almost impossible to eradicate. Young and old leaves are affected and may be dull and reddened, or simply shed from the plant during spells of warmer weather. Red spider mite reproduce rapidly by asexual means when environmental conditions are favourable. Their gossamer webs are to be seen across leaf axils, or on their undersurfaces, where they act as a protection against climatic vagaries and a variety of natural and artificial controls. Females lay eggs at the rate of about six a day and as many as a hundred will be laid in an adult's lifetime. Reproduction rates accelerate with rising temperatures, as with other pests. The potential numbers of offspring are frighteningly large: at temperatures of 30°C (86°F) and within optimum conditions, around thirteen million would be produced during a single female's lifetime (taking into account the offspring of her own young). Population explosions are compounded by the difficulty in applying miticides to the undersides of fuchsia leaves. Unfertilized red spider eggs develop into females with a single set of chromosomes. Because there is no courtship, reproduction is swift and any pesticide resistance is quickly passed to future generations. Red spider mite take about twenty-one days to develop from eggs to adults at temperatures around 18°C (64°F).

A red spider mite is beige in colour with two dark spots on its back that are composed of chlorophyll concentrated in the mite's guts as it has fed on the sap of the plant. When day length falls below thirteen-and-a-half hours and temperatures begin to drop, the mite turns red again as it prepares to go into winter hibernation. If plants are growing actively and sap quality is good, hibernation will be delayed in spite of the reduced length of the day. At this time of the year red spider mite are negatively phototropic; this leads them to withdraw from the upper parts of plants, which can give the impression that they have been eliminated, whereas it may be that they are simply hibernating. It is thought that the reddened form is less attractive to predators: this means that every effort must be made to reduce numbers of the pest before autumn colours brighten. Red spiders overwinter among leaves, branches, soil and greenhouse structures. They resume activities as soon as temperatures rise and plant growth increases. Red spider mite move towards the upper parts of the plants' canopy in the spring, led by positive phototropism and by the likelihood that temperatures will be higher there. Red spider mite will thrive at high temperatures in low humidity levels.

Red spider mite predation Its main predator is *Phytoseiulus persimilis* that is specific to red spider and very aggressive. Adults will eat up to five adults or twenty juveniles and numerous red spider eggs in a day. Pests cannot become resistant to predation. (Incidentally, none of the predators used commercially and mentioned in this chapter harms fuchsias in any way.) *Phytoseiulus* needs a higher humidity level than red spider mites in order to thrive. Plant stress and poor sap will bring about a summer rest (or diapause) in the mites' life, while the predator, not being native to Great Britain, can starve and disappear. As conditions improve, new predators might have to be introduced into greenhouses to avoid an increase in pest numbers. When conditions are poor, red spider will hang by threads from the upper leaves and drift with the wind onto other plants nearby. The *Phytoseiulus* predatory mite has a bright red, pear-shaped body, and is larger than its victims. It moves faster and its reproduction rate is twice as quick. At temperatures around 18°C (64°F) females will lay over fifty eggs that will hatch within five days. The cycle of development is complete in nine to eleven days. The predator lives for up

to twenty-six days. At temperatures around 21°C (70°F) predator populations will increase by three hundred times in thirty days. Introductory rates of about ten thousand to 0.4 hectare (one acre) will soon see phenomenal population levels among predators. *Phytoseiulus* waits until it has eaten all the red spider mite from the undersurface of the leaves and will then move to the upper leaf surfaces, from where it is blown long distances onto other plants out of doors. Predators should be spread evenly among plants and because they are positively phototropic, they should be placed low on the plants at first.

Another predator of red spider mite is *Typhlodromus pyri*.

I   SCIARID FLY
Sciarid flies are just one of the many fungus flies. They are minute, black flying insects and often appear in large numbers around propagating units and young plants. Their larvae are similar to nematodes in appearance and they can eat roots and cause considerable damage, especially among newly-rooted cuttings.

Sciarid fly predation Predation is unknown but also unnecessary for plants under cultivation. Insecticides have remarkably little effect on them or their larvae. The best method of combating them is to allow compost to become very much drier, and to maintain these drier levels for as long as possible by watering minimally on the maxim that, until a cure is achieved, little and often is better than a good soak when sciarid flies are a problem.

J   SLUGS
Small keel slugs are most likely to be a problem in moist areas like propagating benches, where they can kill considerable numbers of small seedlings in the course of an hour or two by nipping them off just above soil level. Larger slugs and snails may cause problems where piles of debris are left near growing plants.

Slug predation Greenhouses, because of their high humidity levels, often attract resident toads and visiting birds; both will help in reducing the numbers of slugs that are also attracted by these conditions. Molluscicides can be applied in liquid form in order to avoid the possible trauma to pets and birds associated with some other methods of treatment.

K   SOLITARY BEE (LEAF-CUTTING)

Solitary bees are widespread but in England their activities are mainly concentrated in the southern counties. *Megachile centuncularis* is the patchwork leaf-cutter, which removes oval sections from the leaves of plants such as roses and fuchsias. Its activities are concentrated during the summer months when leaf sections are removed with shearing jaws and then rolled into cylinders. These are sealed at one end, stocked with pollen and nectar, then have an egg placed in each. A circular section of leaf seals the open end of the chamber. Galleries of these cigar-like egg chambers are sometimes found around the edges of the soil when fuchsias are removed for potting-on. Otherwise, damage is limited to a few plants and for short periods of time, usually in June or July (in the United Kingdom).

Solitary bee predation Nothing is known, and there appears to be no commercial need for it in the United Kingdom.

L   VINE WEEVIL

Vine weevils, *Otiorhynchus sulcatus*, have become a serious pest in recent years. They cause the most critical problems on those fuchsias that are kept over winter as old plants. Adult vine weevils, which appear to be only females, cause little damage to fuchsias as they only cut irregular notches from their leaves. This damage is done mainly at night and it is often possible to find the weevils with a torch during the hours of darkness. In the summer a single adult can lay over five hundred eggs a week over a period of, perhaps, two months. Adults are highly mobile and have only vestigial wings. They are about 1.27 cm (0.5 in) long, with a typical weevil's snout, or beak, and are brown or dark grey in colour. The crescent-shaped larvae are about the size and colour of fishing maggots. They feed on the roots and crowns of plants until they are destroyed; often the first sign of an attack is the sudden collapse of a previously healthy plant. Eggs are laid in about August and September (in the United Kingdom) and these hatch out to cause problems during the following spring. This is only one of a very large group of British beetles numbering almost five hundred species, many of them living on the roots of plants such as nettles. Across the whole world, weevils are the most numerous of all animals, with over forty thousand species identified.

Vine weevil predation Nematodes, which look like thread-like worms, have been produced commercially to combat this pest. *Steinernema feltiae* (previously *bibionis*) has been the main subject chosen as a commercial predator, but *Heterorhabitis* has also shown promise. Under greenhouse conditions these nematodes can travel through capillary matting and invade untreated pots to kill their prey. Bacteria associated with the nematodes cause red discoloration of invaded vine weevils. As numbers of nematodes multiply in the dead weevils, they migrate to find new hosts. Another approach has been to attack the weevil with a naturally occurring fungus, *Maetarhizium anisopliae*.

M   WASPS

Wasps often multiply as the season reaches its peak and flowering is at its height. Holes may be found bored through the tubes of fuchsia flowers. More often, stamens or even pistils are removed from blooms so that they look unusual and are of no value for hybridizing. Even so, the damage done to fuchsias is likely to be less than that done to the people who tend them.

Wasp predation This is unheard of. Instead, locate the nests and use chemicals to eradicate them once they become a problem.

N   WESTERN FLOWER THRIP

The Western Flower Thrip (WFT), or *Frankliniella occidentalis*, has become a serious pest in recent years. The thrips are of the order *Thysanoptera* and are most commonly known to people as thunder flies. Their tiny elongated wings have hairy margins. They suck plant sap but also take pollen and nectar from the flowers. Identifiable damage is often the distortion of young leaf or flower tissue, giving a crinkled appearance. Silvering, deformity, growth malfunctioning and brown oedema-like bumps may be seen. Adults and larvae scrape and rasp leaf surfaces and suck the resulting sap.

Western Flower Thrips survive in greenhouse debris, and overwinter where greenhouse bubble plastic is used to line the inside of the glass and weeds tend to grow. They have a wide host range and often survive at low temperatures on weeds outside greenhouses. Eggs are laid in slits in plant tissues, using the

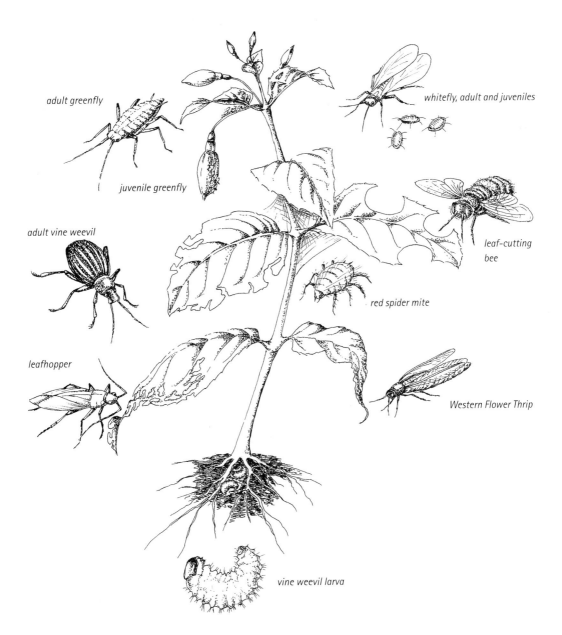

adult greenfly

whitefly, adult and juveniles

juvenile greenfly

adult vine weevil

leaf-cutting
bee

red spider mite

leafhopper

Western Flower Thrip

vine weevil larva

Fig. 26 Garden and greenhouse pests

females' ovipositors. Thrips tend to live on the growing points and around flowers. Eggs hatch in about three days at temperatures of about 25°C (77°F) or at two weeks at 14°C (57°F). Newly hatched nymphs feed on plant tissues and prefer to be enclosed. Within a week they moult and form pre-pupae. At this stage they stop feeding and migrate to the soil where they pupate for about ten days before emerging again as adults. Adults remain active for about six weeks and are about 3 mm (0.12 in) long. They are yellow or brown and are highly active, running, jumping and flying. Twelve to fifteen generations can be produced in a single year. Linsenmaier (1972; see Bibliography) gives an interesting account of the varied instars, or developmental stages, through which thrips must pass before maturity.

Western Flower Thrip predation In the wild, digger wasps and chalcid wasps predate on thrips but *Amblyseius* is the commonest predator of WFT in greenhouse crops, *Amblyseius barkeri* having proved to be the most versatile. The predator that has proved of most interest in commercial glasshouse control of WFT is *Orius laevigatus*, from the order *Hemiptera* and the genus *Anthocoridae*. There are five other naturally occurring species of *Orius* in the British Isles. Adult ones eat up to eighteen thrips a day and, because they can fly, they can spread rapidly throughout greenhouse crops. This predator needs a minimum day length of fourteen hours to remain active. It has five developmental stages, or instars, as well as the egg and adult stages. All instars have red eyes. The adults are colourless at first and change to dark brown or black with white flecks. Mating occurs within three days. Fertilized females hibernate overwinter. *Orius* sucks the body fluids from its prey and is one of the predatory group of bugs. Another control that has been used with commercial success is the predatory fungus *Verticillium lecanii*.

O WHITEFLY

Whiteflies, or *Aleurodina*, are little sap-sucking insects with yellow heads and black eyes. They live on the undersides of leaves where their empty body casings and other unsightly debris may be found on inspection. Their white coats are one of the principal reasons why pesticides have little effect on them. This white wax is not present at first but is produced from small glands on each side of their abdomens. The threads that are produced are gathered by bristles that spread them over the whole body, with the sole exception of their eyes. The wings, when at rest, cover their abdomens to give the small insects a moth-like appearance. Whiteflies go through several stages before they turn into either male or female adults. These adults have curious courtship routines during which dances are performed and males

stroke the females. In spite of all this, young are frequently produced parthenogenetically. Females have an odd way of laying eggs, too. First, a female will stab with her proboscis and start to suck sap. She will simultaneously lay single eggs at about two-hourly intervals. As each egg is laid, the female rotates her proboscis and abdomen slightly, so that eggs are usually distributed in semi-circular formations. It is interesting to speculate that the pressure of the sap entering a female whitefly might actually help her lay her eggs. Whiteflies lay their eggs on the undersides of leaves, where they also live. Infestations appear as 'hot spots' among the plants. During warm weather the little insects become more active and can be seen flying between plants.

Whitefly predation *Trialeurodes vaporariorum* is the species of whitefly usually found in greenhouses; the predator that is most often produced commercially to combat it is *Encarsia formosa*. This predator has no effect on greenfly and, like many of the commercially produced predators, is specific in its action.

PART TWO: DISEASES

P BOTRITIS CINEREA

Botritis cinerea is a common foe of fuchsias grown in dull, dark and cold conditions. It can also cause damage when plants fed with high nitrogen fertilizer have a sudden growth spurt in bright and warm weather and become crowded on the benches. Fluffy grey, gossamer-like botritis threads often attack immature plant growth where moisture collects in leaf axils. Infections may then spread to involve several stems and leaves, but often only one branch on a young plant is affected, the others remaining perfectly healthy. Other soil-borne fungi that cause cuttings and seedlings to rot include *Rhizoctonia*, *Pithium*, *Fusarium* and *Phytophthora*.

Treatment of *Botritis cinerea* Treatment with a variety of fungicides is effective in reducing losses. Seaweed products also seem to have an inhibitory effect on soil-borne fungi.

Q FUCHSIA RUST

Fuchsia rust, *Pucciniastrum epilobii*, can be a serious problem. It is usually acquired with new stock and can spread rapidly unless swift action is taken to combat it. Rusts are closely allied to fungi but have several different forms, and may require two different hosts so that the various forms can grow successfully. Wilfred Sharp (1973) wrote lucidly on the subject in the *British Fuchsia Society Annual*. Fuchsia rust can be found growing on rosebay willow herb. This plant is common on heathland following summer fires; building sites are also places on which to find it. Their long, strap-like leaves frequently have dull red or rusty-looking upper surfaces. When these are turned over, golden or orange spores can be seen in vast quantities, looking as if pepper granules had been spread on the undersides of the leaf. Infected fuchsias are similarly attacked: dull brown upper surfaces are a sign of orange spores under the leaf. Sometimes whole plants will be attacked. At other times, individual leaves are affected. In the latter case, removal of the leaf and regular close inspection will often prevent the disease spreading. It is probably wiser to destroy larger plants in order to avoid the disease passing to other plants nearby. Many of the fungicides currently marketed are not active against fuchsia rust and every effort should be made to obtain the correct product to combat this disease.

PART THREE:
GENETIC CHANGE

R   FASCIATION
Fasciation might look to the ill-informed as if a plant has some strange disease. The mixture of leaf and flower occurs in late summer and often on a very few branches. Coloration is usually bright red and green. It, like gigantism, is a passing aberration.

S   GIGANTISM
Gigantism is often seen on fuchsias like 'Estelle Marie' when two, three or more flowers are joined more firmly than Siamese twins. Using these blooms for hybridizing does not increase the chromosome numbers nor does it change the nature of offspring.

T   SPORTING
Sporting (of flowers and foliage) is also genetically mutated and is not in any way a sign of disease or infection. Hybridizing with such plants does not usually produce variegated leaves or petals of the desired colours. In the same way that sports can occur spontaneously, they can revert to the original again. Sometimes part of a plant will change while the remainder continues as before. All these phenomena will be of interest to the keen fuchsia grower rather than causes for concern.

PART FOUR:
CHEMICAL CONTROLS

The modern horticulturist has to be very safety-conscious and needs to understand a few basic rules if pests and diseases are to be kept under control. These rules apply as much to any other plant as to fuchsias. The first and most important thing for any horticulturist to understand is:

No one method of control should be practised repeatedly on its own.

Pests and diseases reproduce so fast and build up resistance to any chemical substance so quickly that immunity to any pesticide or fungicide is always a hair's breadth away. The answer is to use chemical rotation or, less desirably, chemical clustering. The substances used should always be from distinctly different chemical groups and brand names are less important than generic ones.

Changes in the availability of chemical controls have seen a drastic curtailing of the options open to commercial and amateur fuchsia growers. Here, a second general rule should be followed whenever possible:

Products used for the prevention of pest should combine miticidal and insecticidal properties on every possible occasion.

Systemics are absorbed into the plants' circulatory systems. They kill all pests that attack them but do not prevent that attack in the first place. Contact killers must always be applied to the undersides of the leaves if they are to be effective. Dipping, rather than spraying, is safer for amateurs, provided that strong protective gloves are worn. A third product should be chosen to complete the control programme. This might be any of the different products available, but here a further general rule can be used by amateur growers to supplement the last one and be applied as follows:

Always inspect product bottles to see which pests are affected by their use.

This rule will allow you to make a choice of products. One point should not be forgotten, however: if predators have been introduced, many of these products will kill foe and friend alike. Remember also that many of the natural predators have been produced to be effective in closed environments, so they rarely suit fuchsias as much as they suit food crops like cucumbers.

The same rules about rotation and reading the product information should be applied to fungicides as they are to pesticides. There is little point in buying two products with different brand names that have identical chemical constituents. Resistance is only slowly being recognized as a problem affecting the combating of fungal infections. Rusts are a more serious problem in many of today's plants than ordinary fungi, and are more difficult to combat as fewer products are available which act against them. It may be therefore be necessary to accept partial action in products, rather than the complete and speedy cure we always hope to find. The number of chemically different products available is very restricted and for this reason no recommendations are made here: inspection will show the best ones and, as new products become available, additions to the chemical armoury can be made.

A number of methods can be used to apply pesticides and fungicides. Sometimes one method is better than another. For example, asthmatics would be wise to avoid spraying or smoking, and to concentrate on dipping their fuchsias whenever possible. Spraying can be extremely dangerous and the use of masks, gloves and protective garments is recommended. The stated mixing ratio should never be exceeded and unused surpluses should not be stored. Common sense has now been supplemented by strict legal requirements. In this context, storage of these substances is as important as usage. A number of leaflets have been produced in Great Britain, and these are available from the Health and Safety Executive. These explain the situation cogently and, although every part will not apply equally to amateur and commercial growers, they carry much valuable information on current recommendations and requirements.

PART FIVE: OTHER CONTROLS

Green controls have come to the fore recently and there is still the unspoken assumption among some gardeners that 'natural' methods of pest control must be best. This over-simplification can be very dangerous. Integrated pest control methods are much better and rely on a more detailed knowledge about pest life cycles, natural predators and degradable pesticides that do no harm to beneficial insects.

One method that is advocated is to hang yellow or blue adhesive boards above and near plants in greenhouses. These do not kill pests like whitefly unless they land on them, attracted as they are by the colours, but they do catch insects in a rather random way. Lacewings and other natural predators can be found stuck to their surfaces on close inspection after some days in position. Because of this they are useful in determining the numbers and kinds of insects present in a greenhouse. Cards must also be placed at frequent intervals, usually every few metres, just above plants, if they are to be effective.

In the old days, smell played a large part in persuading pests there were better places to go than in the greenhouse. Moth balls, or naphthalene, were often used. Marigolds placed in the greenhouse are said to have a similar effect. The scent of phenol that some products incorporate is like that of an old-fashioned dentist's surgery. Paraffin can also be placed in saucers to give off inhibitory fumes. Older gardeners often grew onions and carrots together in order to confuse their natural predators. Nowadays, pheromones can be utilized to attract or repel pests such as aphids. Many possibilities are waiting to be discovered in the unending worldwide war against pests.

Pests and predators are affected by changes in temperature and many will go into diapause when conditions are unfavourable. High temperatures increase the rate of reproduction in the majority of pests and their predators. The former seem to be at an advantage, in that they can usually reproduce at slightly lower temperatures than their adversaries; but as the temperature rises, the balance moves in favour of the predators. The latter are nearly always more active and are more mobile in search of their prey.

Highly humid conditions do not suit pests such as red spider as much as hot and arid ones do. It is therefore an advantage, when plants are to be kept under glass during hot weather, to drench floors and benches to raise relative air humidity. At temperatures higher than 30°C (86°F) fuchsias are unable to absorb or transpire water and watering the roots can drown plants. Shade houses or shade paints can help to lower heat levels. Wind helps to spread pests and predators alike, but breezes also help to reduce excessive temperatures. For this reason, fan blowers are often used to circulate greenhouse air and to help with transpiration, which in turn helps to reduce temperatures at leaf level where pests live

Greenhouses, by providing peculiar conditions, also encourage faster rates of pest reproduction. Weeds, some hedges, grass and rubbish of every sort in the vicinity will harbour pests that can then transfer into monoculture crops under glass, like fuchsias. Diseases are encouraged by open-topped water butts within greenhouses, by leaf litter and by the close spacing of developing plants. Dull, dark and damp conditions encourage trouble. Plants bought, or brought in, should be quarantined for at least two weeks before placing them with other plants, as many will have pests or diseases when acquired. At the end of each growing season, when fuchsias are due to be pruned and started into regrowth for commercial purposes, it is often a useful idea to defoliate them totally. This removes pests like whitefly and red spider and destroys rusts and fungal spores. With growing plants there is no substitute for frequent inspection, especially in the corners of greenhouses that are the least accessible places. Plants should be lifted whenever possible and the undersides of the leaf surfaces inspected for the first signs of trouble.

Summary

The whole subject of pests and diseases is a fascinating one. There is no doubt, too, that the people best equipped to deal with any problem are those growers with acute observation who regularly inspect their fuchsias and are prepared to adapt to changing circumstances. Help can always be obtained when it comes to diagnosis and treatment; for instance, organizations such as fuchsia clubs have a wealth of knowledge on the subject. Other organizations, like national horticultural or scientific bodies, may also be contacted for help. Having said all this, fuchsias are more adaptable and less troubled by pathogens, especially viruses, than almost every other ornamental plant.

CHAPTER 16
Hybridizing

PART ONE: SEEDS

Before considering the technicalities of hybridizing, let us consider raising fuchsias successfully from seed. Chapter 4 examined the ways in which fuchsias could be propagated and how to set up propagating units to provide ideal conditions for cuttings. Those needs are repeated when it comes to raising fuchsias from seed. Too much heat, produced by strong sunlight, can be even more harmful than cool conditions. Sufficient moisture should be provided, especially at the surface of compost, to ensure that seed and seedlings never become dry. Enclosing the whole propagating area within a cover made from polythene or fibre-fleece helps maintain this slightly damp condition. Compaction, waterlogging and lack of oxygen will inhibit germination and may kill fuchsia seedlings in their very early stage of growth. Fresh compost should provide a neutral pH (about 7) so that new seedlings are never put under stress. Fungicides and molluscicides can help to prevent fatalities once germination has taken place.

Much early information given in relation to raising fuchsias from seed was misleading, if not untrue. Because of this, experiment as much as possible with any available fuchsia seeds before trying to raise plants from special crosses. A useful way to start is to take seed from *F. procumbens* in order to find out about seedling germination times, appearance, needs and preferences. Seed may also be removed from ripe seedpods on garden plants, which have been fertilized by chance. Species and hardies usually produce seeds most easily.

Colour and size bear little relationship to the ripeness of pods and seeds. Some fuchsias like 'Estelle Marie' will have opalescent or pale green round pods when fully ripe. Others, such as 'Coquet Dale', will have fruit the colour of Victoria plums. Encliandras have small, black, shiny seedpods. Some, like *F. procumbens*, have

pods, which resemble peppers with their hollow spaces. Yet more have gherkin-like pods and some a banana shape. Sizes of ripe pods vary as much as colours. *F. procumbens* has the largest known pod, about the size of a Victoria plum. The smallest is probably to be found on *F. lycioides*, with pods little larger than a match-head. With such a wide variation careful observations are best carried out; these inevitably gather a wealth of experience beyond the narrow scope of hybridizing. Fuchsias, once fertilized, take about ten or twelve weeks to ripen their seeds. Factors such as day length, light levels, warmth, humidity levels and feeding can also affect timing. One amazing feature of many fuchsias is that their seeds will grow, given the ideal conditions, even when they appear to be very immature. Seed size is no guide to viability as I have seen by careful observation over an extended period of time.

One of those fallacies, which have been passed as gospel for many years, is that viable seed will sink when placed in water, while anything that floats is useless. This is plain nonsense. If careful records are kept and all seed, however doubtful-looking, is sown, the most unlikely material will frequently give the best results. With this in mind, seedpods may be cut in half from the pedicel to the place where the inflorescence was attached. These halves should be squashed on newspaper so that excess moisture is absorbed. Seeds are then separated from the skin and flesh of the pod using a sharp knife blade or point. They are placed to one side until they have all been removed.

Fuchsia seed is best sown immediately. The probability of successful germination drops quickly with time and old seed is unlikely to give good results. The seed itself is sown ideally around the edges of pots or pans and only fractionally below the surface of the compost. Sometimes the seeds are best tucked between the side of the pot and the compost, where air and water movement are greatest.

Some crosses produce no more than a single seed. In the past such seeds were probably lost or destroyed, as they are so difficult to find. It is always worth examining an apparently empty seedpod where the pod itself joins the pedicel: there, tucked into the angle of the fruit, a single green seed can sometimes be found, which, when planted, will grow.

Pans or short pots may be prepared in advance of seed sowing and ideally left on the propagator for twenty-four hours or more, so that their temperature rises to 18°C (64°F) before sowing takes place. Compost should be moist like new bread, of a fine texture and should not be allowed to dry out completely once seeds have been sown. In the seedlings' early days, a light spraying with water from a hand-held sprayer will be sufficient to maintain these ideal conditions. Later, as they grow, watering is best done by dipping the pot into dilute liquid feed. No more than half the pot should be immersed, and then only briefly, as the moisture will continue to permeate upwards through the compost for a time after watering in this way. Some marginal benefits are obtained from sieving compost to remove lumps of peat and coarse fibres. A granular structure seems to suit fuchsia seeds best. Covers should be placed over the pots to preserve moisture levels and to retain steady levels of warmth.

Germination times vary considerably from one seed parent to another. Once the seeds have been sown, and given ideal conditions, they should be up within four to eight weeks. They appear as tiny dicotyledons. When seeds germinate irregularly, as they often will when hard crosses are attempted, it can be difficult to ascertain when all the seeds have grown. One way to find out is first to look carefully to check that no seedlings are just coming through, then gently prick the surface of the compost using a fine point (such as you find on a cocktail stick). This will break the surface cap and allow air and moisture levels to fluctuate more freely.

Sometimes seedlings will emerge only to have their seed leaves imprisoned within the capsule, which has protected them up to this stage. Avoid the temptation to remove this case by hand as this will often break the whole top off a seedling. Instead, spray the seedling lightly with tepid water every few hours so that the case becomes soft and can be forced apart by the expanding plant tissues. Once the seedlings have two seed leaves, they can be eased from the compost, holding only the leaves and using something like a cocktail stick as a dibber, and replanted lightly into fresh, warm and moist compost, to grow on in individual pots. Dilute liquid feeds with balanced nutrients will help to maximize growth rates at this stage. The little seedlings will vary a great deal in the speed and strength of their growth. Once in individual pots these differences are catered for more easily.

As soon as the seedlings have grown large enough, perhaps at the six- or eight-leaf stage, their tops can be taken as cuttings. It is an odd fact that the plants from such cuttings are usually better than those from which the material has been taken. A second plant also helps as an insurance against the loss of especially valuable stock. It sometimes assists small cuttings if very small canes are placed next to them at this stage. Quite whether this is just a question of support is in some doubt; it may be that there is something akin to companion planting in the action. Certainly, seedlings transplanted in pairs will often thrive better in the initial stages after transplanting. Unfortunately, this benefit does not last into later life. The benefits do not attach to beneficial bacteria in the soil, and there are no nitrogen-producing nodules on the roots as there are on legumes.

PART TWO: UNDERSTANDING THE NEW

Some of the landmarks in hybridizing were noted in Chapter 1. We saw that few of the species fuchsias have been used in hybridizing, and therefore in producing fuchsias as we know them today. This chapter examines how new fuchsias come into being, but also looks at some of the flowering characteristics which must be understood before hybridizing possibilities are studied.

Understanding distinct differences between fuchsias is made easier by examining pictures of some of the prominent types. Minor differences often have little significance when it comes to the production of new cultivars, although many of them are of great significance when it comes to the identification of fuchsias in the wild. Details of some of the main fuchsia types, relevant to plant breeding, are therefore given below.

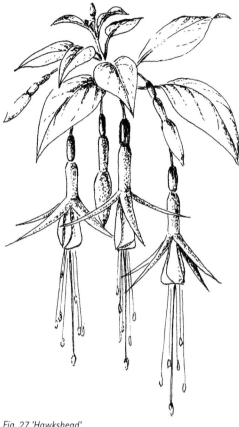

Fig. 27 'Hawkshead'

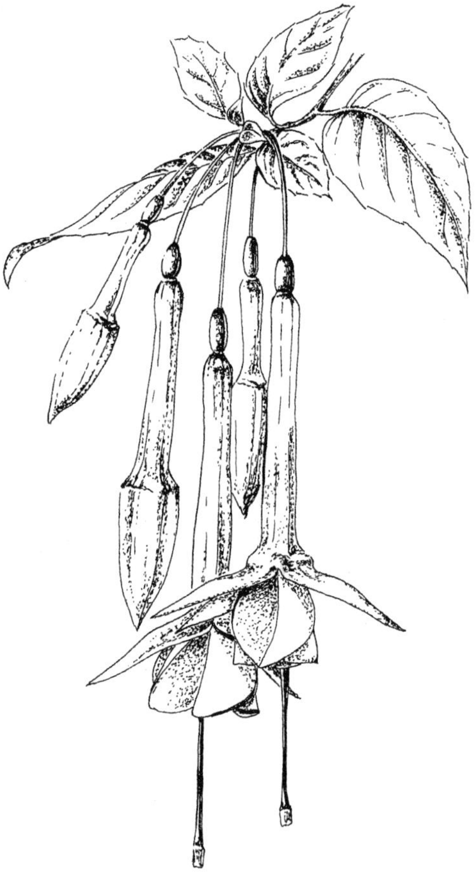

Fig. 28 'Peter Crooks'

F. *magellanica* and its variants have played by far the largest part in the production of today's garden fuchsia. They can be recognized as having originally had relatively small red and purple flowers, which are held in the leaf axils. Because this group of fuchsias has been in cultivation for longer than the others, and has been used by plant breeders extensively, it has developed into quite a varied group. Some plants have finer foliage than others do, while many have ornamental leaves; flower shapes and colours have become more varied. The essence of this group is that they are axillary-flowering.

Triphyllas, and those with long tubes, constitute by far the largest natural grouping of species fuchsias and, yet, they are still a small group when it comes to hybrids. Fuchsias such as 'Mary' provide a benchmark when it comes to identification of essential characteristics. Flowers are long, and their tubes are usually tapered gently out from the ovary. Sepals and petals are commonly short and of less significance. Blooms are held in terminal bundles, corymbs or racemes. Fuchsias in this group withstand heat better than cold.

Fuchsias in the *encliandra* section have been consistently undervalued and little understood. They have fine, fern-like foliage and miniature flowers, which are commonly carried more heavily during the darker months of the year. Blooms are often of one sex only, being pistillate or staminate, but perfect flowers – those that have both sexes within a single flower – are also widespread. All carry axillary blooms and are robust and adaptable, shrubby plants. Obligate out-breeding (unable to self-fertilize), as seen in this group, facilitates greater variability and a stronger genetic base among wild progeny. Facultative breeding (able to be fertilized by itself and by others) helps seed production

Fig. 29 F. encliandra *subsp.* encliandra. *This shows the typical fern-like growth and tiny flowers of the* encliandra *section.*

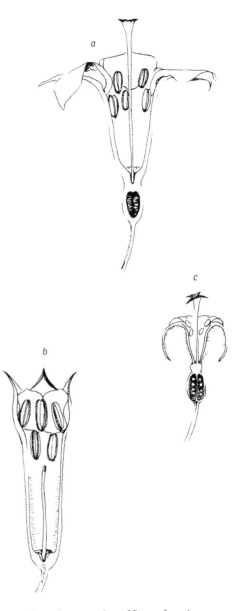

Fig. 30 *Lateral cross-sections of flowers from the* encliandra *section.*
a: A perfect flower, with both male and female parts.
b: A staminate flower. No ovary is present.
c: A pistillate bloom. Single-sex flowers often have subfertile or vestigial parts of the missing sex.

among more stable and isolated plant communities. From a plant-breeding point of view, perfect flowers are larger than those with only one sex and are therefore more desirable for garden displays.

F. procumbens has one characteristic not in keeping with the other fuchsias from New Zealand: it has no petals. Of course, its liana-like branches and small size are also unusual and these make it eminently suitable for use as a rockery plant. It is now commonly recognized that fuchsias such as *F. tilletiana* also have no petals and, although this has little adverse effect on the attractiveness of the flowers, it is unlikely to be something most hybridists would wish to promote. There does seem to be a place for the widening of the colour range within the fuchsias like *F. procumbens*, but this species has been a difficult one to work with and many of its early progeny proved to be sterile.

Fuchsia flowers are also differentiated from each other by the number of petals in their corollas. Single blooms are common among fuchsia hybrids, variants and species. Four petals constitute the basic shape of the corolla. These are variable in size and many form large and attractive bells. As flower size increases, there is also a requirement for a shorter and stronger pedicel to support the extra weight and to ensure that the full beauty of each flower can be seen. As a consequence, more flowers are now produced nearer to the ends of branches than

they were in the first half of the 19th century, and we have seen how upward-looking flowers have been developed. An increase in chromosome numbers often enlarges flower size while maintaining the single nature of blooms.

Fig. 31 F. procumbens:
a: A typical liana-like branch carrying buds and open flowers.
b: A mature bloom of this New Zealand species.

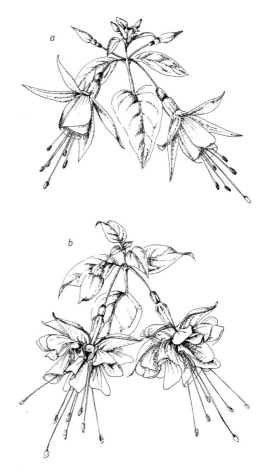

Fig. 32
a: A single-flowered fuchsia.
b: A double-flowered fuchsia.

Doubleness occurs in the corollas of fuchsias. Petal numbers increase from four to as many as eighty in some plants. Double flowers are as sought after among fuchsia growers as they are among the enthusiastic growers of other garden plants but, in the wild, such doubleness inhibits pollination and reduces fertility. It is therefore militated against by natural forces and is rarely seen. Increases in chromosome numbers enhance the probability of doubleness among seedlings. The conscientious hybridist pays attention to such things as pest and disease resistance, which can be compromised by too much concentration on flower size at the expense of other equally desirable characteristics. Doubleness has, so far, been mainly restricted to those fuchsias with *F. magellanica* parentage, but there appears to be no reason why *triphylla* and *encliandra* types could not be developed in this way.

Before moving to more technical matters associated with hybridizing, it is worth considering some of the features found among species fuchsias and examining the implications or benefits associated with them. Hairy, or felty, leaves are common among fuchsias in the terminal-flowering *triphylla* group. *F. boliviana* var. *luxurians* 'Alba' is a good example but there are many others. In the garden, this characteristic makes it difficult for greenfly and other pests to thrive, especially on older leaves. This feature also limits diseases like rust. Glossy- or waxy-textured leaves are found in fuchsias like *F. putumayensis* and this not only looks attractive but also inhibits pests and diseases.

Flower colours are closely associated with specific light wavelengths, because birds and insects are attracted to some colours rather than to others. Humming-birds and a wide variety of insects can act as pollen vectors. In New

Zealand, blue pollen attracts small birds, bees and flies: in South America blue and red are combined in the petals, tubes and sepals to act as attractants. The flash of colour in the flowers is regarded as a flight-path guide which leads the pollinators to copious supplies of nectar, that sugary, high-energy liquid most easily seen in *F. procumbens*. The advantages of a petal-less bloom are less easy to see. Perhaps the blue pollen of the New Zealand species acts as an attractant and, once close, sparrows can see the golden goblets of nectar.

Size is one of those characteristics most clearly associated in the wild with specific pollinators. Flies and bees would have little hope of sipping nectar from the longest tubes unless holes could be cut at their bases: this would prevent pollination and work against the interests of future generations of plants and their insect pollinators. Fuchsia flowers are adapted to combine each species' needs with those of the most helpful animal life in their native habitat.

Sporting obviously occurs in the wild but rarely has major habitat advantages. These same changes, when they happen to plants in cultivation, may provide fascinating variations for garden displays. *F. magellanica* var. *molinae*, with its pale pinkish-white flowers, has provided some interesting examples: *F. magellanica* var. *molinae* 'Enstone' has yellow and green leaves while *F. magellanica* var. *molinae* 'Sharpitor' has leaves with creamy white and green variegation. 'Tom West', a sport from the fuchsia 'Corallina', has leaves which mix red, cream and green on equally hardy stock. 'Lemacto' arrived as a yellow-leaved sport on 'Camelot', while 'Tolemac' provided a clearly variegated yellow and green alternative.

Flower sports are common among fuchsias. They usually occur in a regular movement from dark-coloured petals to light ones. A typical example is 'Graf Witte', a hardy fuchsia with red and violet flowers. This fuchsia sported, introducing 'Pixie' with its red and pink blooms. Eileen and Ted Saunders released 'White Pixie' when it appeared with red and white flowers. Sports do not pass on their characteristics to their seedling offspring in the expected way; progeny are most likely to be affected by the dominant darker colours of the original. Recessive characteristics are obtainable, but with much effort. Thus it is unlikely that *F. boliviana* var. *luxurians* 'Alba' is a sport from *F. boliviana* var.

luxurians, as all the seedlings I have ever raised had white tubes and rosy red petals.

Some very odd things happen in the world of genetics and in the world of fuchsia sports. It can seem as if a genetic time clock is ticking steadily away for a very long period and then, suddenly, changes of the same kind occur at different locations within a very short time of each other. 'Countess of Aberdeen' provides us with a splendid example. Dobbie Forbes introduced it in 1888, having been raised by Cocker. During the 1970s and 1980s changes occurred and several different raisers introduced sports with pale pink corollas. 'Shuna', 'Daphne Arlene' and 'Michelle Wallace' were all released with the same characteristics. Incidentally, this is one occasion when changes moved from a light to a dark.

Some aberrations arise which are of no use to the fuchsia hybridist and cannot be passed on to future generations of seedlings. The first of these, fasciation, occurs at the ends of branches and there are no fertile parts. Gigantism also presents itself in some plants. It might be thought that this would provide an increase in chromosome numbers but this is not so. Another change that happens towards the end of the growing season, when day lengths shorten and light levels fall, occurs on individual plants or branches. Flower size is usually much reduced and colours are noticeably paler; confusion may arise if these are thought to be sports as, if they are grown from cuttings, their characteristics will return to normal in the next flowering season. Bloom size is maximized on standard whips, but this does not herald a permanent change that can be inherited by future progeny. 'Snowcap' and 'Mieke Meursing' are just two of those fuchsias which have flowers on different plants ranging from almost always single on some stock, to small and full doubles on others. The selection of plant material for particularly good characteristics has always been practised by keen gardeners but has no inheritable feature.

Another difference seen sometimes on 'Phyllis', and more obviously on 'Checkerboard', 'Gay Fandango' and 'Twinkling Stars', is an increase in the number of sepals from four to five, six or more. There is no reason why this feature should not be used advantageously by hybridists to increase sepal numbers, and thence flower size and impact. It remains an inheritable characteristic of every plant of 'Phyllis' and is not restricted to those individual flowers, which exhibit the phenomenon.

PART THREE: HYBRIDIZING METHODS

To ensure the pollen parent is the only one allowed to pollinate a prospective seed parent some elementary precautions must be taken. The first and most important one is to protect the stigma and style from accidental pollination by insects or by other means. In the past it was common to enclose the stigma in half a medicine capsule, using cotton wool to complete the seal once deliberate pollination had been carried out. Sometimes foil served the same purpose. Each method was reasonably successful, but also time-consuming and sometimes damaging to the stigma or style.

The alternative is to grow fuchsias in pots and to keep them in greenhouses. Doors and windows are netted to prevent the entry of unwanted pollinators. Fine muslin will do well and there are several synthetic fibres, which are equally suitable for fastening to the greenhouse frame. This has been the preferred method for my own plant breeding work, after an experimental period in which a variety of methods were compared for effectiveness and simplicity.

Certainty of parentage is achieved by a process called 'emasculation'. Stamens are removed from prospective seed-bearing fuchsias before they produce pollen. Sometimes this means that flowers are opened gently and prematurely by hand, usually with finely pointed scissors, in order to avoid self-pollination. It is important to realize that the anthers on some fuchsia flowers are carried inside the tube while others may be displayed externally. It is best to use the flowers at the top of a plant as seed parents, so that pollen cannot fall onto ripe stigmas from blooms hanging above them.

Deliberate pollination is not difficult to achieve. Mature but not over-ripe pollen is taken from the fuchsia chosen as the male parent and placed on the stigma of the plant chosen as the seed-bearing parent. This is usually done by removing one ripe anther and touching it to the mature stigma. Hybridists sometimes remove a whole flower with ripe pollen and touch male and female blooms end to end so that the stigma is covered with pollen grains. Pollen is variable in colour and texture but there is no evidence to show that one colour is more fertile than another. Dusty pollen is harder to see than

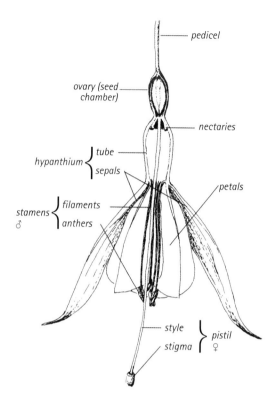

Fig. 33 Lateral cross-section of a single fuchsia flower.

pollen attached to viscine threads. The whole subject of pollen fertility and viability is a fascinating one, but trial and error, combined with keen powers of observation, are more important to prospective fuchsia hybridists than any printed information.

There are several ways in which flowers can be labelled when pollination has taken place. The easiest is to fold a long, thin adhesive computer label around the pedicel so that it sticks to itself. Information can then be written on each side. Care should be taken to see that this information is written in pencil or indelible pen, as damp and light will often fade the writing before the pods are ripe. Essential information includes the name of the female and male fuchsias used, and the date of pollination. This information should also be written on labels inserted in the pots once seed has been sown and should be supplemented on the labels' reverses, with the date of sowing.

One essential tool is a notebook in which to store information. Modern plant breeders also have the benefit of storing and sorting massed information in computer systems once the preliminary fieldwork has been completed.

There are certain conventions regarding hybridizers' notation. The first convention to note is that female parents are always listed before males. The recognized signs for these genders are the planetary symbols for Venus (female, ♀) and Mars (male, ♂). This practice should be adhered to throughout to avoid confusion and to retain credibility. Another useful idea is to group together all of one parent's crosses and subsequent progeny. This helps to show successful lines for future hybridizing and to prevent repetition of the less effective crosses. If only one record book is kept, it is usual to group female crosses only in this way. Entries may be regrouped from rough notebooks used initially to a larger register. A similar register may be kept showing these crosses reversed: each cross made using a particular pollinator is grouped with others from that pollinator.

Each seed parent used can be designated a letter or letters, while numbers can refer to male parentage. Such methods help to shorten written work. Each cross should be designated with the year. Under such a system we could show 'Celia Smedley' (A) crossed with 'Marcus Hanton' (2) thus: '01 A x 2'. As subsequent seedlings are raised and given an individual identity, they are given a further individual letter or letters. If ten seedlings were raised from the cross above, then they would be labelled from '01 A x 2a' to '01 A x 2j'. When more than twenty-six seedlings arise from a single cross, letters are doubled or repeated thus: '01 A x 2 aa' or '01 A x 2 ja'. It is not a good idea to name seedlings unless a firm decision has been taken to release them.

An assessment register can prove valuable as it encourages the factual representation of good and bad points associated with each seedling raised to flower. Facts should be differentiated between those relating to growth and those associated with flowering. Details like habit, self-branching ability and shortness of internodes should be listed with possible drawbacks, if for example the plant is prone to botritis. The number of blooms carried in each internode, continuity of flowering, length of pedicel, nearness to the plant's periphery, colour and shape should be noted with faults, such as whether the flowers are bruised easily by bees. It will become clear that particular parents, either

alone or in combination, repeatedly pass on some of these characteristics, perhaps to advantage but possibly to a seedling's detriment.

Another sort of notebook to keep is one in which to 'think aloud'. Use this to note possible future crosses, with reasons for wanting to try them. They may also provide a list of prospective names for future introduction. This would be a good place to introduce pictograms of fuchsia flowers. Drawings can be made of the possible outlines of tubes, sepals and corollas, coloured to provide targets for future breeding programmes. You should allow yourself to play with the possibilities.

There are some things which can affect the success rate of fuchsia crosses as much as, if not more than, the compatibility or otherwise of chosen parents. Pollen production and viability is adversely affected by excessive wind, sun and low air humidity. The time of day at which pollination takes place can be significant and some crosses are unlikely to succeed unless they are made in the early morning, or possibly in the late evening. Temperatures play a large part in success rates; the ideal temperature is between 18ºC (64ºF) and 26ºC (79ºF). Low temperatures slow the rate of pollen tubule growth to a level which may prove fatal when attempting long-tubed crosses. High temperatures can shorten the life of pollen grains by desiccating them before they have achieved their purpose. Prospective seed parents are also affected, because flower life is prolonged or shortened as temperatures fall or rise: stigmas and ovaries must be receptive to viable pollen. I have found that the most difficult crosses are most likely to be achieved very late in the growing season.

There is a period in the life of all fertile pollen when it is at its optimum viability. This high point is not always easy to assess as pollen characteristics vary considerably from one cultivar to another. Some fuchsias have fine, powdery pollen granules, while others have adhesive, thread-like strands of pollen. Trial and error shows that most pollen is ready about twelve to twenty-four hours after flowers have opened naturally. Stigma receptivity is equally variable. Moist and tacky stigmas usually denote that pollination is possible but many receptive female parents have dry stigmas. Pollen may be applied to stigmas even if blooms have been opened prematurely by hand and for perhaps the next twenty-four hours. A few species, like

F. paniculata, are able to self-pollinate within apparently immature and closed flowers. Such fuchsias will necessarily be difficult to use as seed-bearing parents. Emasculating some fuchsias, and especially species like *F. fulgens*, seriously impairs the possibility of success in pollination. Dieback quickly follows brutalization of their flower tissues. If fuchsias respond in this way, and have pollen sacks that cling to and enclose the stigmas, early and thorough pollination with other parents gives the best chance of success.

Gardening journalists have sometimes had strange ideas, which influence fuchsia growers with little experience of hybridizing. One of these is that starvation helps to make fuchsias flower because they think they are about to die. Most successful crossing is done with parents which are growing strongly and in the very pink of condition. There are more flowers to use and they are healthier and remain fertile for longer than those that are half starved. The best results are obtained by raising mother plants deliberately as large specimens. Pollen may be used from a wide range of cultivars and these only need a single fertile stamen on one flower to be effective. Continuity of blooming helps to ensure that flowers are mutually compatible when the weather and cultural conditions are at their best.

There is considerable evidence that equality of chromosome numbers is neither necessary nor desirable with fuchsias. Certainly equality of numbers gives no guarantee of success in crossing. Some fuchsias, like 'Mary', may be crossed with many other fuchsias and produce no viable seed. 'Stella Ann' and 'Finn' produce vast numbers of empty seedpods. Others, such as 'Cloverdale Jewel' and 'Ting-a-Ling', appear to be fertile with many fuchsia plants although they have vastly different chromosome counts. For the average hybridist with only limited resources, plant breeding is still very much based upon trial and error.

It may be that some of the genetic characteristics within the genus *Fuchsia* are passed via extra-nuclear material. It could be that chromosome counts are variable, even on a single cultivar. It might be that because of the lack of expertise, and their minute size, some chromosome counts have been incorrect. Why, for example, has 'Lye's Unique', with its chromosome count of fifty-five, been so successful with so many cultivars displaying even counts of twenty-two? 'Rolla' has seventy-seven chromosomes and yet has been the parent of many doubles and whites through the years. It sounds like heresy to say that odd-numbered chromosome counts appear to give the best success in providing unusual offspring and yet I have sought such plants and used them successfully for many years. Fuchsias are variable, even as species, and line breeding is less successful than it is with many other flowering plants.

Sources of chromosome counts have been listed (see Appendix 1). It seems that work in this area has only just started and there is much to be accomplished before we fully understand the genetics of fuchsias. In the meantime we can learn and achieve much through experiment. Essentially, the successful hybridist takes nothing for granted and believes little of what he is told, preferring instead to work by trial and error, keeping meticulous records and copious notes, until unexpected and exciting results come almost on their own.

Hybridists need to know what to aim for. Successful hybridists know much about fuchsia culture and the individual quirks of particular cultivars. They also need to be aware of the vast range of cultivars currently available. There is no place for a new red and mauve fuchsia when not only is such a fuchsia a hundred years behind the times but also when many better hybrids have gone out of cultivation already. It has been said that there are too many new seedlings arriving on the market, but this can hardly be true when there is clearly still a need for better or different fuchsias. Perhaps all hybridists should produce so many seedlings that they have to choose which are best and which should be thrown away immediately. If it takes several years to assess a fuchsia, it cannot be much good.

Earliness of flowering is an essential characteristic in providing a long flowering season and in promoting fuchsias to the wider horticultural market. Continuity of flowering is just as vital. Anther colours can add or subtract from the overall effect of the flowers of a fuchsia. Bicoloured, bright red, big and plentiful blooms enhance a fuchsia's impact. Hardiness can be applied to wind resistance as well as to heat and cold. Resistance to pests and diseases will become increasingly important in future years as the numbers of fuchsias grown worldwide increase rapidly.

Fig. 34 A courtyard decorated with fuchsias.

It is worth noting that few fuchsias have absolutely no faults. Sometimes, even with an obvious fault, a new seedling will be worth releasing because it is so much better than or remarkably different from alternatives. For example, 'Display' has split sepals, and 'Swanley Gem' with unobtrusive colours has perfect form and a graceful habit.

Potential marketability needs to be assessed. 'Rina Felix' points the way to further hybrids that might have waxy textures and the unusual colours suitable for the flower arranger. 'Greenpeace' flowers on the ends of long fronds: fuchsias have yet to be developed which can match the need for long-lived cut flowers. Encliandras could be produced with larger flowers on house-tolerant pot plants. Garden hardies could be extended in colour and form. Bedding and basket use demands a much greater variety of plants. Shows require better subjects that appeal more to the general public, moving away from pallid singles in white and mauve and pink; doubles are always in demand.

Fuchsia names often sell plants. Some old favourites are probably kept in circulation because of their name and others have difficulty in surviving for the same reason. Imagine introducing a fuchsia with the title 'Andenken an Heinrich Henkel' (synonym 'Heinrich Henkel') nowadays, if only because of writing out its labels. Attractive names, usually with the suggestion of femininity, tend to sell fuchsia plants. Disreputable nurseries often label their fuchsias with names like 'Ballerina' in order to con a gullible gardening public into purchasing plants. Many keen hybridists own a copy of *The Checklist of Species, Hybrids and Cultivars of the Genus Fuchsia* (1991), by Leo B. Boullemier in order to avoid names already in circulation. The Dutch national society's computerized list of introductions is the best of modern alternatives.

There remains the one vital ingredient in all the best-laid plans: action. Now is a good time to start learning, planning and doing. Only when many seedlings have been thrown away might a genuine gem bear your name.

CHAPTER 17

Species

Species are classified under the genus *Fuchsia* and are part of the order of plants called *Onagraceae*. Information on these wild plants, up to now, has been scattered among a variety of publications. Here, each is described briefly and placed in the botanical section to which it belongs. Each one is given a textual and pictorial reference, which should aid any further research the reader wishes to undertake. References for further study are given in the Bibliography of this book.

This chapter describes all the currently grown fuchsia species. Both their sections and the species themselves are arranged in alphabetical order for ease of reference and there is a full list of each at the start of the chapter. Each section

is summarized briefly before its species are described in detail. Of necessity, some terms will be academic; wherever possible, the entries are jargon-free and erudite terminology has been eliminated. Fuchsia species are referred to throughout in the abbreviated form, for example *F. decussata*.

Cloud forests, the most common natural habitats for fuchsia species, are among the most threatened environments in the world. A map of their distribution, and many others presenting detailed information on soil types, altitude, temperature ranges and much else of relevance to wild fuchsias, are to be found in *The Times Atlas of the World* (1990).

ALPHABETICAL LIST OF FUCHSIA SECTIONS WITH THE NUMBER OF SPECIES IN EACH

Ellobium	3	Pachyrrhiza	1
Encliandra	6	Procumbentes	1
Fuchsia	63	Quelusia	9
Hemsleyella	14	Schufia	2
Jimenezia	1	Skinnera	3
Kierschlegeria	1		

ALPHABETICAL LIST OF SPECIES FUCHSIAS WITH THEIR SECTIONS, PLACE FOUND, YEAR OF INTRODUCTION AND FINDER OR TAXONOMIST

NAME	SECTION	PLACE	YEAR	FINDER/TAXONOMIST
F. abrupta	Fuchsia (5)	Peru	1925	I. M. Johnston
F. alpestris	Quelusia	Brazil	1842	G. Gardner
F. ampliata	Fuchsia (6)	Ecuador	1841-43	Bentham
F. andrei	Fuchsia (5)	Ecuador/Peru	1925	I. M. Johnston
F. apetala	Hemsleyella	Peru	1802	Ruiz & Pavón
F. arborescens	Schufia	Mexico	1825	Sims
F. austromontana	Fuchsia (8)	Peru	1939	I. M. Johnston
F. ayavacensis	Fuchsia (6)	Peru	1802	Humboldt, Bonpland & Kunth
F. boliviana	Fuchsia (12)	Bolivia	1876	Carrière
F. bracelinae	Quelusia	Brazil	1929	P. Munz
F. brevilobis	Quelusia	Brazil	1989	P. Berry
F. campii	Fuchsia (6)	Ecuador	1995	Berry & Brako

F. campos-portoi	Quelusia	Brazil	1935	Pilger & Schulze
F. canescens	Fuchsia (13)	Colombia	1845	Bentham
F. caucana	Fuchsia (6)	Colombia	1982	P. Berry
F. ceracea	Fuchsia (9)	Peru	1982	P. Berry
F. cestroides	Hemsleyella	Peru	1940	Schulze-Menz
F. chloroloba	Hemsleyella	Peru	1939	I. M. Johnston
F. cinerea	Fuchsia (13)	Ecuador	1982	P. Berry
F. coccinea	Quelusia	Brazil	1789	Solander
F. cochabambana	Fuchsia (8)	Bolivia	1982	P. Berry
F. confertifolia	Fuchsia (7)	Peru	1844	Fielding & Gardner
F. coriacifolia	Fuchsia (9)	Peru	1982	P. Berry
F. corollata	Fuchsia (6)	Colombia	1845	Bentham
F. corymbiflora	Fuchsia (12)	Peru	1802	Ruiz & Pavón
F. crassistipula	Fuchsia (13)	Colombia	1972	P. Berry
F. cuatrecasasii	Fuchsia (5)	Colombia	1943	P. Munz
F. cylindracea	Encliandra	Mexico	1838	Lindley
F. cyrtandroides	Skinnera	Tahiti	1942	Moore
F. decidua	Ellobium	Mexico	1929	Standley
F. decussata	Fuchsia (1)	Peru	1802	Ruiz & Pavón
F. denticulata	Fuchsia (8)	Peru	1802	Ruiz & Pavón
F. dependens	Fuchsia (13)	Ecuador	1837	Hooker
F. eileeniana	Fuchsia (2)			Berry
F. encliandra	Encliandra	Mexico	1840	Steudel
F. excorticata	Skinnera	New Zealand	1776	Forster
F. ferreyrae	Fuchsia (1)	Peru	1978	P. Berry
F. fontinalis	Fuchsia (1)	Peru	1940	J. F. Macbride
F. fulgens	Ellobium	Mexico	1828	De Candolle
F. furfuracea	Fuchsia (11)	Bolivia	1925	I. M. Johnston
F. garleppiana	Hemsleyella	Bolivia	1893	Kuntz & Wittmack
F. gehrigeri	Fuchsia (7)	Venezuela	1973	P. Munz
F. glaberrima	Fuchsia (3)	Ecuador	1925	I. M. Johnston
F. glazioviana	Quelusia	Brazil	1888	Taubert
F. harlingii	Fuchsia (8)	Ecuador	1972	P. Munz
F. hartwegii	Fuchsia (13)	Colombia	1845	Bentham
F. hatschbachii	Quelusia	Brazil	1989	P. Berry
F. hirtella	Fuchsia (13)	Colombia	1823	Humboldt, Bonpland & Kunth
F. huanucoensis	Hemsleyella	Peru	1945	P. Berry
F. inflata	Hemsleyella	Peru	1940	Schulze-Menz
F. insignis	Hemsleyella	Ecuador	1867	Hemsley
F. jimenezii	Jimenezia	Costa Rica	1982	Breedlove, Berry & Raven
F. juntasensis	Hemsleyella	Bolivia	1898	O. Kuntz
F. lehmannii	Fuchsia (5)	Ecuador	1943	P. Munz
F. llewelynii	Fuchsia (7)	Peru	1941	J. F. Macbride
F. loxensis	Fuchsia (2)	Ecuador	1823	Humboldt, Bonpland & Kunth
F. lycioides	Kierschlegeria	Chile	1800	Andrews
F. macropetala	Fuchsia (4)	Peru	1831	Presl
F. macrophylla	Fuchsia (4)	Peru	1925	I. M. Johnston
F. macrostigma	Fuchsia (8)	Ecuador	1844	Bentham
F. magdalenae	Fuchsia (8)	Colombia	1943	P. Munz
F. magellanica	Quelusia	Chile	1788	Lamarck
F. mathewsii	Fuchsia (12)	Peru	1941	J. F. Macbride
F. membranacea	Hemsleyella	Venezuela	1876	Hemsley
F. microphylla	Encliandra	Mexico	1823	Humboldt, Bonpland & Kunth

F. nana	Hemsleyella	Bolivia	1950	P. Berry
F. nigricans	Fuchsia (3)	Venezuela	1849	Linden
F. obconica	Encliandra	Mexico	1969	D. E. Breedlove
F. orientalis	Fuchsia (3)	Ecuador	1982	P. Berry
F. ovalis	Fuchsia (4)	Peru	1802	Ruiz & Pavón
F. pachyrrhiza	Pachyrrhiza	Peru	1989	Berry & Stein
F. pallescens	Fuchsia (3)	Ecuador	1938	Diels
F. paniculata	Schufia	Costa Rica	1856	Lindley
F. perscandens	Skinnera	New Zealand	1927	Cockayne & Allan
F. petiolaris	Fuchsia (6)	Colombia	1823	Humboldt, Bonpland & Kunth
F. pilaloensis	Hemsleyella	Ecuador	1985	P. Berry
F. pilosa	Fuchsia (4)	Peru	1844	Fielding & Gardner
F. polyantha	Fuchsia (10)	Colombia	1943	Killip
F. pringsheimii	Fuchsia (14)	Dominican R.	1899	Urban
F. procumbens	Procumbentes	New Zealand	1839	R. Cunningham
F. putumayensis	Fuchsia (5)	Colombia	1943	P. Munz
F. ravenii	Encliandra	Mexico	1969	D. E. Breedlove
F. regia	Quelusia	Brazil	1943	Vandelli
F. rivularis	Fuchsia (7)	Peru	1940	J. F. Macbride
F. salicifolia	Hemsleyella	Peru	1876	Hemsley
F. sanctae-rosae	Fuchsia (1)	Bolivia	1898	O. Kuntz
F. sanmartina	Fuchsia (9)	Peru	1982	P. Berry
F. scabriuscula	Fuchsia (2)	Ecuador	1845	Bentham
F. scherffiana	Fuchsia (7)	Ecuador	1888	André
F. sessilifolia	Fuchsia (10)	Ecuador	1845	Bentham
F. simplicicaulis	Fuchsia (9)	Peru	1802	Ruiz & Pavón
F. splendens	Ellobium	Mexico	1832	Zuccarini
F. steyermarkii	Fuchsia (2)	Ecuador	1982	P. Berry
F. subparamosis	Fuchsia (2)			Berry
F. summa	Fuchsia (2)	Ecuador	1995	Berry & Brako
F. sylvatica	Fuchsia (3)	Ecuador	1845	Bentham
F. thymifolia	Encliandra	Mexico	1823	Humboldt, Bonpland & Kunth
F. tilletiana	Hemsleyella	Venezuela	1972	P. Munz
F. tincta	Fuchsia (11)	Peru	1939	I. M. Johnston
F. triphylla	Fuchsia (14)	Dominican R.	1705	Plumier/Linneus
F. tunariensis	Hemsleyella	Bolivia	1898	O. Kuntz
F. vargasiana	Fuchsia (11)	Peru	1946	Vargas
F. venusta	Fuchsia (7)	Colombia	1823	Humboldt, Bonpland & Kunth
F. verrucosa	Fuchsia (14)	Colombia	1845	T. Hartweg
F. vulcanica	Fuchsia (6)	Colombia	1888	André
F. wurdackii	Fuchsia (12)	Peru	1964	P. Munz

INCORRECT NAMES FOR SPECIES

F. asperifolia	F. hirsuta	F. michoacansis	F. storkii
F. aspiazui	F. hybrida	F. minimiflora	F. striolata
F. asplundii	F. hypoleuca	F. minutifolia	F. tacenensis
F. bacillaris	F. jahnii	F. munzii	F. tetradactyl
F. colensoi	F. killipii	F. osgoodii	F. townsendii
F. colimae	F. kirkii	F. platypetala	F. tuberosa
F. cordifolia	F. leptopoda	F. pringlei	F. unduavensis
F. fischeri	F. macrantha	F. scutchiana	F. woytkowskii
F. hemsleyana	F. mexicae	F. smithii	

DESCRIPTIONS AND REFERENCES FOR ALL KNOWN SPECIES IN ALPHABETICAL AND SECTIONAL ORDER

Section *Ellobium*

This fuchsia section comprises three species that have perfect flowers. Its soft-wooded shrubs either grow in the ground or are epiphytic. Leaves are opposite or ternate. Flower tubes are longer than the sepals and petals. Flowering varies from axillary in *F. splendens* to racemose in *F. fulgens* and *F. decidua*. The latter two have tuberous roots. *F. decidua* is the only one difficult to obtain in cultivation.

F. DECIDUA
Ellobium   Mexico   1929   Standley
F. decidua is found growing among rocks or epiphytically high in trees, on the trunks of oaks in moist forest areas. The leaves on this deciduous fuchsia are opposite each other. Blooms are held in dense racemes. Their long tubes and short sepals are dark pink; the petals are short and red. Blooming occurs during the dry season, from December to May, when the leaves are lost. *F. decidua* is rare. Its tuberous roots help it to cope with seasonally variable moisture levels.
Description: Breedlove, D. E., et al (1982), pp. 218-20.
Illustration: Schnedl, E. & H. (1997), opposite p. 44.

F. FULGENS
Ellobium   Mexico   1828   De Candolle
F. fulgens has a much wider distribution than *F. decidua*. It too is to be found as a terrestrial or an epiphytic plant. Its stems are soft and its tuberous roots allow it to cope with the dry season. Leaves are opposite, and older ones are villous. Flowering occurs when the leaves are present during the rainy season, from June to November. Blooms are held in small terminal racemes. Tubes are long and gently tapered. The sepals and petals are short. References show this fuchsia to have red flowers but the many variants in cultivation in the British Isles have orange blooms with darker orange petals. Plants of *F. fulgens* kept for several years in cultivation are slower to come into regrowth in each succeeding year. Cuttings are best taken in the autumn after earlier pruning.

Description: Breedlove, D. E., et al (1982), pp. 216-18.
Illustration: Goedman-Frankema, M. (1992), p. 10.

F. SPLENDENS
Ellobium   Mexico   1832   Zuccarini
F. splendens has the widest habitat distribution of all species within the section *Ellobium*. It commonly grows terrestrially and, rarely, as an epiphyte. Its leaves are usually opposite but occasionally ternate. Flowers are produced singly in the leaf axils on young growth. Tube length varies considerably; tubes are flattened just beyond the ovary and are orange or red. Sepals are short and green. The petals are green. *F. splendens* can be found in flower throughout the year in its native habitat but in Great Britain it tends to bloom during the darker months. *F. splendens* is naturally so variable that the fuchsia known as *F. cordifolia* is sometimes classified within this species; opinions vary. It flowers throughout the year. Both *F. splendens* and *F. cordifolia* are widely available under cultivation.
Description: Breedlove, D. E., et al (1982), pp. 213-16.
Illustration: Goedman-Frankema, M. (1992), p. 13.

Section *Encliandra*

Species within the section *Encliandra* may be gynodioecious – that is, with perfect and pistillate blooms. They may also often be dioecious, having staminate and pistillate flowers on separate plants. Epipetalous filaments always reflex into the hypanthia. This variability has led to considerable confusion in naming individual plants. Flies, bees and humming-birds act as pollinators and are often specific to particular flower types. Encliandras are numerous throughout the range of their habitats but are less common in arid or cloud forest areas. Most fuchsias in this section have wiry, shrubby growth and fine, fern-like foliage with small leaves. The fuchsias that have the largest blooms, and are therefore most likely to be popular with gardeners and hybridists in the future, are those encliandras with perfect flowers. Identification within this group is exceptionally difficult. All are thought to be in cultivation but many are grown erroneously under the name *F.* x *bacillaris*.

F. CYLINDRACEA

Encliandra Mexico 1838 Lindley
F. cylindracea was renamed from *F. parviflora* by Paul Berry to avoid confusion between *F. parviflora* and its synonym *F. lycioides*. The description given by Dennis Eugene Breedlove remains the same. The flowers are dioecious. Staminate blooms have cylindric tubes of about 1 cm in length. The tubes are usually dark orange or red but, like the petals, may be white or red. Pistillate flowers are similarly coloured but slightly smaller, with hosts of black berries. Leaves are opposite and branchlets ascending. The erect shrubs grow to a height of up to 4 metres in forests. There appear to be three distinctly different kinds of *F. cylindracea* with slight differences in the foliage and flower colours.
Description: Breedlove, D. E. (1969), pp. 56-7.
Illustration: Goedman-Frankema, M. (1992), p. 18.

F. ENCLIANDRA

Encliandra Mexico 1840 Steudel
F. encliandra has three subspecies (Breedlove): *F. encliandra* subsp. *encliandra*, *F. encliandra* subsp. *microphylloides* and *F. encliandra* subsp. *tetradactyla*. *F. enc.* subsp. *microphylloides* can be differentiated from *F. encliandra* subsp. *encliandra* by its divaricating branch pattern and by its serrulate leaves. *F. encliandra* subsp. *tetradactyla* has larger leaves and hairy tubes. All have dioecious flowers that are held in whorls. Each staminate bloom has a cylindrical hypanthium, about 1 cm long but pistillate flowers are considerably shorter; all are predominantly red. Some variation in petal colour occurs among the different populations and pink or white corollas are common. Shrubs reaching 2 metres in height may be found growing in forests among wild strawberry trees, pine and oak.
Description: Breedlove, D. E. (1969), pp. 51-4.
Illustration: Goedman-Frankema, M. (1992), p. 16.

F. MICROPHYLLA

Encliandra Mexico 1823 Humboldt, Bonpland & Kunth
F. microphylla is highly variable and six subspecies have been described: *F. microphylla* subsp. *aprica*, *F. microphylla* subsp. *chiapensis*, *F. microphylla* subsp. *hemsleyana*, *F. microphylla* subsp. *hidalgensis*, *F. microphylla* subsp. *microphylla* and *F. microphylla* subsp. *quercetorum*. It has been suggested that some, like *F. mic.* subsp. *hidalgensis*, are really seedlings resulting from chance crosses but this has yet to be proved. *F. mic.* subsp. *microphylla* can be found growing in the wild as a shrub up to 2 metres tall in mixed forests. Branchlets occur at right angles to the stems. Perfect flowers have cylindrical tubes about 1 cm in length, and petals of about half that size. Pistillate blooms are approximately half the size of perfect ones. Both are red and may have a purple cast. *F. mic.* subsp. *hidalgensis* forms spreading shrubs; it is different from the others in this species because its blooms are white and smaller. *F. mic.* subsp. *quercetorum* is recognized by its dark green leaves and small red flowers. Its habit is upright and bushy. *F. mic.* subsp. *aprica* has a more spreading growth, although shrubs of up to 3 metres in height may be found. Perfect and pistillate blooms are red or purplish-red: the former are about 1.5 cm long and the latter about half that size. *F. microphylla* subsp. *chiapensis* has larger leaves and more pubescent leaves and stems than *F. mic.* subsp. *aprica* which it resembles, but which grows at a higher elevation. *F. mic.* subsp. *hemsleyana* has slightly glazed leaves and can form shrubs up to 4 metres tall: these may be epiphytic. The flowers are about 1 cm long or smaller, and are red, pink or white in colour. Insects and humming-birds act as pollinators.
Description: Breedlove, D. E. (1969), pp. 40-7.
Illustration: Goedman-Frankema, M. (1992), p. 20.

F. OBCONICA

Encliandra Mexico 1969 D. E. Breedlove
F. obconica has ascending branchlets on shrubs up to 3 metres tall. It inhabits oak and pine forests along parts of the Trans-Mexican Volcanic Belt. This dioecious fuchsia has drooping pedicels and an obconic hypanthium. Staminate flowers are about 0.75 cm long and white. Pistillate blooms are only about 0.25 cm in length and slightly narrower at about 1.25 mm.
Description: Breedlove, D. E. (1969), pp. 54-6.
Illustration: Goedman-Frankema, M. (1992), p. 22.

34 'Brighton Belle'

35 'Edwin J. Goulding'

36 'Lechlade Potentate'

37 'Martin's Yellow Surprise'

38 'Orient Express'

39 'Our Ted'

40 'Sophie's Surprise'

41 'Beryl Shaffery'

42 'Canny Bob'

43 'Excalibur'

44 'Look East'

45 'Aalt Groothuis'

46 'Anjo'

47 'Delta's Bride'

48 'Delta's Drop'

49 'De Groot's Happiness'

50 'Earre Barré'

51 'Gay Parasol'

52 'Golden Vergeer'

53 'Graf Christian'

54 'Hathor'

55 'Hidden Treasure'

56 'Marlea's Vuurbol'

57 'Martin's Tiny'

58 Fuchsias in a Suffolk Garden

59 Mr J. v. d. Hee's 'Leverkusen'

60 Mr Hee's border

61 Mr G. Stals's 'Nettala'

62 Mr M. Appel's standards and tubs

63 Martin Appel's half-round baskets

64 Mr A. Bouw's garden with 'Gartenmeister Bonstedt'

65 Fuchsias displayed in Keukenhof Gardens

66 'Grietje'

67 'Panache'

68 'Ton Goedman' 69 'Wapenveld's Bloei'

70 'Fuksie Foetsie'

71 'Katinka'

72 'Marlies de Keijzer'

73 'Obcylin'

74 'Martin's Choice'

75 'Très Long'

76 'Alison Ruth Griffin'

77 'Anne Strudwick'

78 'Barry M. Cox'

79 'Betty Jean'

80 'Brian A. McDonald'

81 'Byron Rees'

82 'Captain Al Sutton'

83 'Cecile'

84 'Cheers'

85 'Chris'

86 'Daisy Bell'

87 'Gipping'

88 'Goldrezie'

89 'Gwendoline'

90 'Gwen Wallis'

91 'Irene van Zoeren'

92 'Jack Rowlands'

93 'Lavender Ann'

94 'Martin's Double Delicate'

95 'Pinto de Blue'

96 'Rohesse New Millennium'

97 'Ron Chambers Love'

98 'Snow Goose'

99 'Suffolk Punch'

100 'Wally Yendell'

F. RAVENII

Encliandra   Mexico   1969   D. E. Breedlove

F. ravenii will make shrubs up to 4 metres tall, with ascending branches and a gynodioecious flowering pattern. The tubes are less than 1 cm long and under 0.5 cm wide. Blooms are red. Female flowers are slightly shorter and wider. Leaves are larger than those of many plants in this section, and are green touched with grey.

Description: Breedlove, D. E. (1969), pp. 57-9.
Illustration: Goedman-Frankema, M. (1992), p. 23.

F. THYMIFOLIA

Encliandra   Mexico   1823   Humboldt, Bonpland & Kunth

F. thymifolia has been split into two subspecies (Breedlove). The first, *F. thymifolia* subsp. *thymifolia*, is said to have the widest variation and distribution of any species in this section. Both subspecies are gynodioecious, make shrubs up to 3 metres tall, and have ascending branchlets. *F. thym.* subsp. *thymifolia* has perfect flowers with obconic tubes about 0.5 cm long. Tubes are white turning to pink. Petals are white or pink at first but they turn to purple once fertilized. Pistillate flowers are about half the size of perfect ones. *F. thym.* subsp. *minimiflora* is differentiated by its larger leaves, shorter and wider flowers, and separated sepal tips when in bud.

Description: Breedlove, D. E. (1969), pp. 48-51.
Illustration: Goedman-Frankema, M. (1992), p. 24.

Section Fuchsia

Fuchsias in this section were originally placed in the section *Eufuchsia* by Phillip A. Munz (1970). His work, *A Revision of the Genus Fuchsia (Onagraceae)*, has been referred to in compiling this section. Paul Berry (1982) has reorganized them into fourteen groups that have broadly similar features. His work has proved immensely useful. There are many species within this section and their descriptions are necessarily brief, not least because several are not in cultivation and have been seen only rarely. Information shows that this section is the one under greatest threat from habitat destruction. It seems quite possible that more new species will be found, but only if there is sufficient time left for the research. Most of these fuchsias live in elevated cloud forests among moist scrub, or along the sides of streams.

1   F. decussata group

F. DECUSSATA

Fuchsia   Peru   1802   Ruiz & Pavón

F. decussata grows as suberect shrubs up to 3 metres high and densely branched. Leaves are usually opposite or ternate, small and lanceolate. Numerous flowers are produced in the leaf axils near the branch ends. The floral tubes are up to 2 cm long and spread to 0.6 cm at their rims. Sepals reach 2 cm in length and, like the tubes, are dark red. Petals are bright orange-red and up to 0.9 cm long. *F. decussata* is common in cultivation and flowers on mature wood.

Description: Berry, P. (1982), pp. 76-9.
Illustration: Goedman-Frankema, M. (1992), p. 35.

F. FERREYRAE

Fuchsia   Peru   1978   P. Berry

F. ferreyrae may be found as an erect or clambering shrub that can reach 3 metres in height. Its leaves are produced in ternate or quaternate whorls and have a furry texture: they may have dark purple undersides. Flowers are held in the leaf axils near the branch ends. The narrowly funnelform tubes reach 2.8 cm in length and 0.9 cm at their widest. Sepals are some 1.6 cm long and, like the tubes, are a dark bluish-red. The petals are almost violet and about 0.9 cm long.

Description: Berry, P. (1982), pp. 79-80.
Illustration: Berry, P. (1982), p. 50, fig. 27.

F. FONTINALIS

Fuchsia   Peru   1940   J. F. Macbride

F. fontinalis may be seen as an erect shrub or scandent, growing to 4 metres high. Its leaves are usually ternate or quaternate but occasionally opposite, and elliptic. The numerous flowers are held in leaf axils, terminal racemes or many-branched panicles. Floral tubes are narrowly funnelform and some 2.8 cm in length. They are somewhat bulbous, and up to 0.4 cm wide. Sepals may be 1.3 cm long but the petals are only 0.9 cm in length. Blooms are dark pink or red.

Description: Berry, P. (1982), pp. 80-81.
Illustration: Schnedl, E. & H. (1997), p. 26.

F. SANCTAE-ROSAE

Fuchsia   Bolivia   1898   O. Kuntz

F. sanctae-rosae may grow as a herbaceous plant, or reach as much as 3 metres as a self-branching shrub. It carries its leaves ternately or quaternately; these have a bluish-green and rather metallic cast when young. Blooms may be carried in the upper leaf axils or appear in more complex pendant groupings. Floral tubes are narrowly funnelform, some 2.2 cm long and 0.6 cm wide near the rims. Sepals reach 1.3 cm in length. Petals are about 0.9 cm long. Blooms are orange-red throughout. This is an adaptable species that is widely grown under cultivation.

Description: Berry, P. (1982), pp. 81-3.
Illustration: Saunders, E. (1987), p. 64.

2   *F. loxensis group*

F. LOXENSIS
Fuchsia   Ecuador   1823   Humboldt, Bonpland & Kunth
F. loxensis grows as a bushy, upright shrub some 6 metres tall. Its leaves are ternate or quaternate. The blooms are carried in the upper leaf axils. The funnelform tubes are 3.3 cm long and up to 0.8 cm wide. Spreading sepals are 1.6 cm in length. Petals are almost 1.1 cm long. The whole flower is scarlet but the petals are rather dull. *F. loxensis* is plentiful and variable in the wild. Berry talks of a white layer of fungal mycelia which covers the leaves of one population near Loja in Ecuador. Examples of this species are in cultivation but not those bearing fungal mycelia.

Description: Berry, P. (1982), pp. 83-6.
Illustration: Goedman-Frankema, M. (1992), p. 41.

F. SCABRIUSCULA
Fuchsia   Ecuador   1845   Bentham
F. scabriuscula can grow as a shrub to 2.5 metres high. Its leaves are usually opposite and have a rough, hairy texture; their undersides are darkly stained. Blooms are few in number and occur in the upper leaf axils. Floral tubes are narrowly funnelform, up to 2.7 cm long, and widen to 0.7 cm near their rims. Sepals spread as they ripen and are up to 1.2 cm in length. Petals reach 1 cm long. The whole flower may be pink or red. *F. scabriuscula* is found in cultivation but is not easy to establish.

Description: Berry, P. (1982), pp. 86-8.
Illustration: Berry, P. (1982), p. 47.

F. STEYERMARKII
Fuchsia   Ecuador   1982   P. Berry
F. steyermarkii forms hairy shrubs of, perhaps, 2 metres in height with multiple branches. The leaves may be opposite, ternate or quaternate; they are small and spiky with glossy upper surfaces and pale, pilose undersides. Blooms are produced a few at a time in leaf axils near branch ends. Narrowly funnelform tubes are 3.7 cm long and 0.6 cm at their rims. Sepals are 1.5 cm in length. Petals, 1 cm long, are a brighter and darker red than the tubes and sepals.

Description: Berry, P. (1982), pp. 88-9.
Illustration: None.

Note: Two more species have been listed within this group. As yet they have not been described in any publication by Paul Berry. They are *F. eileeniana* and *F. subparamosis*.

3   *F. nigricans group*

F. GLABERRIMA
Fuchsia   Ecuador   1925   I. M. Johnston
F. glaberrima grows as minimally branched shrubs to a height of 3 metres. The opposite leaves are carried near the branch ends and are membranous and oblanceolate; they also have dark undersides. Blooms are held in terminal, bracteate, drooping racemes. Floral tubes reach 3.5 cm long and 0.7 cm at their widest. Sepals are 1.1 cm in length. Both are orange-red. Petals are rather darker red, and some 0.1 cm long.

Description: Berry, P. (1982), pp. 97-8.
Illustration: Munz, P. A. (1970), p. 125, fig. 55.

F. NIGRICANS
Fuchsia   Venezuela   1849   Linden
F. nigricans will make erect, self-branching bushes up to 3 metres high. Its leaves are mostly ternate and elliptic with hairy, dark green surfaces. Flowers may be produced in the upper leaf axils but are also commonly found in terminal bracteate racemes. Tubes reach 2.2 cm in length and 0.5 cm in width. The spreading sepals may be 1 cm long. Both are red. The dark purple petals are 1 cm long. *F. nigricans* is available in cultivation.

Description: Berry, P. (1982), pp. 89-92.
Illustration: Goedman-Frankema, M. (1992), p. 45.

F. ORIENTALIS
Fuchsia Ecuador 1982 P. Berry
F. orientalis will make shrubs of some 2 metres tall. Its leaves are opposite or occasionally ternate, and elliptic. The flowers are held in bracteate racemes at the ends of branches or in upper leaf axils. Floral tubes reach 2.1 cm long and 0.5 cm wide. Sepals are 0.8 cm in length. Both are orange-red. Petals are similar in colour and 0.8 cm long. *F. orientalis* lives in the lower levels of the Andean cloud forests and is found in cultivation.
Description: Berry, P. (1982), pp. 95-7.
Illustration: Schnedl, E. & H. (1997), p. 34.

F. PALLESCENS
Fuchsia Ecuador 1938 Diels
F. pallescens grows as a herb or sub-shrub. The leaves may be opposite or ternate and are dark green with velvety surfaces. Small numbers of drooping blooms are carried in the upper leaf axils or terminally in subracemose groups. Narrowly funnelform tubes reach 2.5 cm in length and 0.5 mm in diameter. The sepals are about 1.5 cm long. Both may be pink or pale red. The petals are maroon and are 0.8 cm long. This species is occasionally found in cultivation, flowering throughout the year.
Description: Berry, P. (1982), pp. 94-5.
Illustration: None.

F. SUMMA
Fuchsia Ecuador 1995 Berry & Brako
F. summa forms shrubs up to a metre tall. All except the tips of branches are bare of leaves; the latter are held in whorls of three or four to an axil: they are sub-coriaceous and broadly elliptic. Flowers are borne in the axillae, often more than one to a node. Narrowly funnelform tubes may be up to 3 cm long. Sepals are 1.4 cm long. Petals are red, like the rest of the flower, and are 1.2 cm in length. *F. summa* is still rare in cultivation.
Description: Berry, P. E. (1995), pp. 320-23.
Illustration: Schnedl, E. & H. (1997), opposite p. 34.

F. SYLVATICA
Fuchsia Ecuador 1845 Bentham
F. sylvatica will grow into erect or scandent shrubs reaching 2.5 metres in height. Leaves are usually ternate but sometimes opposite or quaternate and finely-haired. The many blooms are carried in long, pendant, terminal racemes.

Floral tubes are 2.2 cm long and up to 0.7 cm wide at their rims. Sepals may be 1.3 cm in length. Both are rose red. Petals are a dark crimson, and 1 cm long.
Description: Berry, P. (1982), pp. 92-4.
Illustration: Munz, P. A. (1970), p. 127, fig. 58.

4   *F. macrophylla group*

F. MACROPETALA
Fuchsia Peru 1831 Presl
F. macropetala forms upright or scandent shrubs up to 3 metres in height. Its large leaves are usually opposite, elliptic, and stained purple on their undersides. The few flowers may be carried on sparse lateral racemes part way up the plants. Hypanthia measure 4.5 cm by 0.7 cm at the maximum. Spreading sepals measure 1.3 cm. Petals are 1.2 cm long. Tubes, sepals and corollas are red. *F. macropetala* is rare in cultivation.
Description: Berry, P. (1982), pp. 99-100.
Illustration: None.

F. MACROPHYLLA
Fuchsia Peru 1925 I. M. Johnston
F. macrophylla makes scandent or erect shrubs up to 3 metres tall. Its leaves are usually opposite, narrowly elliptic, and have paler lower surfaces. Blooms are produced in small lateral racemes and not at the ends of branches. Tubes, which are red, are 2.5 cm in length and up to 0.6 cm in width. The 0.9-cm long sepals are similarly coloured except that they have green tips. The petals are 1 cm long, and scarlet. *F. macrophylla* has been greatly affected by the destruction of its habitat but is occasionally found in cultivation.
Description: Berry, P. (1982), pp. 98-9.
Illustration: Saunders, E. (1987), p. 62.

F. OVALIS
Fuchsia Peru 1802 Ruiz & Pavón
F. ovalis grows as erect or scandent shrubs up to 3 metres in height. Its hairy leaves are opposite, ternate or quaternate. Blooms are carried in terminal or lateral panicles and racemes. Their narrowly funnelform red tubes are up to 2 cm long and 0.45 cm wide. Sepals are 1.3 cm in length and they, too, are red. Similarly coloured petals may be 0.9 cm long. This species has been severely affected by habitat destruction.
Description: Berry, P. (1982), pp. 100-101.
Illustration: Munz, P. A. (1970), p. 125, fig. 54.

F. PILOSA

Fuchsia   Peru   1844   Fielding & Gardner

F. pilosa grows as a hairy shrub to 2 metres high in cloud forest pockets. Leaves, too, are pilose and may be opposite, ternate or quaternate. The many flowers are held in long, terminal, pendant racemes. Tubes are narrowly funnelform, 2 cm long, and bright orange-red. The sepals are lanceolate, 0.8 cm in length, and similar in colour to the tubes, as are the petals which measure 0.8 cm long.

Description: Berry, P. (1982), pp. 101-3.
Illustration: None.

5   *F. putumayensis group*

F. ABRUPTA

Fuchsia   Peru   1925   I. M. Johnston

F. abrupta makes a deciduous, scandent shrub of up to 3 metres, usually with opposite lance-shaped leaves. Floral tubes are 4.5 cm in length and some 1 cm wide. Sepals are 1.5 cm long. Each flower part is orange-red. Petals are similar in length to the sepals, and spreading. Flowers are produced in pendant terminal racemes on the branch ends.

Description: Berry, P. (1982), pp. 109-10.
Illustration: Berry, P. (1982), p. 47, fig. 20.

F. ANDREI

Fuchsia   Ecuador/Peru   1925   I. M. Johnston

F. andrei forms shrubs up to 4 metres tall. Its leaves may be opposite or occasionally ternate, and are narrowly elliptic to obovate, with a waxy texture. Floral tubes may be 3.5 cm long, and taper from 0.1 cm near the ovary to 0.6 cm at their widest. Petals are 1 cm long and spread widely with maturity. Blooms are waxy orange and are held in numerous terminal racemes. *F. andrei* is common in cultivation.

Description: Berry, P. (1982), pp. 106-8.
Illustration: Goedman-Frankema, M. (1992), p. 29.

F. CUATRECASASII

Fuchsia   Colombia   1943   P. Munz

F. cuatrecasasii makes infrequent sub-shrubs up to 1.5 metres tall. The elliptical glossy leaves are opposite with a purple shade on their undersides. Blooms are held in terminal, drooping racemes. Their tubes are funnelform, some 5 cm long, and up to 0.8 cm at their widest. The sepals may reach 2 cm and the petals about 0.5 cm shorter. Flowers are bright red.

Description: Berry, P. (1982), pp. 108-9.
Illustration: Munz, P. A. (1970), p. 119, fig. 40.

F. LEHMANNII

Fuchsia   Ecuador   1943   P. Munz

F. lehmannii grows as erect or scandent shrubs, with plentiful side shoots, to a height of 3 metres. Leaves are produced in whorls of three or four and are narrowly lanceolate. Large numbers of orange blooms are carried in terminal racemes. Floral tubes are funnelform and 3.5 cm long; their width is 0.9 cm at its widest. Spreading sepals measure 1.3 cm in length and the frilly, delicate petals, which are slightly paler in colour, are 1.1 cm long. *F. lehmannii* appears to be in cultivation, but is difficult to distinguish from *F. andrei*.

Description: Berry, P. (1982), pp. 104-6.
Illustration: Goedman-Frankema, M. (1992), p. 41.

F. PUTUMAYENSIS

Fuchsia   Colombia   1943   P. Munz

F. putumayensis forms shrubs up to 3 metres tall. Its opposite leaves have glabrous upper surfaces. Blooms are carried in small but dense terminal racemes. Their funnelform tubes are up to 2.7 cm in length and about 0.7 cm in diameter. Sepals are 1.1 cm long, and lanceolate. Petals are 0.9 cm in length. The whole flower is orange-red and has a waxy texture. This species is widely available in cultivation but is difficult to tell apart from *F. andrei*.

Description: Berry, P. (1982), pp. 103-4.
Illustration: Saunders, E. (1987), p. 64.

6   *F. petiolaris group*

F. AMPLIATA

Fuchsia   Ecuador   1841-43   Bentham

F. ampliata grows as an erect or scandent shrub, up to 3 metres high, with ternate or quaternate leaves. These are narrowly lanceolate and drooping. Flowers are produced in small numbers in the leaf axils and are funnelform in shape. Tubes are up to 5 cm long and 0.45 cm at their widest near their sepals, which reflex with maturity and reach up to 2.3 cm long. The broadly-rounded petals are about 0.18 cm long. Flowers are orange-red throughout.

Description: Berry, P. (1982), pp. 125-7.
Illustration: Berry, P. (1982), p. 49, fig. 23.

F. AYAVACENSIS

Fuchsia   Peru   1802   Humboldt, Bonpland & Kunth

F. ayavacensis grows as a semi-scandent shrub

up to 3 metres high, where forest-clearing has taken place. Its large leaves are ternate or quaternate, elliptic-lanceolate, with white surface hairs. Flowers are produced in the upper leaf axils. Their tubes are almost 6 cm long and broaden out to 0.8 cm near the sepals that are 0.15 cm in length. The rounded petals are about 1 cm long and the whole flower is orange-red. This fuchsia is rare in cultivation.
Description: Berry, P. (1982), pp. 121-2.
Illustration: Munz, P. A. (1970), p. 111, fig. 18.

F. CAMPII

Fuchsia   Ecuador   1995   Berry
F. campii forms shrubs between 1.5–4 metres high. Young branches are hairy; older ones are purple with exfoliating bark. Leaves are produced in whorls; they are narrowly elliptic. Flowers are produced in terminal leaf axils: tubes are 4 cm long, 0.25 cm at the base and widening to 0.8 cm near the sepals. Sepals are triangular and pink like the tubes, except for their green tips: 1.5 cm long. Petals are 1 cm in length, and orange.
Description: Berry, P. E. (1995), pp. 318-20.
Illustration: Goedman-Frankema, M. (1992), p. 32.

F. CAUCANA

Fuchsia   Colombia   1982   P. Berry
F. caucana forms sparse shrubs up to 2 metres high. Its leaves are usually ternate but not invariably so; they are narrowly lanceolate. Flowers are produced in small numbers in the upper leaf axils. Their hypanthia are narrowly funnelform, 4.5 cm long and 0.4 cm wide. The partially spreading, and pointed, sepals may be as much as 1.7 cm long. Both are light red. The petals are a darker red and reach just over 1 cm in length.
Description: Berry, P. (1982), pp. 118-21.
Illustration: Berry, P. (1982), p. 49, fig. 26.

F. COROLLATA

Fuchsia   Colombia   1845   Bentham
F. corollata produces erect or scandent shrubs up to 5 metres high with exfoliating bark. The leaves are ternate or quaternate and elliptic to oblanceolate, dark and glossy green. The floral tubes are up to 5.5 cm long, swell bulbously to 0.8 cm wide, and are pink or red. The sepals are 1.7 cm long, red with green tips. Petals are scarlet and some 1.8 cm long.
Description: Berry, P. (1982), pp. 114-18.
Illustration: None.

F. PETIOLARIS

Fuchsia   Colombia   1823   Humboldt, Bonpland & Kunth
F. petiolaris can be seen as a shrub growing to 2 metres tall or climbing through trees to a height of 5 metres. Its leaves are often carried in dense whorls and are narrowly lanceolate. Flowers are carried in leaf axils near the perimeter of plants. Floral tubes are some 5 cm long, 1.1 cm wide, and funnelform. Sepals are widely spread and reach 2.3 cm in length. The former are rose pink while the latter are paler and green-tipped. Petals may be 1.6 cm long and bright pink. *F. petiolaris* is available in cultivation.
Description: Berry, P. (1982), pp. 110-4.
Illustration: Saunders, E. (1987), p. 63.

F. VULCANICA

Fuchsia   Colombia   1888   André
F. vulcanica is a shrub that grows up to 3.5 metres high, and is also a partially epiphytic fuchsia on mossy trees. The narrowly elliptic leaves are carried in whorls of three, four or less commonly, five. Pendant flowers are held near the branch ends in the leaf axils. Their tubes are 5 cm long and 0.7 cm at their widest. Sepals may be 2 cm in length. Broadly obovate petals are 1.5 cm long. The tubes and sepals are sometimes paler than the corollas that are red. *F. vulcanica* is in general cultivation.
Description: Berry, P. (1982), pp. 122-5.
Illustration: Goedman-Frankema, M. (1992), p. 53.

7   *F. venusta group*

F. CONFERTIFOLIA

Fuchsia   Peru   1844   Fielding & Gardner
F. confertifolia forms densely branched, brown and hairy-stemmed shrubs up to 2 metres high. Its coriaceous leaves may be opposite, ternate or quaternate, and oblong-ovate in shape. The few flowers are subterminal and pendant. Their dark red tubes are about 5 cm long and, perhaps, 0.8 cm at their widest. The sepals are narrow, about 1.8 cm long, and red. Corollas are comprised of narrowly tapered red petals that reach 1.3 cm in length.
Description: Berry, P. (1982), pp. 136-7.
Illustration: Munz, P. A. (1970), p. 117, fig. 30.

F. GEHRIGERI

Fuchsia   Venezuela   1973   P. Munz
F. gehrigeri forms erect or scandent shrubs up to 5 metres high with pendant branches. Leaves are mostly ternate and narrowly elliptic with felty

surfaces. Flowers are nearly always axillary or corymbose near the ends of branches. Floral tubes are narrowly funnelform, 5 cm long and up to 0.9 cm wide near the sepals which are 2.1 cm in length; both are red. Petals are scarlet, and up to 2.1 cm long. *F. gehrigeri* is in cultivation.
Description: Berry, P. (1982), pp. 132-5.
Illustration: Goedman-Frankema, M. (1992), p. 38.

F. LLEWELYNII

Fuchsia   Peru   1941   J. F. Macbride
F. llewelynii is to be found as a shrub no more than a metre high with spiny projections on its stems. Its narrowly oblanceolate leaves are opposite or ternate. The few flowers are produced in the upper leaf axils or in sparse racemes. The hypanthium is 5.4 cm long and widens to 0.8 cm near its mouth. Sepals are 1.7 cm in length. Tubes and sepals are pink. The petals, which are some 2 cm long and rather spreading, are a brighter pink. This species is not in cultivation.
Description: Berry, P. (1982), p. 135.
Illustration: Munz, P. A. (1970), p. 115, fig. 25.

F. RIVULARIS

Fuchsia   Peru   1940   J. F. Macbride
F. rivularis produces lianas, with purple stems and few side shoots, which can scramble through trees to a height of 10 metres. The leaves are usually ternate or quaternate with paler green undersides. Flowers are sparse and hang from the upper leaf axils. Floral tubes may reach 6.5 cm long and 1 cm in diameter. They and the sepals, which are 2 cm long, are red. Petals are 2.2 cm in length, frilly in appearance and are orange-red.
Description: Berry, P. (1982), pp. 131-2.
Illustration: Schnedl, E. & H. (1997), p. 38.

F. SCHERFFIANA

Fuchsia   Ecuador   1888   André
F. scherffiana forms spreading shrubs with purple stems that may grow up to 3 metres tall. The leaves are usually opposite but occasionally ternate. They have a dark metallic hue and are narrow. Blooms are not numerous but they are axillary and drooping. Floral tubes may be up to 5 cm long and 0.8 cm at their widest. Sepals are 1.4 cm in length and spreading when mature. Tubes and sepals are orange-red. Petals are also red, and are some 1.1 cm long.
Description: Berry, P. (1982), pp. 136-7.
Illustration: None.

F. VENUSTA

Fuchsia   Colombia   1823   Humboldt, Bonpland & Kunth
F. venusta will grow to a height of 10 metres with lianas climbing through trees, or it may be seen as a shorter upright shrub. Its numerous branches droop at their extremities. Leaves are usually ternate, small and glossy green. Flowers are axillary or subracemose towards the ends of branches. Their tubes are 6 cm long and 1 cm in width, while sepals are 2 cm in length. Petals may reach 2.2 cm in length. Each part of the bloom is orange-red although some green may be present. This species is in general cultivation.
Description: Berry, P. (1982), pp. 127-30.
Illustration: Goedman-Frankema, M. (1992), p. 52.

8   *F. denticulata group*

F. AUSTROMONTANA

Fuchsia   Peru   1939   I. M. Johnston
F. austromontana grows as floppy or semi-scandent shrubs up to 4 metres in height. Leaves may be opposite or produced in whorls. The hypanthium is funnelform, about 4 cm long, and red. The sepals are red and up to 0.17 cm long. The obovate red petals are about 0.15 cm long. This deciduous shrub carries its few blooms in the upper leaf axils. There is doubt about its authenticity in cultivation.
Description: Berry, P. (1982), pp. 142-3.
Illustration: Munz, P. A. (1970), p. 107, fig. 8.

F. COCHABAMBANA

Fuchsia   Bolivia   1982   P. Berry
F. cochabambana grows as a low shrub to 1.5 metres tall. Leaves are ternate or, less frequently, quaternate and elliptic with a purple flush on their undersides. Blooms are produced near the branch ends in the leaf axils or subracemosely. The narrowly funnelform tubes may be up to 5.8 cm long and, at their widest, 1 cm. Sepals are some 1.8 cm in length and, like the tubes, scarlet. Petals become a darker red as they age and are about 1.3 cm long.
Description: Berry, P. (1982), pp. 144-5.
Illustration: None.

F. DENTICULATA

Fuchsia   Peru   1802   Ruiz & Pavón
F. denticulata will   form   erect   or   scandent

shrubs up to 10 metres tall. Leaves are usually ternate or quaternate, and oblanceolate. Flowers are produced in the leaf axils towards the branch ends. The straight tubes are 4.7 cm long and 1.2 cm wide. The former are waxy red and the latter are a mixture of red and green. Petals are 1.8 cm long and bright orange. This species, which is widely found growing in cloud forests, is also frequently found in cultivation.

Description: Berry, P. (1982), pp. 137-42.
Illustration: Goedman-Frankema, M. (1992), p. 36.

F. HARLINGII

Fuchsia   Ecuador   1972   P. Munz

F. harlingii forms scandent or erect shrubs: the former may reach a height of 3 metres. Leaves are opposite or ternate and have membranous surfaces and a narrowly elliptical shape. The few drooping flowers are held in the upper leaf axils. Their broad tubes are up to 5.3 cm long and 1.2 cm wide. Sepals are 1.7 cm long. Tubes and sepals are orange or red. Petals are 1.5 cm long and a darker red.

Description: Berry, P. (1982), pp. 143-4.
Illustration: Berry, P. (1982), p. 49, fig. 25.

F. MACROSTIGMA

Fuchsia   Ecuador   1844   Bentham

F. macrostigma is to be found as an upright shrub growing to 1.5 metres. Its leaves are alternate or occasionally ternate and they are dark green above and stained purple below. The few flowers are produced in the upper leaf axils. They are held horizontally and have a bend in their tubes. The floral tubes are 8 cm long and 1 cm wide. Sepals are fleshy and 2.3 cm in length. Both are dark red but the latter have green tips. The petals are 1.8 cm long and a brighter red. *F. macrostigma* is in cultivation but is a difficult plant from which to take cuttings, does not like nipping and exhibits circadian rhythm in its young shoots.

Description: Berry, P. (1982), pp. 145-7.
Illustration: Munz, P. A. (1970), p. 111, fig. 17.

F. MAGDALENAE

Fuchsia   Colombia   1943   P. Munz

F. magdalenae forms spreading shrubs up to 5 metres tall. Its leaves are opposite, ternate or quaternate. The few pendant flowers are produced in the upper leaf axils. Floral tubes may be as long as 6 cm and, perhaps, 1 cm wide; they have a constriction just above the nectaries. The spreading sepals are 1.8 cm in length. Petals may be 1.9 cm long. Tubes are dark at the base lightening to orange-red. The sepals and petals are similarly coloured but the former have green tips. *F. magdalenae* can be found in cultivation and has proved useful to hybridists such as Henk Waldenmaier, in recent years, although it is not easy to grow. It will only really tolerate pinching when there are lots of new shoots.

Description: Berry, P. (1982), pp. 147-8.
Illustration: Goedman-Frankema, M. (1992), p. 43.

9   *F. simplicicaulis group*

F. CERACEA

Fuchsia   Peru   1982   P. Berry

F. ceracea grows as a climbing shrub with lianas reaching 6 metres above the ground. Leaves may be opposite or ternate and narrowly ovate. Pendant racemes of blooms are sheathed at their base with brackets of leaves. Floral tubes may be 13 cm long, bulbous, and up to 0.9 cm wide at their rim. The pendant sepals are, perhaps, 3 cm in length. Both tubes and sepals are light red. Petals reach 0.7 cm and are dark purple.

Description: Berry, P. (1982), pp. 149-50.
Illustration: Berry, P. (1982), p. 51, fig. 31.

F. CORIACIFOLIA

Fuchsia   Peru   1982   P. Berry

F. coriacifolia forms shrubs up to 2 metres high. Its leathery leaves may be opposite or ternate on the branchlets, and have paler undersurfaces. These funnelform flowers are produced in loose terminal racemes. Tubes are 5.8 cm by 1cm. Sepals are 1.9 cm long. Lanceolate petals are about 1.2 cm in length. Flowers are rosy red. It has only just come into cultivation.

Description: Berry, P. (1982), pp. 150-2.
Illustration: None.

F. SANMARTINA

Fuchsia   Peru   1982   P. Berry

F. sanmartina may be found as a shrub or spreading its lianas to 10 metres through surrounding trees. Its leaves are usually ternate but occasionally opposite, and narrowly elliptic-ovate. Blooms are plentiful and hang in terminal panicles. Their floral tubes are 7.6 cm long and up to 0.8 cm wide near the sepals, which are about 2.5 cm long. Petals are 1.6 cm in length and the whole flower is red.

Description: Berry, P. (1982), pp. 152-3.
Illustration: None.

F. SIMPLICICAULIS

Fuchsia Peru 1802 Ruiz & Pavón

F. simplicicaulis forms scandent shrubs that may reach 5 metres high. Its leaves are ternate or quaternate and linear-lanceolate. Whorls of blooms are held in long, drooping racemes at the ends or the highest branches. The narrowly funnelform tubes may be 5 cm long by 0.7 cm in diameter. Sepals are about 2 cm in length. Both are pink-red. Petals are brighter red and are 1.3 cm long. This species, rare in the wild, is common in cultivation.

Description: Berry, P. (1982), pp. 148-9.
Illustration: Goedman-Frankema, M. (1992), p. 49.

10 F. sessilifolia group

F. POLYANTHA

Fuchsia Colombia 1943 Killip

F. polyantha forms erect shrubs up to 2 metres tall. Its leaves, which are dark above and light green beneath, are quaternate and elliptic. Blooms are carried in large numbers in terminal pendant panicles. Funnelform tubes are up to 4.3 cm long and 0.7 cm at their widest. Sepals are 1.5 cm in length. Both are red. Petals are a slightly darker red, and are 1.4 cm long.

Description: Berry, P. (1982), pp. 155-7.
Illustration: Munz, P. A. (1970), p. 119, fig. 37.

F. SESSILIFOLIA

Fuchsia Ecuador 1845 Bentham

F. sessilifolia grows with few branches to a height of 3 metres. Younger branchlets are dark red. Leaves are quaternate, large and sessile. Flowers are held in pendant panicles on the branch ends. The floral tubes are narrowly funnelform and some 1.8 cm long by 0.5 cm wide. Sepals are 1.1 cm long and petals are 0.9 cm: their scarlet colour contrasts with the paler pink, green or light red of the tubes and sepals. *F. sessilifolia* is found in cultivation.

Description: Berry, P. (1982), pp. 153-5.
Illustration: Goedman-Frankema, M. (1992), p. 48.

11 F. tincta group

F. FURFURACEA

Fuchsia Bolivia 1925 I. M. Johnston

F. furfuracea can be found as an erect or scandent shrub reaching 2.5 metres in height. It is usually found in especially wet and forested areas. Its leaves are commonly opposite but occasionally ternate or ovate. The few flowers are usually held in terminal pendant racemes. Narrowly funnelform tubes reach a length of 4.8 cm and a width of 0.9 cm: they are orange-red. Sepals may be 1.8 cm long, similar in colour, but with darker tips. Petals are 0.9 cm long and dark red. *F. furfuracea* is in cultivation but is difficult to grow.

Description: Berry, P. (1982), pp. 159-61.
Illustration: Schnedl, E. & H. (1997), p. 27.

F. TINCTA

Fuchsia Peru 1939 I. M. Johnston

F. tincta forms erect sub-shrubs up to 1.5 metres tall. Branchlets are covered with white hairs that turn brown with age. The ovate leaves are nearly always opposite; they are pale green above and flushed purple beneath. Blooms are held in dense terminal corymbose racemes. Their narrowly funnelform tubes are about 2.3 cm long and up to 0.5 cm wide. Sepals are 0.9 cm in length. Petals, like the rest of the flower, are bright red, and are 0.9 cm long.

Description: Berry, P. (1982), pp. 157-9.
Illustration: Munz, P. A. (1970), p. 117, fig. 32.

F. VARGASIANA

Fuchsia Peru 1946 Vargas

F. vargasiana grows in moist, shady thickets to a height of 2 metres. Young growth is covered with fine white hairs that turn brown as they age. Leaves are usually opposite and narrowly ovate-elliptic. Blooms are held in terminal corymbose racemes. Their narrowly funnelform tubes are 4 cm long and 0.8 cm at their widest. Sepals are 1.6 cm in length. Petals are 1.2 cm long. Tubes and petals are red; sepals are almost entirely green. *F. vargasiana* was thought to be in cultivation but its authenticity is doubtful.

Description: Berry, P. (1982), pp. 161-2.
Illustration: Goedman-Frankema, M. (1992), p. 51.

12 F. boliviana group

F. BOLIVIANA

Fuchsia Bolivia 1876 Carrière

F. boliviana forms strong, erect shrubs and small trees up to 4.5 metres high. Its leaves are commonly opposite but sometimes alternate or ternate; they are elliptic to ovate in shape, with a soft pubescence on upper and lower surfaces. Young shoots exhibit clear circadian rhythms. Flowers are produced in large terminal, pendulous panicles or corymbs. Their tubes are 6 cm long and taper out to 0.7 cm at their rims. Sepals are about 2 cm long and quickly become fully reflexed. Petals are 1.3 cm in length and, like the tubes and sepals, scarlet. Variants are: *F. boliviana* var. *boliviana*, *F. boliviana* var. *luxurians* and *F. boliviana* var. *luxurians* 'Alba'. All are easy to grow.

Description: Berry, P. (1982), pp. 162-70.
Illustration: Goedman-Frankema, M. (1992), p. 31.

F. CORYMBIFLORA

Fuchsia Peru 1802 Ruiz & Pavón

F. corymbiflora forms erect or scandent shrubs up to 4 metres tall. Young growth is hairy. Leaves are opposite or occasionally ternate. Flowers are usually produced in terminal, pendant racemes. The funnelform tubes reach 6.5 cm long and 0.8 cm at their widest. Sepals are 1.5 cm long. Both are bright pink or scarlet. Petals are 1.7 cm in length and rather darker in colour. This species has only recently come back into cultivation and is most easily differentiated from *F. boliviana* and its variants by the plum-like shape of its seed pods.

Description: Berry, P. (1982), pp. 170-71.
Illustration: Munz, P. A. (1970), p. 119, fig. 38.

F. MATHEWSII

Fuchsia Peru 1941 J. F. Macbride

F. mathewsii can be found as a semi-erect shrub up to 3 metres tall, with exfoliating bark. The elliptic leaves are ternate or quaternate on the branchlets. Its many blooms are held in terminal, pendant racemes or panicles. Funnelform tubes may be 6.3 cm long and 0.8 cm in diameter. The sepals reach 1.6 cm in length as do the petals. Tubes and sepals may be lavender, pink or red. Petals may be crimson or darker. This species is in cultivation.

Description: Berry, P. (1982), pp. 173-4.
Illustration: Schnedl, E. & H. (1997), p. 33.

F. WURDACKII

Fuchsia Peru 1964 P. Munz

F. wurdackii grows as an erect shrub up to 1.5 metres high. Young branches are covered with fine white hairs that turn brown with age. The dark green leaves are opposite or ternate and are softly pilose. Blooms are carried in terminal corymbose racemes. Narrowly funnelform tubes are 5 cm long and 0.8 cm at their most bulbous. Sepals are obtuse and 1.6 cm long. Petals are 2 cm in length. All are red. *F. wurdackii* is available in cultivation.

Description: Berry, P. (1982), p. 172.
Illustration: Goedman-Frankema, M. (1992), p. 54.

13 F. dependens group

F. CANESCENS

Fuchsia Colombia 1845 Bentham

F. canescens makes shrubby, sometimes climbing, plants up to 4 metres tall and grows in high-rainfall terrain. Leaves are produced in whorls and are narrowly elliptic in shape. Blooms are produced in the upper leaf axils and may appear in subterminal or terminal leafy racemes. Orange funnelform tubes may reach 5 cm long and widen to 0.9 cm. The triangular green sepals are up to 1.8 cm in length. Petals are almost 2 cm long and are a slightly darker red than the rest of the flower.

Description: Berry, P. (1982), pp. 182-4.
Illustration: Munz, P. A. (1970), p. 109, fig.13.

F. CINEREA

Fuchsia Ecuador 1982 P. Berry

F. cinerea forms terrestrial shrubs up to 5 metres high. Leaves are carried in whorls, ternately or more commonly quaternately, are narrowly elliptic in shape, and are covered in ash-coloured hairs. Flowers are produced in leaf axils near the ends of the upper branches. Their funnelform tubes are about 5 cm long and 0.6 cm wide. The narrow sepals spread with maturity. They and the tubes are dull orange. The petals are rather darker, about 1.5 cm in length and spreading with maturity. There is doubt about the authenticity of the species in cultivation.

Description: Berry, P. (1982), pp. 184-5.
Illustration: None.

F. CRASSISTIPULA

Fuchsia Colombia 1972 P. Berry

F. crassistipula grows as a scandent shrub to 3 metres high. Leaves are produced in dense whorls and are oblanceolate, flushed purple on

their undersides, this coloration being enhanced during the darker months of the year. Flowers are usually produced in terminal racemes. Floral tubes are 4.6 cm long and 0.5 cm at their widest and bright pink or scarlet. The sepals are 1.4 cm long, and spreading when mature; they are similarly coloured but darken at their tips. Petals are a darker red and some 1.6 cm long. *F. crassistipula* is in cultivation.
Description: Berry, P. (1982), pp. 181-2.
Illustration: Goedman-Frankema, M. (1992), p. 34.

F. DEPENDENS
Fuchsia   Ecuador   1837   Hooker
F. dependens can form a scandent shrub up to 10 metres high, with pendant branches and mainly quaternate, narrowly elliptic and hairy leaves. Flowers are usually held in pendant terminal racemes or panicles. The thin funnelform tubes can grow to 5 cm long and 0.8 cm wide. Sepals are 1.3 cm in length. Both are orange-red, like the petals that are up to 1.4 cm long. *F. dependens* is readily found in cultivation.
Description: Berry, P. (1982), pp. 174-6.
Illustration: Goulding, E. J. (1995), plates 42-3.

F. HIRTELLA
Fuchsia   Colombia   1823   Humboldt,
Bonpland & Kunth
F. hirtella grows as a low semi-scandent shrub up to 5 metres high with exfoliating bark. Its leaves are carried in whorls of four or more; they are pubescent and elliptic. They also have pale undersides. Flowers are produced in large numbers in terminal, pendant panicles. The floral tubes are bulbous, 4 cm long and 0.9 cm at their maximum width. These and the sepals, which are 1.6 cm in length, are lavender to red. Petals are crimson, and 1.6 cm long.
Description: Berry, P. (1982), pp. 176-8.
Illustration: Munz, P. A. (1970), p. 119, fig. 36.

F. HARTWEGII
Fuchsia   Colombia   1845   Bentham
F. hartwegii forms small shrubs or trees up to 4 metres tall. Its leaves are olive green, felty, broadly elliptic and held in whorls of four or more to a joint. Flowers are held in terminal racemes or panicles and may be hermaphroditic or gynodioecious. Male-sterility is unknown among other fuchsias in this section. Their funnelform tubes are 2 cm long and up to 0.5 cm wide. These, like the sepals that are 0.4 cm long,

are scarlet. Petals are red and are 0.9 cm in length. *F. hartwegii* is common in cultivation and it may be seen with orange and red variants.
Description: Berry, P. (1982), pp. 178-81.
Illustration: Goedman-Frankema, M. (1992), p. 40.

14 *Anomalous species*

F. PRINGSHEIMII
Fuchsia   Dominican Republic   1899   Urban
F. pringsheimii grows as an erect shrub to about 2 metres high. Leaves are opposite or ternate, small and narrowly lanceolate. The drooping blooms appear in leaf axils near the periphery of the plants. Their floral tubes are 3.1 cm long and gradually widen to 1.6 cm near the sepals, which are about 2.5 cm in length. Petals are 2.4 cm long. The whole flower is bright red. *F. pringsheimii* is occasionally found in cultivation.
Description: Berry, P. (1982), pp. 191-2.
Illustration: Berry, P. (1982), p. 50.

F. TRIPHYLLA
Fuchsia   Dominican Republic   1705
Plumier/Linneus
F. triphylla forms low sub-shrubs. Its leaves are opposite, ternate or quaternate, and narrowly lanceolate. Flowers are plentiful and are carried in terminal racemes or occasionally subracemes. Floral tubes are up to 4 cm long and 1.1 cm at their most bulbous. Sepals are 1.3 cm in length and petals reach, perhaps, 0.9 cm. Blooms may be orange or orange-red. This variable species is in general cultivation and is more easily grown from seed than from cuttings.
Description: Berry, P. (1982), pp. 185-91.
Illustration: Goedman-Frankema, M. (1992), p. 50.

F. VERRUCOSA
Fuchsia   Colombia   1845   T. Hartweg
F. verrucosa forms erect or scandent sub-shrubs which are sometimes 2 metres tall. Young branches are stained darkly, as are the undersides of the otherwise green leaves that are held opposite each other. The few drooping blooms are carried in the upper leaf axils. Their tubes are obconic and 0.6 cm long, considerably shorter than the ovaries. Sepals are longer, at 1.1 cm. Petals reach 0.9 cm in length. Tubes and sepals are bright scarlet but corollas are orange-red. This species is occasionally found in cultivation.
Description: Berry, P. (1982), pp. 192-4.
Illustration: Goedman-Frankema, M. (1992), p. 52.

Section *Hemsleyella*

The *Hemsleyella* section of fuchsias, which is characterized by the absence of petals, is native to South America. Some are epiphytes and most have tuberous roots that help them to survive the dry season each year. All are thinly dispersed in difficult terrain where they are hard to find, chiefly because of their deciduous and seasonal habit. Plants at the lower end of their altitudinal range are usually epiphytic while those at higher altitudes are more likely to be terrestrial with scandent branches. Paul Berry warns that this section of fuchsias is the one most threatened by deforestation in its native habitat. Humming-birds with especially long bills act as pollinators. Tubes that are slightly restricted near the ovaries and hairy further down help to keep nectar within the flower. Their thickened lower stems, and tubers, act as reservoirs of moisture and allow plants to survive during the dry seasons. Many from this section are in cultivation.

F. APETALA

Hemsleyella   Peru   1802   Ruiz & Pavón

F. apetala forms a low-growing shrub among rocks, on moist tree trunks and on mossy banks. Its flowers are held in small, dense racemes on short lateral stems in the dry season. Its leaves are alternate and clustered at the ends of the branchlets during the wet months. Young leaves are hairy. Flower tubes vary in length from 4 cm to 16 cm and about 0.5 cm wide. Sepals are wide and short. Blooms are rose to orange-red. Petals are occasionally formed: this seems to be especially related to those in cultivation. This species is in cultivation.

Description: Berry, P. E. (1985), pp. 223-9.
Illustration: Berry, P. E. (1985), p. 225.

F. CESTROIDES

Hemsleyella   Peru   1940   Schulze-Menz

F. cestroides forms shrubs up to 3 metres tall, with leaves that are opposite or ternate. The floral tubes are up to 2 cm long and 0.2 cm wide. The flowers are produced in dense clusters during the dry months. Tubes are rose pink to lavender. Sepals are green, at first, turning to purple. Unlike the other fuchsias in this section, *F. cestroides* inhabits the dry, open scrubland bordering the Pacific slopes of the Peruvian Andes.

Description: Berry, P. E. (1985), pp. 229-31.
Illustration: None.

F. CHLOROLOBA

Hemsleyella   Peru   1939   I. M. Johnston

F. chloroloba grows in rocky outcrops or epiphytically on trees in Peruvian cloud forests. It can reach up to 2 metres in height with leaves growing alternately on the stems. Bulbous flower tubes are about 5 cm long and 0.5 cm wide; shiny orange in colour. The vivid green sepals are up to 2.5 cm long. Blooms are produced in clusters on the ends of young shoots or in axillae.

Description: Berry, P. E. (1985), pp. 231-3.
Illustration: Berry, P. E. (1985), p. 232.

F. GARLEPPIANA

Hemsleyella   Bolivia   1893   Kuntz & Wittmack

F. garleppiana grows among rocks or epiphytically, up to a height of 4 metres. Its habit is upright and its leaves alternate. Flowers are produced in the leaf axils or in larger numbers at the ends of branches, when leaves are absent. Their tubes may be as long as 14 cm and up to 0.5 cm wide. Sepals are around 1.5 cm long. Each part of the flower is pale pink.

Description: Berry, P. E. (1985), p. 233.
Illustration: Berry, P. E. (1985), p. 234.

F. HUANUCOENSIS

Hemsleyella   Peru   1945   P. Berry

F. huanucoensis produces low, scandent shrubs with narrow, opposite leaves and stems. No tubers are formed. Flowering is axillary and near to the ends of branches. The funnelform tubes are nearly 3.5 cm long and about 0.5 cm wide. Both tubes and reflexed sepals are bright pink or red.

Description: Berry, P. E. (1985), p. 235.
Illustration: None.

F. INFLATA

Hemsleyella   Peru   1940   Schulze-Menz

F. inflata is a variable species that may grow epiphytically or among rocks, and produces tubers. Leaves are commonly alternate although opposite ones can be found. Floral tubes may be up to 12 cm long and narrowly constricted above the ovary before opening to about 1 cm or more in width. The short sepals become slightly recurved. Tubes are pale orange, while sepals are green. *F. inflata* is in cultivation.

Description: Berry, P. E. (1985), pp. 235-8.
Illustration: Goedman-Frankema, M. (1992), p. 58.

F. INSIGNIS

Hemsleyella Ecuador 1867 Hemsley

F. insignis forms terrestrial or epiphytic plants as shrubs or having scandent branches. Tubers are formed and leaves are alternate. Flowers are grouped on the ends of new branchlets when leaves are absent. Funnelform tubes are about 6 cm long and 0.5 cm wide. The sepals are larger than others in this section and reflexed. Both the tubes and the sepals are bright orange.

Description: Berry, P. E. (1985), p. 238.
Illustration: Schnedl, E. & H. (1997), opposite p. 52.

F. JUNTASENSIS

Hemsleyella Bolivia 1898 O. Kuntz

F. juntasensis often has small tubers on terrestrial or, more commonly, epiphytic shrubs up to 1.5 metres tall. Flowers may be produced in the leaf axils or in clusters on the ends of branches. Flowers have funnel-shaped tubes up to 5 cm in length and almost 1 cm in width. Tubes and short, slightly recurved sepals are dark lavender to violet. Blooms and leaves may appear together on *F. juntasensis*, the latter being alternate on the branches. This species is in cultivation and has proved to be quite vigorous.

Description: Berry, P. E. (1985), pp. 238-40.
Illustration: Goedman-Frankema, M. (1992), p. 56.

F. MEMBRANACEA

Hemsleyella Venezuela 1876 Hemsley

F. membranacea grows as a shrub up to 2 metres tall, with lianas among rocks or epiphytically in cloud forests. Small tubers are sometimes present. Leaf position is variable with opposite, ternate and sub-opposite ones produced. Blooms are produced in leaf axils and in small groups near the ends of branches. Funnelform flower tubes reach 5 cm in length and about 1 cm at their widest. These are pink or red; the short sepals are green.

Description: Berry, P. E. (1985), pp. 240-3.
Illustration: Berry, P. E. (1985), p. 242.

F. NANA

Hemsleyella Bolivia 1950 P. Berry

F. nana can be found as a creeping sub-shrub, or most often as an epiphyte among trees where it produces multiple small tubers. Its leaves are alternate and grow in the wet season. The flowers have funnelform tubes that may be almost 3 cm long and about 0.3 cm wide. Tubes and short, pointed sepals are bright pink or red. There is usually a dark violet ring around the entrance to the tube. It is rare in cultivation.

Description: Berry, P. E. (1985), pp. 243-4.
Illustration: Berry, P. E. (1985), p. 243.

F. PILALOENSIS

Hemsleyella Ecuador 1985 P. Berry

F. pilaloensis sometimes grows as an epiphyte: at other times it can be seen as a shrub up to 1 metre high, or with long, pendulous branches. It may have tubers or thickened stems and its leaves may be produced opposite each other, ternately or sub-oppositely. Flowers are pale pink. Their tubes are about 5 cm long and about 1 cm at their widest. Blooms are sometimes present with reduced leaves and in small numbers on the peripheral branches. This species is found in cultivation where it grows considerably taller, with support, than it would in the wild.

Description: Berry, P. E. (1985), pp. 244-6.
Illustration: Goedman-Frankema, M. (1992), p. 60.

F. SALICIFOLIA

Hemsleyella Peru 1876 Hemsley

F. salicifolia is most often to be found as an epiphyte growing on trees and, less commonly, among rocks as a terrestrial shrub up to 2 metres high. Tubers sometimes form. The plant carries alternate, narrow leaves. Small numbers of blooms are carried either in the leaf axils or clustered near the ends of branches. Flower tubes may be 5 cm or more long and are funnelform: they widen to, perhaps, 1 cm. Tubes and sepals are pink or red. The former have dark purple rings near their junctions with the sepals.

Description: Berry, P. E. (1985), pp. 246-7.
Illustration: Schnedl, E. & H. (1997), opposite p.52

F. TILLETIANA

Hemsleyella Venezuela 1972 P. Munz

F. tilletiana will form a shrub up to 2 metres in height when growing in the ground. Sometimes it is found as an epiphyte or climbing up trees to a height of 10 metres with thickened stems and pendulous branches. It has opposite or ternate leaves and large terrestrial shrubs may produce small tubers. Flower tubes are about 3.5 cm long and funnelform to almost 1 cm wide. Sepals are short, being about 0.5 cm, and reflexed. Tubes and sepals are pink or cherry red. Subracemose clusters of blooms appear at the tips of branches when leaves are absent. This species is in cultivation.

Description: Berry, P. E. (1985), pp. 247-9.
Illustration: Berry, P. E. (1985), p. 248.

F. TUNARIENSIS

Hemsleyella Bolivia 1898 O. Kuntz

F. tunariensis grows as a shrub with alternate leaves, up to 1.5 metres high. The plants may grow as epiphytes, in humus-rich sites, or among rocks. Tubers are usually present. Leaves may be opposite or alternate and may grow with flowers. The few blooms are produced in leaf axils near the periphery of plants. Their tubes are about 5.5 cm long, and funnelform to about 1 cm at their widest. The short sepals, like the tubes, are usually bright pink or orange-red in colour.

Description: Berry, P. E. (1985), pp. 249-51.
Illustration: Berry, P. E. (1985), p. 250.

Section Jimenezia

F. JIMENEZII

Jimenezia Costa Rica 1982 Breedlove, Berry & Raven

This South American section has only one representative species and is a relatively recent discovery. *F. jimenezii* grows into a scandent sub-shrub, up to 1.5 metres tall, with opposite leaves. Flowers are usually produced in plentiful terminal racemes although they may be found in leaf axils or in few branched panicles. Flower tubes are up to 0.45 cm long and widen from 0.15 cm near the ovaries to 0.45 cm near the sepals that are about 0.5 cm long. Tubes and sepals are red; petals are pink. Antipetalous stamens reflex into the flower tubes. Plants are to be found among secondary vegetation in Panamanian and Costa Rican cloud forests. This species is in cultivation.

Description: Breedlove, D. E., et al (1982), pp. 220-23.
Illustration: Goedman-Frankema, M. (1992), p. 63.

Section Kierschlegeria

F. LYCIOIDES

Kierschlegeria Chile 1800 Andrews

F. lycioides is the sole representative of this fuchsia section. It is found only in a narrow coastal belt of central Chile that has a semi-arid Mediterranean type of climate. Its only known pollinator is a tiny humming-bird that appears to be entirely dependent on this fuchsia species. Flowering is continuous throughout the year. It is thought that sexual differentiation in species such as this comes about because of the shortage of water and nutrients in the native environment. *F. lycioides* exhibits a state of subdioecy in which some hermaphroditic flowers are female fertile while others are female sterile, or functionally male. Small-flowered female blooms are also present and nectar production is severely limited in these. Perfect blooms are rose-coloured, up to 0.5 cm long and about 0.1 cm wide in the tube. Female-only flowers measure up to 0.3 cm in length and are narrower still; fruit is most freely produced on these blooms. Tubes are frequently pierced to obtain nectar and this reduces successful pollination among hermaphroditic flowers. Plants grow into stiffly upright bushes that intermittently shed their leaves to retain moisture. This gives them a spiky appearance that is exaggerated by the spines left behind as the leaves are shed. *F. lycioides*, with its slightly bulbous lower stem, is freely available in cultivation.

Descriptions: Munz, P. A. (1970), pp. 69-71. Atsatt, P. R., & Rundel, P. W. (1982), pp. 199-208.
Illustration: Goedman-Frankema, M. (1992). p. 64.

Section Pachyrrhiza

F. PACHYRRHIZA

Pachyrrhiza Peru 1989 Berry & Stein

F. pachyrrhiza grows into a shrubby plant up to 2 metres tall and has substantial tuberous roots. It grows in rocky ground where other shrubs predominate and has leaves that are opposite or ternate. Flowers are axillary, hermaphroditic, solitary and pendant. They are carried in the dry season when the leaves are normally absent. Flower tubes are up to 0.75 cm long and tapered outward from the ovaries to a width of 0.45 cm. The triangular sepals are about 1 cm long. Tubes and sepals are bright orange-red. Petals are up to 0.65 cm long and maroon-coloured. This species is rarely found in cultivation, flowering in the spring when in leaf and occasionally in the summer. It is difficult to take cuttings from and is most successfully propagated from pieces of tuber, in winter, once the leaves have fallen off.

Description: Berry, P. E., et al (1988), p. 483.
Illustration: Goedman-Frankema, M. (1992), p. 69.

Section *Procumbentes*

F. PROCUMBENS

Skinnera New Zealand 1839 R. Cunningham
F. procumbens is the only (apetalous) fuchsia in its section. Its fine, prostrate stems usually carry alternate rounded leaves. Solitary flowers are carried in the leaf axils. The golden yellow hypanthium is filled with nectar and often topped with stamens carrying blue pollen. Pollination is by bees, flies or small birds. Hypanthia are 0.8 cm long and 0.5 cm wide. The fully reflexing sepals, which are 0.6 cm in length, change from green to dark chocolate brown. It is thought some populations may be hermaphroditic and others female-sterile. The pattern is unclear; there is some evidence that _plants in cultivation may change the sex of their flowers (or some of their flowers) at different times in their lives, perhaps as a result of temperature or cultural changes. *F. procumbens* is freely available in cultivation and is easily raised from seed.
Description: Godley, E. J. & Berry, P. E. (1995), pp. 473 & 502-3.
Illustration: Goedman-Frankema, M. (1992), p. 86.

Section *Quelusia*

F. ALPESTRIS

Quelusia Brazil 1842 G. Gardner
F. alpestris grows as a spreading shrub with long branches, to a height of 5 metres. It can be found in rocky, moist and bushy areas. Its leaves are usually opposite but occasionally ternate, and broadly ovate. Branchlets and leaves are pilose. A few pendant blooms are carried in the upper leaf axils. Floral tubes are cylindrical-fusiform, 0.8 cm long and 0.4 cm at their widest. The partially spreading sepals may be 2.6 cm in length. Tubes and sepals are red or rose pink. Petals are 1.4 cm long, and violet. This species is in cultivation.
Description: Berry, P. (1989), pp. 547-50.
Illustration: Berry, P. (1989), p. 548.

F. BRACELINAE

Quelusia Brazil 1929 P. Munz
F. bracelinae sometimes forms scandent shrubs up to 2 metres tall in dense undergrowth; otherwise it creates sub-shrubs of 60 cm or so high. Young branches are purple and pilose. Leaves form whorls of three, four or five to a joint and are narrowly elliptic-lanceolate. Solitary blooms are carried towards the ends of branchlets in the leaf axils. Their tubes are cylindrical-fusiform, 0.7 cm long, and pale red. Sepals are 2.6 cm in length and are also red. The petals are dark violet, about 1.5 cm long. *F. bracelinae* is subject to frosts in its native habitat and is quite hardy. It is rare in cultivation.
Description: Berry, P. (1989), pp. 550-51.
Illustration: Berry, P. (1989), p. 551.

F. BREVILOBIS

Quelusia Brazil 1989 P. Berry
F. brevilobis grows in swamp forests where it may form scandent shrubs up to 8 metres high, with lianas climbing among other trees. Leaves may be opposite, ternate or quaternate, and lanceolate. The solitary blooms are found in leaf axils near the ends of branches. Floral tubes are subcylindric to fusiform, 1 cm long and pale red. The sepals are similarly coloured, form a cone around the petals, and are 2.5 cm in length. The petals are almost entirely enclosed and are dark violet. This species is now in cultivation.
Description: Berry, P. (1989), pp. 552-4.
Illustration: Berry, P. (1989), p. 552.

F. CAMPOS-PORTOI

Quelusia Brazil 1935 Pilger & Schulze
F. campos-portoi forms sub-shrubs or grows as a scandent bush to 2 metres tall. Its leaves are most often ternate and are carried in whorls. Solitary flowers are carried towards the ends of branchlets in leaf axils. Floral tubes are subrhombic, 0.6 cm long and 0.25 cm at their widest. Sepals are only partially separated and spreading when mature. Tubes and sepals are pale red. The partially-hidden corollas are 1.2 cm long, and dark violet. *F. campos-portoi* is available in cultivation but its authenticity is in doubt.
Description: Berry, P. (1989), pp. 554-5.
Illustration: Berry, P. (1989), p. 554.

F. COCCINEA

Quelusia Brazil 1789 Solander
F. coccinea may be found as an increasingly rare, upright shrub of 1.5 metres. It also grows with scandent branches climbing to 6 metres. It is unusual in having numerous underground stems. Ovate leaves are usually ternate although they can be seen as opposite or quaternate held close to the stems. Flowers droop from arching pedicels in the upper leaf axils. Their fusiform tubes are 1 cm in length and 0.45 cm at their widest. Sepals may be

2.4 cm long. Both tubes and sepals are pale red. The obovate petals are violet, and 1 cm long. This species is in general cultivation.
Description: Berry, P. (1989), pp. 555-7.
Illustration: Berry, P. (1989), p. 557.

F. GLAZIOVIANA
Quelusia Brazil 1888 Taubert
F. glazioviana will form shrubs up to 4 metres tall with spreading branches as much as 6 metres in length. It produces many densely-packed branchlets with opposite or ternate shiny leaves. Upper leaf axils carry the solitary blooms whose cylindrical tubes are 0.7 cm long and 0.4 cm wide. The partially spreading sepals measure 2.2 cm, much longer than the petals that are 1.2 cm in length. Tubes and sepals are pale red. Corollas are violet. This species is in cultivation.
Description: Berry, P. (1989), pp. 57-9.
Illustration: Berry, P. (1989), p. 558.

F. HATSCHBACHII
Quelusia Brazil 1989 P. Berry
F. hatschbachii may grow as an erect shrub but more commonly pushes its scandent branches to heights of 5 metres. Dry sandstone or limestone regions are its native habitat. Narrowly lanceolate leaves are opposite although they may sometimes be found as ternate or quaternate. Solitary blooms are found in the upper leaf axils. The cylindrical floral tube may be 1.5 cm long and 0.5 cm wide, while drooping sepals are 2.6 cm in length. Both are red. Petals are 1.7 cm long, and violet. *F. hatschbachii* is in cultivation.
Description: Berry, P. (1989), pp. 559-61.
Illustration: Berry, P. (1989), p. 560.

F. MAGELLANICA
Quelusia Chile 1788 Lamarck
F. magellanica forms erect or semi-scandent shrubs up to 3 metres high, in moist areas. Its elliptic-ovate leaves are usually opposite or ternate but occasionally quaternate. Solitary or possibly paired flowers are held in the upper leaf axils. Their floral tubes are 1.5 cm long by 0.35 cm wide. These and the partially spreading sepals, which are 2.5 cm long, are usually red but may be paler. The corollas are 2 cm long and violet although these, too, may be paler sometimes. *F. magellanica* is widely cultivated, as are its many variants.
Description: Berry, P. (1989), pp. 561-8.
Illustrations: Berry, P. (1989), p. 562. Goedman-Frankema, M. (1992), pp. 75 & 76.

F. REGIA SUBSP. REGIA
Quelusia Brazil 1843 Vandelli
F. regia subsp. *regia* may be found spreading its lianas as high as 15 metres among adjacent trees. Leaves may be opposite, ternate or quaternate and lance-elliptic. Solitary flowers, or occasionally paired ones, occur in the upper leaf axils. Their floral tubes are 1.6 cm long and 0.6 cm wide. The partially drooping sepals measure 4.5 cm. Tubes and sepals are red. Violet petals are 2.2 cm in length. This fuchsia is found in general cultivation.
Description: Berry, P. (1989), pp. 570-73.
Illustrations: Berry, P. (1989), p. 571. Goedman-Frankema, M. (1992), p. 77.

F. REGIA SUBSP. REITZII
F. regia subsp. *reitzii* sometimes grows as erect shrubs but may also be seen with its scandent branches reaching 4 metres high. Leaves are carried in whorls of three or more and are narrowly elliptic with gland-serrate edges. Solitary or paired flowers are carried in the upper leaf axils. Floral tubes are 0.9 cm long by 0.4 cm wide. These, and the partially spreading sepals that are 2.8 cm in length, are red. Petals are 1.5 cm long and violet. This fuchsia is also plentiful in cultivation.
Description: Berry, P. (1989), pp. 577-80.
Illustrations: Berry, P. (1989), p. 578. Goedman-Frankema, M. (1992), p. 78.

F. REGIA SUBSP. SERRAE
F. regia subsp. *serrae* forms lianas that clamber through surrounding trees to 15 metres in height. Its branchlets are covered in fine hairs. Its leaves are opposite or in whorls, have crassate stipules, and are ovate. Solitary blooms are found pendant in the upper leaf axils. Their tubes are 1.5 cm long. Sepals may be recurved or reflexed after pollination, partially connate, and are 3.4 cm in length. Tubes and sepals are red. Petals are 2 cm long and violet. *F. regia* subsp. *serrae* is also found in cultivation.
Description: Berry, P. (1989), pp. 573-7.
Illustrations: Berry, P. (1989), p. 574. Goedman-Frankema, M. (1992), p. 79.

Section Schufia

F. ARBORESCENS
Schufia Mexico 1825 Sims
F. arborescens grows to 8 metres as a shrub or small tree. Branchlets are ascending, leaves are

opposite or sometimes in whorls of three or four and have a glazed appearance. Its habitat is in the highest rainfall areas. Flowers are hermaphroditic and held in terminal panicles. Flower tubes are up to 0.6 cm long and widening to 0.4 cm at the entrance. Sepals are about 1 cm long. Tubes and sepals are rose or purple. The spreading petals are lavender-coloured, and up to 0.9 cm in length. There are several markedly different strains of *F. arborescens* in cultivation.

Description: Breedlove, D. E., et al (1982), pp. 224-7.

Illustrations: Breedlove, D. E., et al (1982), p. 225. Goedman-Frankema, M. (1992), p. 83.

F. PANICULATA

Schufia   Costa Rica   1856   Lindley

F. paniculata, unlike *F. arborescens*, is gynodioecious or subdioecious. It forms shrubs or trees, some of which may reach 8 metres in height, and are to be found in cloud forests. Leaves on the ascending branchlets are opposite or in whorls and have shiny surfaces. The erect flowers are held in terminal panicles. Hermaphroditic ones have flower tubes up to 1.2 cm long and 0.3 cm wide at their entrance. Sepals may reach 1 cm in length and recurve when mature. Tubes and sepals are rose-purple. Petals, which are up to 1 cm long and spreading, are lavender-coloured. Pistillate blooms are similar in colour but smaller. Fewer seeds are set on perfect flowers than on pistillate ones. *F. paniculata* is available in cultivation and its flowers often have a notable scent. Berry and Breedlove have described a new subspecies of *F. paniculata*. Known formerly as *F. arborescens* var. *zempoalt*, it is now known as *F. paniculata* subsp. *mixensis*. The leaves and flowers are large and hairy. It has hermaphrodite and female plants. Flowers are darker and redder than on normal *F. paniculata* specimens: growth is long with few branchlets.

Description: Breedlove, D. E., et al (1982), pp. 227-32.

Illustrations: Breedlove, D. E., et al (1982), p. 225. Goedman-Frankema, M. (1992), pp. 82 & 83.

Section *Skinnera*

The *Skinnera* section of fuchsias comes almost exclusively from New Zealand, the exception being *F. cyrtandroides* that is found in Tahiti. All have bright blue pollen and are commonly visited by small birds, bees and flies for their nectar and pollen. Corollas are rudimentary. The habit of growth in this section is variable.

F. CYRTANDROIDES

Skinnera   Tahiti   1942   Moore

F. cyrtandroides is to be found as a small tree growing to a height of about 4 metres, high in the island's mountains and some 3,000 miles north-east of New Zealand. Its leaves have a leathery texture and are commonly alternate. Flowers are carried in the leaf axils. Their tubes are 1 cm long and spread to 0.6 cm at their rims. Sepals spread with maturity and measure 1.4 cm in length. Dark purple petals are up to 0.4 cm. Blooms start as a waxy green and ripen to rose magenta. This species is rare in cultivation.

Description: Godley, E. J., & Berry, P. E. (1995), pp. 503-5.

Illustration: Godley, E. J., & Berry, P. E. (1995), p. 504.

F. EXCORTICATA

Skinnera   New Zealand   1776   Forster

F. excorticata grows as a tree, with exfoliating bark, to 10 metres. The leaves are alternate, glabrous, lance-ovate and have white undersurfaces. Pendant flowers are produced in solitary leaf axils. The tubes are 1.5 cm long and widen to 1 cm. Sepals spread to 1.4 cm. Petals are dark purple and some 0.4 cm long. As with all the New Zealand species, pollen is bright blue. *F. excorticata* is available in cultivation.

Description: Godley, E. J., & Berry, P. E. (1995), pp. 508-9.

Illustration: Munz, P. A. (1970), p. 127, fig. 60.

F. PERSCANDENS

Skinnera   New Zealand   1927   Cockayne & Allan

F. perscandens produces long, scandent branches. Leaves are sometimes opposite but more commonly alternate and are orbicular-ovate. Floral tubes are 0.9 cm long and expand to 0.7 cm at their rims. Sepals are about 0.7 cm in length, spreading or slightly reflexed. Petals are 0.25 cm long. Tubes and sepals start as waxy green and ripen to dark red. The corollas are dark purple. *F. perscandens* is similar to *F. x colensoi* which is thought to be a naturally occurring interspecific hybrid and both are in general cultivation.

Description: Godley, E. J., & Berry, P. E. (1995), pp. 505-8.

Illustration: Goedman-Frankema, M. (1992), p. 88.

Chromosome References and Plant Genetics

Gregor Mendel postulated two laws of genetic theory on which most modern plant breeding is based. The first is the law of segregation and the second is the law of independent assortment.

Law of segregation: Alleles, pairs of genes occupying the same position on two homologous chromosomes, which have been brought together in the F1 generation, can be segregated in the F2 generation.

Law of independent assortment: Most parental characteristics can appear, in different combinations, in the parents' offspring.

Chromosomes are thread-like bodies in the nucleus of all cells. They become visible during cell division, when they shorten and broaden. All the cells in a species contain the same number of chromosomes. Homologous, or similar, chromosomes are paired during meiosis (formation of reproductive cells) and their centromeres (the attachment of the chromatids or sister chromosomes) and loci (locations and, to some extent, purposes) have identical positions.

Genes are contained on chromosome chains and define the code for particular characteristics. Haploid chromosome numbers (half the parent's genetic material) exist in pollen granules and in the ovaries. Fertilization raises the number again to diploid numbers (the full genetic complement for the species). In fuchsias the haploid number is eleven but tetraploid, triploid and other polyploid sets of chromosomes exist. Most single-flowered types have diploid counts of twenty-two or forty-four. Larger doubles, such as 'Rolla' with seventy-seven as its diploid count, exhibit polyploidy.

Numbers of chromosomes are not the only important factor when undertaking plant breeding programmes. The information stored in the genes is probably of greater importance. It is also possible that some characteristics are passed on via cytoplasmic inheritance and plasmagenes (genetic material contained in cell cytoplasm and not in nuclear material), as some aspects of fuchsia breeding do not appear to obey the Mendelian laws in predictable ways.

Chromosomes are best studied during meiosis or when haploid numbers allow the strands and their configuration to be studied under high-powered microscopes following selective staining procedures. Darlington and La Cour (1969) discuss techniques in detail. Fuchsias have small chromosomes by comparison with many other plants; this makes their study difficult. It may also go some way towards explaining the discrepancies that exist in the counts obtained from some hybrids. Chromosome studies of hybrids, with their greater numbers of chromosomes, are less reliable than those that have been carried out more recently on species fuchsias. Many advances in the hybridizing field have been made where there has been some variability of chromosome characteristics already evident within a species. Much of my own work has been based upon the search for this instability, so that the Mendelian laws can be used in more than merely conventional ways. It is as necessary to split and recombine characteristics as it is to join them in the first place, if variety is to be introduced into hybrids. This also introduces hybrid vigour.

Pollen grains have been studied for their chromosome content and their viability. It was thought at one time that the number of poles present on each grain was related to the chromosome numbers but a direct relationship has not been established. Within some species it is possible to find bi-polar and tri-polar grains obtained from the same anther. However, variability and instability are closely allied where plant breeding is concerned.

Viscine threads help some pollen to attach itself more successfully to receptive stigmas. If the two plants involved are incompatible, fertilization will not occur. Other fuchsias have dust-like pollen grains that are highly fertile. Pollination itself operates on a 'first-past-the-post-system': success by one pollen grain prevents the passage of further pollen tubules towards the ovary. Fertility, especially in pollen grains, is affected by many different factors such as air humidity and temperature.

The following table lists chromosome numbers and their sources (see Bibliography). Haploid and gametic chromosome numbers are identical but somatic numbers, when two gametes join and form a new individual, are doubled hence the terms n and 2 × n (sexual reproduction requires the joining of two halves). Research based on somatic counts seems to have produced the least reliable figures in the following list, although this could be because higher numbers are more difficult to count.

CHROMOSOME INDEX

NAME	GAMETIC CHROMOSOME NUMBER = N	BIBLIOGRAPHY NUMBER
Section Ellobium		
F. decidua	11	Berry, P. E., et al 1982, p.220
F. fulgens	11	Berry, P. E., et al 1982, p.217
F. splendens	11	Berry, P. E., et al 1982, p.215
Section Encliandra		
F. encliandra subsp. *encliandra*	11	Breedlove, D. E., 1969, p.53
F. encliandra subsp. *tetradactyla*	11	Breedlove, D. E., 1969, p.54
F. microphylla subsp. *aprica*	11	Breedlove, D. E., 1969, p.47
F. microphylla subsp. *hemsleyana*	11	Breedlove, D. E., 1969, p.48
F. microphylla subsp. *hidalgensis*	11	Breedlove, D. E., 1969, p.43
F. microphylla subsp. *microphylla*	11	Breedlove, D. E., 1969, p.41
F. microphylla subsp. *quercetorum*	11	Breedlove, D. E., 1969, p.44
F. obconica	11	Breedlove, D. E., 1969, p.56
F. parviflora	11	Breedlove, D. E., 1969, p.57
F. ravenii	11	Breedlove, D. E., 1969, p.59
F. thymifolia subsp. *minimiflora*	11	Breedlove, D. E., 1969, p.51
F. thymifolia subsp. *thymifolia*	11	Breedlove, D. E., 1969, p. 50
F. × *bacillaris*	11	Breedlove, D. E., 1969, p. 60
Section Fuchsia		
F. abrupta	11	Berry, P. E., 1982, p.34
F. ampliata	11	Berry, P. E., 1982, p.34
F. andrei	11	Berry, P. E., 1982, p.34
F. austromontana	11, 22 (2 × n)	Berry, P. E., 1982, p.34
F. ayavacensis	11	Berry, P. E., 1982, p.34
F. boliviana	11	Berry, P. E., 1982, p.34
F. campii	11	Berry, P. E., 1995, p.320
F. canescens	11	Berry, P. E., 1982, p.34
F. caucana	11	Berry, P. E., 1982, p.34
F. ceracea	11	Berry, P. E., 1982, p.34
F. cinerea	11	Berry, P. E., 1982, p.34
F. corollata	11, 22 (2 × n)	Berry, P. E., 1982, p.34
F. corymbiflora	11	Berry, P. E., 1982, p.34
F. crassistipula	11	Berry, P. E., 1982, p.34
F. denticulata	11, 22 (2 × n)	Berry, P. E., 1982, p.34
F. dependens	11	Berry, P. E., 1982, p.35
F. ferrerae	11	Berry, P. E., 1982, p.35
F. fontinalis	11	Berry, P. E., 1982, p.35
F. gehrigeri	11	Berry, P. E., 1982, p.35
F. hartwegii	11	Berry, P. E., 1982, p.35
F. hirtella	11	Berry, P. E., 1982, p.35
F. lehmannii	11	Berry, P. E., 1982, p.35
F. loxensis	11	Berry, P. E., 1982, p.35

F. macrophylla	11	Berry, P. E., 1982, p.35
F. magdalenae	22	Berry, P. E., 1982, p.147
F. mathewsii	11	Berry, P. E., 1982, p.35
F. nigricans	11, 22 (2 x n)	Berry, P. E., 1982, pp.35-6
F. orientalis	11	Berry, P. E., 1982, p.36
F. pallescens	11	Berry, P. E., 1982, p.36
F. petiolaris	11	Berry, P. E., 1982, p.36
F. pilosa	11	Berry, P. E., 1982, p.36
F. polyantha	11	Berry, P. E., 1982, p.36
F. pringsheimii	22	Berry, P. E., 1982, p.36
F. rivularis	11	Berry, P. E., 1982, p.36
F. sanctae-rosae	11	Berry, P. E., 1982, p.36
F. sessilifolia	11	Berry, P. E., 1982, p.36
F. sylvatica	11	Berry, P. E., 1982, p.36
F. tincta	11	Berry, P. E., 1982, p.36
F. triphylla	22, 44 (2 x n)	Berry, P. E., 1982, p.36
F. vargasiana	11	Berry, P. E., 1982, p.36
F. venusta	11	Berry, P. E., 1982, p.36
F. verrucosa	22	Berry, P. E., 1982, p.37
F. vulcanica	22, 44 (2 x n)	Berry, P. E., 1982, p.37
F. wurdackii	11	Berry, P. E., 1982, p.37

Section Hemsleyella

F. apetala	22, 44 (2 x n)	Berry, P. E., 1985, p.216
F. cestroides	11	Berry, P. E., 1985, p.216
F. chloroloba	11, 22 (2 x n)	Berry, P. E., 1985, p.216
F. garleppiana	11, 22 (2 x n)	Berry, P. E., 1985, p.233, p.216
F. inflata	11, 22 (2 x n)	Berry, P. E., 1985, p.216
F. juntasensis	22	Berry, P. E., 1985, p.216
F. membranacea	11	Berry, P. E., 1985, p.216
F. tilletiana	11	Berry, P. E., 1985, p.216
F. tunariensis	11, 22 (2 x n)	Berry, P. E., 1985, p.251, p.216

Section Jimenezia

| F. jimenezii | 11 | Berry, P. E., et al 1982, p.222 |

Section Kierschlegeria

| F. lycioides | 11 | Hoshino, T. & Berry, P. E., 1989, p.588 |

Section Pachyrrhiza

| F. pachyrrhiza | 11 | Berry, P. E., et al 1988, p.488 |

Section Procumbentes

| F. procumbens | 11 | Godley, E. J. & Berry, P. E., 1995, p.503 |

Section Quelusia

F. alpestris	22, 44 (2 x n)	Berry, P., 1989, p.549
F. bracelinae	22	Berry, P., 1989, p.550
F. brevilobis	22	Berry, P., 1989, p.553
F. campos-portoi	22	Berry, P., 1989, p.555
F. coccinea	22	Berry, P., 1989, p.556
F. glazioviana	22	Berry, P., 1989, p.559
F. hatschbachii	22	Berry, P., 1989, p.559
F. magellanica	22	Berry, P., 1989, p.563
F. regia subsp. regia	22, 44 (2 x n)	Berry, P., 1989, p.571
F. regia subsp. reitzii	44	Berry, P., 1989, p.578
F. regia subsp. serrae	44	Berry, P., 1989, p.574

Section Schufia

F. arborescens	11	Berry, P. E., et al 1982, p.226
F. paniculata	11	Berry, P. E., et al 1982, p.228

Section Skinnera

F. cyrtandroides	11	Godley, E. J., & Berry, P. E., 1995, p.505.
F. excorticata	11	Godley, E. J., & Berry, P. E., 1995, p.508.
F. perscandens	11	Godley, E. J., & Berry, P. E., 1995, p.507

Fuchsia chromosomes are always present in multiples of eleven. Large doubles may have counts of more than seventy-seven. As the numbers increase, so do the difficulties in interpreting chromosome count results. Much early work on chromosomes was carried out on root tip cells, and consequently the documentation is more difficult to locate and the figures harder to substantiate. Much of the material listed below draws on earlier sources; thus it should be regarded only as a starting point. While the low counts and highly scientific methods employed in recent years on species fuchsias is of great significance, work on the complex world of hybrid chromosomes is long overdue.

NAME AND RAISER	CHROMOSOME NUMBER	BIBLIOGRAPHY NUMBER
'Alice Hoffman' (Klese 1911)	66	Manthey, G., 1983, p.103
'Amy Lye' (Lye 1885)	55	Manthey, G., 1983, p.103
ditto	55	Bergmans, M., et al 1991, p.157
'Annie Earle' (Lye 1887)	55	Manthey, G., 1989, p.103
'Balkonkönigin' (Neubronner 1895)	66	Manthey, G., 1983, p.103
'Ballet Girl' (Veitch 1894)	77	Manthey, G., 1983, p.103
ditto	77	Bergmans, M., et al 1991, p.103
'Beauty' (Banks 1866)	66	Manthey, G., 1983, p.103
'Boerhaave' (van Wieringen 1970)	44	Bergmans, M., et al 1991, p.157
'Bon Accord' (Crousse 1861)	77	Manthey, G., 1983, p.103
'Caledonia' (Lemoine 1899)	33	Manthey, G., 1983, p.103
'Carnea' (Smith 1861)	44	Manthey, G., 1983, p.103
'Charming' (Lye 1895)	77	Manthey, G., 1983, p.103
'Checkerboard' (Walker & Jones 1948)	44	Manthey, G., 1983, p.103
ditto	44	Bergmans, M., et al 1991, p. 157
'Clipper' (Lye 1897)	77	Manthey, G., 1983, p.103
'Coachman' (Bright 1910 approx.)	66	Manthey, G., 1983, p.103
'Conspicua' (Smith 1863)	88	Manthey, G., 1983, p.103
'Countess of Aberdeen' (Cocker 1888)	55	Manthey, G., 1983, p.103
ditto (formerly attributed to Dobbie Forbes)	55	Wilson, S. J., 1965, p.131
'Display' (Smith 1881)	66	Manthey, G., 1983, p.103
'Dollar Princess' (Lemoine 1912)	88	Manthey, G., 1983, p.103
ditto	88	Bergmans, M., et al 1991, p. 157
'Dolores' (Neiderholzer 1944)	66	Manthey, G., 1983, p.103
'Dominiana' (Dominy 1852)	22	Manthey, G., 1983, p.102
'Dorothy' (Wood 1946)	66	Manthey, G., 1983, p.103
'Duchess of Albany' (Rundle 1891)	55	Manthey, G., 1983, p.103
'E. A. Babbs' (Wood 1942)	44	Manthey, G., 1983, p.103
'Elegans' (Bull 1866)	66	Manthey, G., 1983, p.103
'Epsii' (Epps 1840)	66	Manthey, G., 1983, p.103
F. coccinea	44	Manthey, G., 1983, p.102
F. cordifolia	22	Manthey, G., 1983, p.102
F. denticulata	22	Manthey, G., 1983, p.102
F. fulgens	11	Wilson, S. J., 1965, p.130
ditto	22	Manthey, G., 1983, p.102
F. lycioides	22	Wilson, S. J., 1965, p.130
ditto	44	Manthey, G., 1983, p.102
F. magellanica	22	Wilson, S. J., 1965, p.130

ditto	44	Manthey, G., 1983, p.102
ditto	44	Nederlandse Kring, 1985, p.16
F. magellanica var. 'Longipedunculata'	44	Manthey, G., 1983, p.102
F. magellanica var. 'Pumila'	44	Manthey, G., 1983, p.102
F. magellanica var. 'Globosa'	55	Manthey, G., 1983, p.103
F. magellanica var. molinae	44	Manthey, G., 1983, p.102
F. microphylla	22	Manthey, G., 1983, p.102
F. procumbens	22	Manthey, G., 1983, p.102
F. regia	44	Nederlandse Kring, 1985, p.16
F. splendens	11	Wilson, S. J., 1965, p.130
ditto	22	Manthey, G., 1983, p.102
F. triphylla	44	Nederlandse Kring, 1985, p.17
'Fanfare' (Reiter 1941)	22	Manthey, G., 1983, p.102
ditto	22	Bergmans, M., et al 1991, p. 157
'Fascination' (Lemoine 1905)	66	Manthey, G., 1983, p.103

Note: 'Fascination' is synonymous with 'Emile de Wildemann'

'Gartenmeister Bonstedt' (Bonstedt 1905)	33	Manthey, G., 1983 p. 103
ditto	33	Bergmans, M., et al 1991, p. 157
'General Gallieni' (Lemoine 1899)	77	Manthey, G., 1983, p.103
'Georgana' (Tiret 1955)	66	Bergmans, M., et al 1991, p.157
'Golden Glow' (Munkner 1958)	44	Bergmans, M., et al 1991, p.157
'Golden Marinka' (Weber 1955)	44	Bergmans, M., et al 1991, p.157
'Golden Treasure' (Carter 1860)	77	Manthey, G., 1983, p.103
'Gustave Doré' (Lemoine 1880)	55	Manthey, G., 1983, p.103
'Hamburger Market' (Unknown)	88	Manthey, G., 1983, p.103
'Heinrich Henkel' (Rehnelt 1897)	44	Manthey, G., 1983, p.103

Note: 'Heinrich Henkel' is sometimes called by its full name 'Andenken an Heinrich Henkel.'

'Henri Poincaré' (Lemoine 1905)	66	Manthey, G., 1983, p.103
'Hidcote Beauty' (Webb 1949)	66	Manthey, G., 1983, p.103
'Immaculate' (Wood 1943)	66	Manthey, G., 1983, p.103
'Jubilee' (Lye 1897)	66	Manthey, G., 1983, p.103
'Jules Daloges' (Lemoine 1907)	88	Manthey, G., 1983, p.103
'Koralle' (Bonstedt 1905)	33	Manthey, G., 1983, p.103
'Lady Boothby' (Raffill 1939)	66	Manthey, G., 1983, p.103
'Letty Lye' (Lye 1877)	55	Manthey, G., 1983, p.103
'Lord Lonsdale' (Unknown)	66	Manthey, G., 1983, p.103
'Loveliness' (Lye 1869)	44	Manthey, G., 1983, p.103
'Marinka' (Rozaine-Boucharlat 1902)	44	Manthey, G., 1983, p.103
ditto	44	Bergmans, M., et al 1991, p. 157
'Masterpiece' (Henderson 1891)	55	Manthey, G., 1983, p.103
'Mme Cornelissen' (Cornelissen 1860)	77	Manthey, G., 1983, p.103
'Mme Danjoux' (Salter 1843)	77	Manthey, G., 1983, p.103
'Mme Lantelme' (Lemoine 1912)	88	Thorne, T., 1964, p.42
'Morning Mist' (Berkeley Nursery 1951)	66	Manthey, G., 1983, p.103
'Mrs C. J. Howlett' (Unknown)	66	Manthey, G., 1983, p.103
'Mrs Marshal' (Jones 1862)	55	Manthey, G., 1983, p.103
'Mrs Popple' (Elliot 1899)	88	Manthey, G., 1983, p.103
'Mrs W. P. Wood' (Wood 1949)	44	Manthey, G., 1983, p.103
'Mrs W. Rundle' (Rundle 1883)	55	Manthey, G., 1983, p.103
'Multa' (van Suchtelen 1968)	44	Bergmans, M., et al 1991, p.157
'Muriel' (Unknown)	77	Manthey, G., 1983, p.103
ditto	77	Bergmans, M., et al 1991, p.157
'Normandy Bell' (Martin 1961)	55	Bergmans, M., et al 1991, p.157
'Ophelia' (Unknown)	66	Manthey, G., 1983, p.103
'Pacific Grove' (Niederholzer 1947)	88	Manthey, G., 1983, p.103
ditto	88	Wilson, S. J., 1965, p.131
'Pee Wee Rose' (Niederholzer 1939)	55	Manthey, G., 1983, p.103
'Pink Galore' (Fuchsia-La 1958)	55	Bergmans, M., et al 1991, p.157
'Pres. Roosevelt' (Garson 1942)	77	Manthey, G., 1983, p.103

'Prince of Orange' (Banks 1872)	55	Manthey, G., 1983, p.103
'Purple Heart' (Walker & Jones 1950)	88	Manthey, G., 1983, p.103
ditto	88	Wilson, S. J., 1965, p.131
'Riccartonii' (Young 1833)	44	Manthey, G., 1983, p.103
'Rolla' (Lemoine 1913)	66	Bergmans, M., et al 1991, p.157
ditto	77	Manthey, G., 1983, p.103
ditto	77	Wilson, S. J., 1965, p.131
'Rose of Castile' (Banks 1855)	77	Bergmans, M., et al 1991, p.157
'Rose of Castile Improved' (Banks 1869)	77	Manthey, G., 1983, p.103
'Royal Purple' (Lemoine 1896)	77	Manthey, G., 1983, p.103
ditto	77	Bergmans, M., et al 1991, p.157
'San Leandro' (Brand 1949)	88	Manthey, G., 1983, p.103
ditto	88	Bergmans, M., et al 1991, p.42
ditto	88	Wilson, S. J., 1965, p.131
'Serena' (Whiteman 1944)	77	Manthey, G., 1983, p.103
'Snow Cap' (Henderson 1880)	77	Manthey, G., 1983, p.103
'Speciosa' (Unknown)	22	Manthey, G., 1983, p.102
'Starlight' (Bull 1868)	66	Manthey, G., 1983, p.103
'Sunray' (Milne 1872)	55	Manthey, G., 1983, p.103

Note: The introducer and year as published are in some doubt.

'Tangerine' (Tiret 1949)	44	Manthey, G., 1983, p.103
'Telegraphe' (Lemoine 1886)	77	Manthey, G., 1983, p.103
'Thalia' (Bonstedt 1906)	22	Manthey, G., 1983, p.102
'Theroigne de Mericourt' (Lemoine 1903)	88	Bergmans, M., et al 1991, p.42
'Thompsonii' (Thompson 1840)	44	Manthey, G., 1983, p.103
'Ting-a-Ling' (Schnabel & Paskesen 1959)	66	Manthey, G., 1983, p.103
ditto	66	Bergmans, M., et al 1991, p.157
'Tom Thumb' (Baudinat 1850)	44	Manthey, G., 1983, p.103
'Venus Victrix' (Gulliver 1840)	44	Manthey, G., 1983, p.103
'Walz Estafette' (Waldenmaier 1981)	33	Bergmans, M., et al 1991, p.157
'Walz Floreat' (Waldenmaier 1981)	55	Bergmans, M., et al 1991, p.157
'Walz Toorts' (Waldenmaier 1981)	77	Bergmans, M., et al 1991, p.157
'Whitemost' (Niederholzer 1942)	77	Manthey, G., 1983, p.103
'White Phenomenal' (Lemoine 1869)	88	Manthey, G., 1983, p.103
ditto	88	Thorne, T., 1964, p.42

The reference material on this subject is growing at an increasing rate, in terms both of its sophistication and its quantity. This trend is likely to continue as fuchsias become more popular. Their adaptability to a wide range of situations combined with long flowering seasons will ensure a successful future for them as garden plants. An expanding range of flower shapes and colours, as well as the possibility of scented flowers and their houseplant potential, will accentuate scientific interest of a high calibre.

APPENDIX 2
Fuchsia Research International

This major new organization was founded in June 1998. It is dedicated to the study, conservation, authentication and dissemination of knowledge about species fuchsias. It will be especially valuable in helping to preserve those species that are threatened by extinction in their native Andean cloud forest.

Fuchsia Research International has its base at Margam Country Park, near Port Talbot in South Wales. Neath Port Talbot Borough Council, owners of the historic estate, have invested substantial sums in the refurbishing of the large Victorian Citrus House that is being used to house the largest collection of *Fuchsia* species in the world.

Rainfall from the greenhouse roof is collected in a large sub-floor reservoir. From there it is re-used for fogging units and waterfalls. An organic system will be operated and biological control methods will be used for pests.

Authentication of species will be aided by DNA fingerprinting and Flavonoid fingerprinting. Each specimen will be given a voucher number. An archive will include photographs as well as a wide range of documents from around the world. A seed bank and herbarium collection are being expanded. Bulletins will be published twice yearly and the *Journal of Fuchsia Research* will be published annually if possible.

Membership (2001) costs £15. This entitles members to free access to the National Collection and to the Fuchsia Research International facilities at Margam Park. Copies of the constitution, Bulletin and Journal are additional bonuses. Advice and information on scientific and technical aspects of Fuchsia species will be free. Information on all projects concerning F.R.I. will be made readily available. Affiliated Societies can receive the publications for £25 a year. The Membership Secretary is Dr P. F. Parker, 14 Chitterne Road, Codford St. Mary, Warminster, Wiltshire, BA12 0PG, U.K. Residents

in the United States of America can send their subscriptions to Salli Dahl, 2130A Little Hannaford Road, Centralia, WA 98531-8913.

A list of those fuchsias held in the Fuchsia Research International collection can be found on their web site. Much other useful information can be found there and this is regularly updated and clearly presented. The site also shows high-quality photographs of fuchsias and their habitats. A very attractive video of the Citrus House and the Andean conditions provided for *Fuchsia* species can be seen if the correct software is available.

Access to view the collection can be made by e-mail: arthur.tickner@ukonline.co.uk or by phone: 01792 893250.

The *Journal of Fuchsia Research International* carries the most technical articles on fuchsias. A scientific and analytical approach is applied to the subjects covered. Vol.1, No.2 (January 2001) covered a number of articles relating to species identification and cultivation. It also had papers by a number of eminent authors. Titles included 'Molecular biological techniques in the determination of relations between *Fuchsia* species.', 'Identification of Fuchsia species using AFLP.' and 'Flow cytometry, a useful tool in determining the genome formula of a hybrid'.

Vol.1, No. 1 (January 2000) carried, in particular, articles on pollen-staining techniques and applications. The information gained provides an extra method of checking on the veracity of species. It also provides valuable information for those hybridists who are interested in applying a more scientific approach to their work with fuchsias. Equipment and materials used are relatively cheap and easy to use.

Fuchsia Research International can be found on the following web site: www.FuchsiaResInt.org

The editor's e-mail address is: leslie.blaber@ukonline.co.uk

APPENDIX 3

Picture References

The following list of picture references is designed to be used in conjunction with the Bibliography. Fuchsia names are located in alphabetical order; they are followed by source and page references. (Species fuchsias are confined to Chapter 17.) Only the best picture or pictures of each fuchsia have been listed. Each photograph is given a quality rating. A rating of 4 denotes a first-class picture, and 1 is the lowest rating. These numbers relate to film content and colour quality.

The practice of photographing one flower on its own has major disadvantages for identification and naming. There are currently about twenty thousand different named fuchsias in cultivation. This number is rising all the time. Some efforts have been made to distil colours and measurements into computer databases. To be useful, such data **must** be studied in conjunction with pictorial information (which can be stored on compact disc). Details such as branch angle, leaf shape, length of internode and quantity of flowers held in each leaf axil are essential means of identification, requiring top-quality photographs. A word of warning: the presence of a particularly photogenic bloom has trapped many an unwary enthusiast into trying to grow an outdated introduction with many cultural faults. The presence of a photographic reference is not a recommendation to grow a plant. It is an aid to identification only.

Abbreviations: pl.: plate number; FC: front cover illustration; BC: back cover illustration.

NAME	BOOK	PAGE	RATING
Abbé Farges	Clark, D., 1990	33 pl.1	1
Abigail	Nijhuis, M., 1994	pl.410	2
Achievement	Nijhuis, M., 1994	pl.637	1
Aladna's Sander	Nijhuis, M., 1994	pl.412	2
Alde	Goulding, E. 1995	pl.31	4
Alison Ewart	Manthey, G., 1983	15 pl.2	2
Alma Hulscher	Nijhuis, M., 1994	pl.415	1
Alton Water	Goulding, E. 1995	pl.14	4
Alwin	Nijhuis, M., 1994	pl.703	2
Amelie Aubin	Birch, M. V., 1992	3 pl.3	2
Amy Marie	Boullemier, L. B., 1985	44	2
Andrew Hadfield	Bartlett, G., 1996, *Colour Guide*	27	1
Angela Lesley	Ewart, R., 1990	pl.69	1
Angela Rippon	Clark, D., 1985	11 pl.1	2
Angel's Dreams	Manthey, G., 1983	118 pl.1	2
Anjo	Nijhuis, M., 1994	pl.46	2
Annabel	Clark, D., 1985	11 pl.2	2
Ann Roots	Goulding, E., 1995	pl.30	3
Anthonetta	Nijhuis, M., et al, 1990	89	1
Applause	Clark, D., 1985	11 pl.3	2
Aquarius	Nijhuis, M., 1994	pl.240	2
Arabella	Boullemier, L. B., 1989	45	2
Archie Owen	Nijhuis, M., 1994	pl.242	2
Army Nurse	Clark, D., 1990	33 pl.5	1
Atlantis	Clark, D., 1985	11 pl.4	1
Aunty Jinks	Ewart, R., 1990	pl.57	2

Aurora Superba	Ewart, R., 1990	pl.177	1
Autumnale	Ewart, R., 1990	pl.22	1
Avalanche	Nijhuis, M., 1994	pl.773	1
Baby Chang	Nederlandse Kring, 1985	pl.102	1
Baby Pink	Saunders, E., 1973	21 pl.5	2
Balkonkönigin	Manthey, G., 1989	23	2
Barbara	Nijhuis, M., 1994	245	1
Baroque Pearl	Nijhuis, M., 1994	pl.418	1
Beacon	Nijhuis, M., 1994	pl.776	1
Beacon Rosa	Clark, D., 1990	34 pl.2	1
Bealings	Bartlett, G., 1988	pl.10	2
Belinda Allen	Clark, D., 1990	34 pl.3	1
Bella Forbes	Clapham, S., 1982	131	2
Belle de Lisse	Nederlandse Kring, 1985	pl.116	2
Belvoir Beauty	Clark, J. R., 1988	108 pl.2	3
Berba	Nederlandse Kring, 1985	pl.56	2
Berba's Francis Femke	Nijhuis, M., 1994	pl.341	1
Berba's Trio	Manthey, G., 1983	119 pl.1	2
Bergnimf	Nederlandse Kring, 1985	pl.25	2
Beverley Hills	Nijhuis, M., 1994	pl.547	2
Bianco	Puttock, A. G., 1959	pl.1	3
Bicentennial	Clark, J. R., 1988	94 pl.1	3
Big Charles	Nijhuis, M., et al, 1990	116 pl.2	2
Billy Green	Clark, J. R., 1988	72	3
Bland's New Striped	Ewart, R., 1990	pl.141	2
Blue Gown	Clark, D., 1990	34 pl.4	2
Blue Pearl	Clark, D., 1985	12 pl.2	2
Blue Petticoat	Nijhuis, M., 1994	pl.90	1
Blue Pinwheel	Dreyer, G., 1986	41	1
Blue Waves	Bartlett, G., 1990	96	2
Blush of Dawn	Bartlett, G., 1990	99	2
Bobby Dazzler	Bartlett, G., 1996, *Colour Guide*	51	1
Bobby Shaftoe	Jennings, K. et al, 1979	pl.15	3
Bobby Wingrove	Bartlett, G., 1996, *Colour Guide*	51	1
Boerhaave	Nijhuis, M., 1994	pl.642	2
Bon Accord	Clark, J. R., 1988	77	4
Bonita	Bartlett, G., 1996, *Colour Guide*	53	1
Border Queen	Boullemier, L. B., 1989	33	2
Bornemann's Beste	Nijhuis, M., 1994	pl.249	2
Bouffant	Clark, J. R., 1988	70	3
Bountiful	Clark, D., 1985	12 pl.4	2
Bouquet	Clark, D., 1990	34 pl.5	2
Bow Bells	Dale, A. D., 1986	44	2
Brenda White	Nijhuis, M., 1994	pl.346	2
Brookwood Joy	Clark, D., 1985	12 pl.5	2
Brutus	Clark, J. R., 1988	92	2
Burning Bush	Saunders, E., 1972	97 pl.2	2
Buttercup	Clark, D., 1987	66	3
Caesar	Clark, D., 1985	12 pl.6	1
Cambridge Louie	Waddington, A., 1988	106	2
Can Can	Nijhuis, M., 1996	pl.262	1
Candlelight	Clark, D., 1985	12 pl.7	2
Cannenburgh Floriant	Nijhuis, M., 1994	pl.548	1

Cardinal Farges	Clark, D., 1990	35 pl.4	2
Carl Wallace	Bartlett, G., 1990	103	1
Carmel Blue	Nederlandse Kring, 1985	pl.11	2
Carmen	Clark, D., 1990	35 pl.5	2
Carnival	Manthey, G., 1983	123	3
Carnoustie	Bartlett, G., 1996, *Colour Guide*	61	1
Caroline	Clark, D., 1985	FC	3
Cascade	Heinke, R., 1989	30	3
Caspar Hauser	Nijhuis, M., 1988	55	2
Catherine Bartlett	Bartlett, G., 1988	pl.2	1
Cecile	Nijhuis, M., 1994	pl.435	1
Celadore	Clark, J. R., 1988	38 pl.2	3
Celia Smedley	Boullemier, L. B., 1989	48	2
Ceri	Clark, J. R., 1988	74	3
Chang	Ewart, R., 1990	pl.191	2
Chaos	Nijhuis, M., 1994	pl.436	1
Checkerboard	Bartlett, G., 1990	104	2
Chickadee	Nijhuis, M., 1994	pl.234	2
Chillerton Beauty	Nijhuis, M., 1988	76	2
China Doll	Dale, A. D., 1986	37	2
Christ Driessen	Nijhuis, M., et al, 1990	117 pl.1	2
Cinpetio	Nijhuis, M., 1994	pl.200	1
Cinvenu	Nijhuis, M., 1994	pl.928	2
Citation	Clapham, S., 1982	113	2
City of Adelaide	Clark, J. R., 1988	55	1
C. J. Howlett	Clark, J. R., 1988	71	3
Clair de Lune	Nijhuis, M., 1994	pl.929	2
Claret Cup	Puttock, A. G., 1959	pl.2	2
Cliantha	Heinke, R., 1989	50 pl.1	2
Cliff's Hardy	Clark, D., 1990	36 pl.4	1
Cliff's Own	Nijhuis, M., 1994	pl.93	2
Cliff's Unique	Clark, D., 1985	13 pl.3	2
Clifton Beauty	Clark, D., 1985	13 pl.4	2
Clifton Belle	Clark, J. R., 1988	107	2
Clifton Charm	Nijhuis, M., 1994	pl.788	1
Cloth of Gold	Saunders, E., 1972	99	2
Cloverdale Jewel	Clark, J. R., 1988	51	3
Cloverdale Pearl	Clark, D., 1987	63	2
Cloverdale Pride	Nijhuis, M., 1994	pl.440	1
Coachman	Clark, D., 1985	24 pl.2	2
Collingwood	Clark, J. R., 1988	61 pl.3	3
Conspicua	Goulding, E. 1995	pl.15	4
Constance	Clark, J. R., 1988	110 pl.1	2
Constellation	Clark, D., 1985	24 pl.3	2
Coquet Bell	Clark, D., 1985	22 pl.1	2
Corallina	Clark, D., 1990	36 pl.5	1
Corsair	Clark, J. R., 1988	38 pl.1	3
Cosmopolitan	Nijhuis, M., 1988	91	1
Cotton Candy	Clark, D., 1987	26	3
Countess of Aberdeen	Clark, J. R., 1988	58	3
Countess of Maritza	Clark, D., 1985	13 pl.8	2
Crescendo	Dreyer, G., 1986	71	1
Crinoline	Ewart, R., 1990	pl.35	2

Fiery Spider	Manthey, G., 1983	140 pl.1	2
Fiona	Clark, J. R., 1988	95	2
Firecracker	Bartlett, G., 2000, *The New Cult.*	95	2
First Success	Nijhuis, M., et al, 1990	73 pl.2	1
Flirtation Walz	Clark, J. R., 1988	39 pl.2	2
Floral City	Saunders, E., 1972	19 pl.1	2
Florence Mary Abbott	Nijhuis, M., 1994	pl.13	2
Florence Turner	Clark, D., 1990	37 pl.5	1
Florentina	Dreyer, G., 1986	99	2
Flying Cloud	Clapham, S., 1982	56	2
Foxtrot	Nijhuis, M., 1988	72	2
Frank Unsworth	Waddington, A., 1988	39	2
Fuchsiade '88	Goulding, E. 1995	pl.29	4
Galadriel	Nijhuis, M., et al, 1990	74	1
Garden News	Bartlett, G., 1990	106	2
Gartenmeister Bonstedt	Nederlandse Kring 1985	pl.87	2
Gay Fandango	Clark, J. R., 1988	59	3
Genii	Clark, D., 1987	78	3
Georgeana	Nijhuis, M., 1994	pl.385	2
George Johnson	Nijhuis, M., 1996	pl.235	2
Giant Pink Enchanted	Bartlett, G., 1996, *Colour Guide*	125	1
Glenby	Nijhuis, M., 1994	pl.817	1
Glow	Clark, D., 1990	38 pl.1	2
Gold Brocade	Clark, D., 1990	38 pl.2	2
Golden Arrow	Goulding, E. 1995	pl.37	3
Golden Lena	Clark, J. R., 1988	34	3
Golden Marinka	Clark, D., 1987	23	3
Golden Treasure	Clark, J. R., 1988	75	3
Golondrina	Clark, D., 1990	38 pl.4	2
Göteborgskan	Nijhuis, M., 1994	pl.714	1
Göttingen	Nijhuis, M., 1994	pl.947	1
Graf Witte	Goulding, E., 1995	pl.11	4
Grandma Sinton	Bartlett, G., 1996, *Colour Guide*	131	1
Grasmere	Nijhuis, M., 1994	pl.273	1
Grayrigg	Nijhuis, M., 1994	pl.61	2
Greatham Mill	Clark, D., 1990	38 pl.8	2
Greenpeace	Nijhuis, M., et al, 1990	69	1
Gregor Mendel	Nijhuis, M., 1994	pl.822	2
Gretna Chase	Bartlett, G., 1996, *Colour Guide*	133	1
Groenekan's Glorie	Nijhuis, M., 1994	pl.948	1
Grus aus dem Bodethal	Boullemier, L. B., 1989	57	1
Gustave Doré	Clark, D., 1990	39 pl.1	2
Hampshire Beauty	Clark, J. R., 1988	43	2
Hampshire Blue	Clark, D., 1987	31	3
Hampshire Prince	Clark, D., 1985	15 pl.4	1
Hampshire Treasure	Clark, D., 1985	15 pl.5	2
Happy	Clark, D., 1990	39 pl.2	2
Happy Wedding Day	Nijhuis, M., 1994	pl.16	2
Harlow Car	Waddington, A., 1988	119	2
Harry Gray	Clark, D., 1985	15 pl.6	2
Haute Cuisine	Goulding, E. 1995	pl.22	4
Hawkshead	Clark, D., 1987	95	2
Heidi Ann	Clark, D., 1985	15 pl.8	2

Heinrich Henkel	Ewart, R., 1990	18	2
Herald	Bartlett, G., 1988	pl.4	1
Herjan de Groot	Nijhuis, M., 1996	pl.27	1
Hermiena	Nijhuis, M., et al, 1990	109 pl.2	2
Hidcote Beauty	Clark, J. R., 1988	46 pl.2	2
Hidden Treasure	Bartlett, G., 2000, *The New Cult.*	115	1
Hobson's Choice	Jennings, J. et al, 1979	pl.10	2
Hokusai	Nijhuis, M., 1994	pl.561	1
Honnepon	Nijhuis, M., et al, 1990	118 pl.2	1
Howlett's Hardy	Clark, D., 1990	39 pl.5	2
Humboldt Holiday	Dale, A. D., 1986	42	3
Ian Leedham	Boullemier, L. B., 1989	60	1
Iceberg	Boullemier, L. B., 1985	pl.8	2
Iced Champagne	Clark, D., 1985	16 pl.1	2
Igloo Maid	Clark, D., 1985	16 pl.2	2
Impala	Nijhuis, M., 1994	pl.64	2
Indian Maid	Clark, J. R., 1988	78	2
Insulinde	Nijhuis, M., 1994	pl.562	1
Interlude	Clark, J. R., 1988	90 pl.2	2
Isle of Mull	Clark, D., 1985	16 pl.4	1
Jaap Brummel	Nijhuis, M., 1996	pl.424	1
Jack Acland	Nijhuis, M., 1994	pl.275	1
Jack King	Nederlandse Kring, 1985	pl.49	2
Jack Shahan	Clark, D., 1985	16 pl.5	2
Jackqueline	Nijhuis, M., 1996	pl.317	1
Janna	Nijhuis, M., 1996	pl.316	2
Jenny Sorenson	Waddington, A., 1988	194	1
Joan Pacey	Waddington, A., 1988	91	2
Joe Kusber	Dreyer, G., 1986	127	1
John Maynard Scales	Nijhuis, M., 1994	pl.950	2
Joseph Holmes	Nijhuis, M., 1994	pl.611	2
Joy Patmore	Clark, D., 1987	99	2
Julchen	Bartlett, G., 2000, *The New Cult.*	129	1
Julie Horton	Ewart, R., 1990	pl.73	1
Katrina	Birch, M. V., 1992	24 pl.3	2
Kegworth Carnival	Clark, D., 1985	22 pl.4	2
Kolding Perle	Clark, D., 1985	16 pl.8	2
Koralle	Ewart, R., 1990	pl.13	2
L'Arlesienne	Ewart, R., 1990	pl.85	2
La Campanella	Bartlett, G., 1988	pl.11	2
La Rosita	Nijhuis, M., 1994	pl.742	2
Lace Petticoats	Ewart, R., 1990	pl.33	2
Lady Isobel Barnet	Bartlett, G., 1990	92	2
Lady Kathleen Spence	Clark, J. R., 1988	103	2
Lady Thumb	Clark, D., 1987	103	3
Lark	Nijhuis, M., 1994	pl.281	2
Lavender Kate	Clark, J. R., 1988	46 pl.1	2
Le Berger	Nijhuis, M., 1988	17 pl.1	3
Lechlade Apache	Goulding, E. 1995	pl.38	3
Lechlade Magician	Nijhuis, M., 1994	pl.631	1
Lechlade Marchioness	Nijhuis, M., 1994	pl.952	1
Lechlade Tinkerbell	Goulding, E. 1995	pl.49	4
Lena	Dale, A. D., 1986	39	3

Morning Light	Clark, D., 1987	102	2
Mr A. Huggett	Clark, J. R., 1988	47	3
Mrs Lovell Swisher	Bartlett, G., 1996, *Colour Guide*	209	1
Mrs Popple	Clark, D., 1990	42 pl.3	1
Mrs W. Rundle	Boullemier, L. B., 1989	37	2
Nancy Lou	Clark, D., 1985	18 pl.3	2
Nellie Nuttall	Clark, D., 1987	35	3
Nettala	Heinke, R., 1989	54 pl.2	1
Nicky Veerman	Nijhuis, M., 1996	pl.18	1
Nicola Jane	Clark, D., 1990	42 pl.4	1
Nimue	Goulding, E. 1995	pl.32	2
Nina Wills	Clark, J. R., 1988	pl.75	2
Northumbrian Belle	Clark, D., 1985	22 pl.5	2
Olive Moon	Bartlett, G., 1996, *Colour Guide*	217	1
Onna	Nijhuis, M., 1994	pl.578	1
Oranje Boven	Manthey, G., 1983	152	2
Orange Crush	Nederlandse Kring, 1985	pl.33	2
Orange Crystal	Clark, D., 1985	18 pl.5	1
Orange Glow	Nijhuis, M., 1996	pl.487	1
Orange Drops	Clark, J. R., 1988	102	2
Oranje van Os	Nederlandse Kring, 1985	pl.31	2
Orient Express	Goulding, E. 1995	pl.36	4
Ortenburger Festival	Manthey, G., 1989	54	2
Orwell	Nijhuis, M., 1994	pl.616	2
Ostfriesland	Nijhuis, M., 1996	pl.150	2
Other Fellow	Waddington, A., 1988	206	2
Our Ted	Boullemier, L. B., 1989	77	3
Pacquesa	Clark, D., 1985	BC pl.4	3
Papillon	Nijhuis, M., et al, 1990	93 pl.2	2
Papoose	Clark, D., 1990	42 pl.5	2
Party Frock	Nederlandse Kring, 1985	pl.107	1
Paul Roe	Ewart, R., 1990	27	2
Pee Wee Rose	Clark, D., 1990	42 pl.6	1
Peppermint Stick	Clark, D., 1985	22 pl.6	2
Petit Fleur	Nijhuis, M., 1994	pl.507	2
Phyllis	Clark, J. R., 1988	109 pl.2	2
Phyrne	Clark, D., 1990	43 pl.3	1
Piet Heemskerk	Nijhuis, M., 1994	pl.617	2
Piet Hein	Nijhuis, M., 1986	94 pl.2	2
Pinch Me	Jennings, J. et al, 1979	pl.22	2
Pink Darling	Ewart, R., 1990	pl.99	1
Pink Fairy	Ewart, R., 1990	pl.70	2
Pink Fantasia	Bartlett, G., 1996, *Colour Guide*	231	1
Pink Galore	Nederlandse Kring, 1985	pl.80	2
Pink Jade	Clark, J. R., 1988	66 pl.1	2
Pink Marshmallow	Boullemier, L. B., 1989	80	2
Pink Quartet	Waddington, A., 1988	122	2
Pixie	Goulding, E., 1995	pl.12	4
Postiljon	Manthey, G., 1983	160	2
Powder Puff	Ewart, R., 1990	pl.72	2
President	Saunders, E., 1972	111 pl.2	2
President Elliot	Clark, D., 1990	43 pl.6	1
President Leo Boullemier	Bartlett, G., 1990	60	2

President Margaret Slater	Bartlett, G., 1990	112	2
President Walter Morio	Fessler, A., 1980	16	2
Preston Guild	Clark, D., 1987	62	3
Prosperity	Clark, J. R., 1988	33	3
Pukkie	Nijhuis, M., 1994	pl.986	1
Purperklokje	Nijhuis, M., 1994	pl.633	1
Purple Splendour	Clark, D., 1990	44 pl.5	1
Pussycat	Nijhuis, M., 1994	pl.307	2
Put's Folly	Ewart, R., 1990	pl.37	2
Quasar	Nijhuis, M., 1994	pl.172	1
R.A.F.	Clark, J. R., 1988	41	2
Radcliffe Bedder	Clark, J. R., 1988	53	3
Rambling Rose	Clark, D., 1985	22 pl.8	2
Reading Show	Clark, D., 1990	45 pl.2	1
Red Ace	Clark, D., 1990	45 pl.3	1
Red Spider	Waddington, A., 1988	126	2
Regina van Zoeren	Nijhuis, M., 1994	pl.513	1
Reverend Dr Brown	Manthey, G., 1983	175	2
Ridestar	Ewart, R., 1990	pl.150	2
Rika	Nederlandse Kring, 1985	pl.55	2
Robbie	Waddington, A., 1988	143	2
Rodeo	Goulding, E. 1995	pl.23	4
Roos Breytenbach	Goulding, E. 1995	pl.27	3
Rosecroft Beauty	Ewart, R., 1990	pl.20	3
Rose of Castile	Clark, D., 1985	19 pl.3	2
Rose of Castile Imp.	Clark, J. R., 1988	86	2
Rose of Denmark	Clark, J. R., 1988	54	3
Rose Phenomenal	Clark, D., 1990	45 pl.6	1
Rose van der Berg	Nijhuis, M., 1994	pl.314	2
Rough Silk	Clark, D., 1985	19 pl.4	1
Roy Walker	Boullemier, L. B., 1989	85	2
Royal Purple	Clark, D., 1990	46 pl.1	2
Royal Velvet	Clark, J. R., 1988	52	3
Ruddigore	Nijhuis, M., 1996	pl.482	1
Rufus	Ewart, R., 1990	pl.115	1
Ruth King	Clark, D., 1985	19 pl.6	2
Salmon Queen	Nijhuis, M., 1994	pl.967	1
Samson	Saunders, E., 1972	107 pl.1	2
Santa Cruz	Clark, D., 1990	46 pl.2	2
Sarina	Nijhuis, M., et al, 1990	120 pl.1	1
Satellite	Clark, J. R., 1988	67 pl.1	2
Schneeball	Clark, D., 1990	46 pl.3	2
Schneewitchen	Clark, D., 1990	46 pl.4	2
Sea Shell	Ewart, R., 1990	pl.38	2
Sealand Prince	Clark, D., 1990	46 pl.5	1
Shanley	Nijhuis, M., 1994	pl.620	1
Sharon Allsop	Nijhuis, M., 1994	pl.727	1
Sharpitor	Clark, J. R., 1988	63 pl.1	3
Silver Breckland	Clark, D., 1997	108	2
Silverdale	Clark, D., 1990	47 pl.1	1
Sleighbells	Clark, J. R., 1988	68	3
Slippery Horn	Nijhuis, M., 1996	pl.151	1
Small Pipes	Goulding, E. 1995	pl.28	4

Snowcap	Bartlett, G., 1988	pl.16	2
Snowfire	Clark, J. R., 1988	76	2
Son of Thumb	Clark, D., 1985	20 pl.1	1
Sonata	Clark, J. R., 1988	39 pl.1	2
Sophisticated Lady	Clark, D., 1985	20 pl.2	2
Southgate	Clark, D., 1985	20 pl.3	2
Space Shuttle	Nijhuis, M., 1988	59 pl.2	2
Spion Kop	Clark, D., 1985	20 pl.4	2
Spitsneus	Nijhuis, M., 1994	pl.519	2
Stad Elburg	Nijhuis, M., 1988	61	2
Stanley Cash	Bartlett, G., 1990	9	3
Stella Ann	Nijhuis, M., 1994	pl.588	2
Strawberry Delight	Saunders, E., 1972	101 pl.2	2
String of Pearls	Clark, J. R., 1988	69 pl.1	3
Sugar Blue	Nederlandse Kring, 1985	pl.117	2
Sunray	Nijhuis, M., 1994	pl.885	2
Sunset	Nijhuis, M., 1994	pl.590	1
Super Sport	Nijhuis, M., 1994	pl.370	2
Susan Travis	Clark, D., 1990	47 pl.2	2
Swanley Gem	Ewart, R., 1990	pl.170	1
Swanley Yellow	Ewart, R., 1990	pl.178	2
Sweetie Dear	Nijhuis, M., 1994	pl.888	2
Swingtime	Bartlett, G., 1990	32	2
Tangerine	Nederlandse Kring, 1985	pl.100	1
Tarra Valley	Nijhuis, M., 1994	pl.998	1
Television	Nijhuis, M., 1988	37 pl.1	3
Tennessee Waltz	Clark, D., 1987	27	3
Texas Longhorn	Goulding, E. J., 1973	pl.36	2
Texas Star	Nijhuis, M., 1994	pl.401	1
Thalia	Bartlett, G., 1988	pl.5	2
The Doctor	Clark, D., 1985	21 pl.1	2
The Small Woman	Saunders, E., 1972	103 pl.1	2
The Tarns	Clark, D., 1990	47 pl.4	1
Thornley's Hardy	Clark, D., 1987	111	3
Tiffany	Nijhuis, M., 1994	pl.33	2
Timlin Brened	Nijhuis, M., 1994	pl.323	1
Tineke	Nijhuis, M., 1994	pl.324	2
Ting-a-ling	César, J., 1981	64	3
Tinkerbell	Nijhuis, M., 1994	pl.84	1
Tolling Bell	Ewart, R., 1990	pl.121	2
Tom Thumb	Clark, D., 1985	21 pl.3	2
Toos	Nijhuis, M., et al, 1990	66 pl.2	2
Torville and Dean	Bartlett, G., 1990	114	2
Tourtonne	Nederlandse Kring, 1985	pl.67	1
Trail Blazer	Clark, D., 1987	118	2
Trailing King	Nijhuis, M., 1994	pl.594	2
Trase	Clark, J. R., 1988	89	2
Traudchen Bonstedt	Nijhuis, M., 1994	pl.327	2
Trewince Twilight	Ewart, R., 1990	pl.36	2
Très Long	Bartlett, G., 2000, *The New Cult.*	219	2
Tristesse	Nederlandse Kring, 1985	pl.21	3
Troika	Nederlandse Kring, 1985	pl.113	2
Tropic Sunset	Saunders, E., 1972	97 pl.1	2

Trumpeter	Clark, D., 1987	18	2
Tsjiep	Nijhuis, M., 1994	pl.232	1
Tuonela	Nijhuis, M., 1994	pl.403	1
Tutone	Clark, J. R., 1988	90 pl.1	3
Twiggy	Nijhuis, M., et al, 1990	67 pl.1	1
Twink	Goulding, E. 1995	pl.25	3
Upward Look	Ewart, R., 1990	pl.168	1
Venus Victrix	Boullemier, L. B., 1989	17	2
Vincent van Gogh	Nijhuis, M., 1994	pl.330	2
Vivienne Davis	Goulding, E., 1995	pl.24	4
Vobeglo	Nijhuis, M., 1994	pl.528	2
Walz Blauwkous	Nijhuis, M., 1994	pl.529	1
Walz Brandaris	Nijhuis, M., 1994	pl.595	1
Walz Clarinet	Nijhuis, M., 1994	pl.407	1
Walz Epicurist	Nijhuis, M., 1988	64	2
Walz Fagot	Nijhuis, M., 1994	pl.532	1
Walz Fanfare	Nijhuis, M., 1994	pl.701	1
Walz Floreat	Nederlandse Kring, 1985	pl.75	2
Walz Gigolo	Nijhuis, M., 1994	pl.900	2
Walz Harp	Nijhuis, M., et al, 1990	122 pl.1	1
Walz Hoorn	Nijhuis, M., et al, 1990	97 pl.1	2
Walz Kattesnor	Nijhuis, M., 1994	pl.186	2
Walz Klarinet	Nijhuis, M., 1994	pl.407	2
Walz Lucifer	Bartlett, G., 1996, *Colour Guide*	305	1
Walz Luit	Nijhuis, M., 1994	pl.975	1
Walz Meermin	Nijhuis, M., 1994	pl.993	1
Walz Nugget	Nijhuis, M., et al, 1990	98	1
Walz Parasol	Nijhuis, M., 1994	pl.332	1
Walz Sprietje	Nijhuis, M., 1994	pl.601	1
Walz Toorts	Nijhuis, M., et al, 1990	71 pl.2	1
Walz Tuba	Nijhuis, M., et al, 1990	99 pl.1	2
Walz Vuurpijl	Nijhuis, M., 1994	pl.999	1
Walz Waterval	Nijhuis, M., et al, 1990	88	1
Walz Xylofoon	Nijhuis, M., et al, 1990	99 pl.2	2
Waternymph	Nijhuis, M., 1994	pl.225	1
Wave of Life	Nijhuis, M., 1994	pl.903	2
Waveney Gem	Goulding, E. 1995	pl.35	4
Westminster Chimes	Clark, D., 1985	21 pl.8	2
Whirlaway	Goulding, E. J., 1973	pl.38	2
Whistling Rufus	Nijhuis, M., 1994	pl.702	1
White Gold	Saunders, E., 1972	103 pl.2	2
White King	Butler, L. A., undated	47	1
White Pixie	Goulding, E. 1995	pl.13	3
White Spider	Butler, L. A., undated	47	1
Whiteknight's Amethyst	Clark, D., 1990	48 pl.5	2
Whiteknight's Pearl	Nijhuis, M., 1994	pl.87	1
Whiteknight's Ruby	Nederlandse Kring, 1985	pl.62	2
Wibke	Nijhuis, M., 1994	pl.337	1
Willemien	Nijhuis, M., 1994	pl.907	2
Willie Tamerus	Nederlandse Kring, 1985	pl.43	1
Winston Churchill	Clark, D., 1985	21 pl.8	2
Yolanda Franck	Nijhuis, M., et al, 1990	123 pl.1	2
Yuletide	Boullemier, L. B., 1985	pl.1	3

Bibliography

This bibliography consists of books or articles on fuchsias that are of special value. It is a selection of those books that have been published since the fuchsia's introduction to Europe; some readers may find it useful for starting or building a collection of fuchsia-related books. Some material will only be available through reference or similar libraries. Any publication which has been produced outside the United Kingdom gives the country of origin in its entry.

ATSATT, P. R., and RUNDEL, P., 'Pollinator Maintenance vs. Fruit Production: Partitioned Reproductive Effort in Subdioecious *Fuchsia lycioides*', in *Annals of the Missouri Botanical Garden*, Vol. 69, 1982, pp 199-208, ISSN 0026-6493-82-0001-0198.

BARTLETT, G., *Fuchsias*, Royal Horticultural Society, 2000, ISBN 0-7513-0754-8.

BARTLETT, G., *Fuchsias, A Colour Guide*, Crowood Press, Marlborough, Wiltshire, 1996, ISBN 1-85223-927-1.

BARTLETT, G., *Fuchsias for House and Garden*, Crowood Press, Marlborough, Wiltshire, 1990, ISBN 1-85223-259-5.

BARTLETT, G., *Fuchsias, Step By Step to Growing Success*, Crowood Press, Marlborough, Wiltshire, 1996, ISBN 1-85223-971-9.

BARTLETT, G., *Fuchsias, The Complete Guide to Cultivation, Propagation and Exhibition*, Crowood Press, Marlborough, Wiltshire, 1988, ISBN 1-55223-029-0.

BARTLETT, G., *Fuchsias, The New Cultivars*, Crowood Press, Marlborough, Wiltshire, 2000, ISBN 1-86126-338-4.

BARTLETT, G., *Hardy Fuchsias, Step By Step to Growing Success*, Crowood Press, Marlborough, Wiltshire, 2000, ISBN 1-86126-332-5.

BECKETT, K. A., *Fuchsias*, Collins, London, Reprinted 1989, ISBN 0-00-412374-3.

BERGMANS, M., and VAN DE SANDE, K., and VAN DER TAK, I., *Fuchsia Onder De Loep Genomen*, Landbouwuniversiteit Wageningen, The Netherlands, Unpublished, 1991.

BERRY, P., 'A Systematic Revision of the Genus *Fuchsia* Section *Quelusia* (Onagraceae)', in *Annals of the Missouri Botanical Garden*, Vol.76, 1989, pp 532-84, ISSN 0026-6493.

BERRY, P., 'Nomenclatural Changes in the Genus *Fuchsia* (Onagracea)', in *Annals of the Missouri Botanical Garden*, Vol. 75: p. 1150, 1988.

BERRY, P., 'The Systematics and Evolution of *Fuchsia* Section *Fuchsia*', in *Annals of the Missouri Botanical Garden*, Vol.69, 1982, pp 1-198, ISSN 0026-6493-82-0001-0198.

BERRY, P. E., 'The Systematics of the Apetalous Fuchsias of South America, *Fuchsia* Sect. *Hemsleyella* (Onagraceae)', in *Annals of the Missouri Botanical Garden*, Vol.72, 1985, pp 213-51, ISSN 0026-6493.

BERRY, P. E., 'Two New Species of *Fuchsia* section *Fuchsia* (Onagracea) from Southern Ecuador', in Novon 5, pp. 318-22, 1995.

BERRY, P. E., and BREEDLOVE, D. E., 'New Taxa of *Fuchsia* from Central America and Mexico', *Novon*, Vol.6, pp. 135-41.

BERRY, P. E., and STEIN, B. A., and CARLQUIST, S., and NOWICKE, J., '*Fuchsia pachyrrhiza* (Onagraceae), a Tuberous New Species and Section of *Fuchsia* from Western Peru', in *Systematic Botany*, 13(4), 1988.

BIRCH, M. V., *The Fuchsia Album Volume One*, Arcadia Nurseries, Middlesborough, 1992.

BIRCH, M. V., *The Fuchsia Album Volume Two*, Arcadia Nurseries, Middlesborough, 1992.

BIRCH, M. V., *The Fuchsia Album Volume Three*, Arcadia Nurseries, Middlesborough, 1994.

BIRCH, M. V., *The Fuchsia Album Volume Four*, Arcadia Nurseries, Middlesborough, 1994.

BOULLEMIER, L. B., *Addendum No 1 to the 1991 Edition of The Check List Of Species, Hybrids and Cultivars of the Genus Fuchsia*, British Fuchsia Society, 1995.

BOULLEMIER, L. B., *A Plantsman's Guide to Fuchsias*, Ward Lock, London, 1989, ISBN 0-7063-6738-3.

BOULLEMIER, L. B., *Fuchsias*, Grange Books, London, 1995, ISBN 1-85627-703-8.

BOULLEMIER, L. B., *Growing and Showing Fuchsias*, David & Charles, Newton Abbot, Devon, 1985, ISBN 0-7153-8592-5.

BOULLEMIER, L. B., *The Checklist of Species, Hybrids and Cultivars of the Genus Fuchsia*, Blandford, London, Revised Edition 1991, ISBN 0-7137-2165-0.

BREEDLOVE, D. E., 'The Systematics of *Fuchsia* Section *Encliandra* (Onagraceae)', University of California Press, Vol.53, 1969, Library of Congress Catalog Card No.: 72-626140.

BREEDLOVE, D. E., and BERRY, P. E., and RAVEN, P. H., 'The Mexican and Central American Species of *Fuchsia* (Onagraceae) except for Sect. *Encliandra*', in *Annals of the Missouri Botanical Garden*, Vol.69, 1982, pp 209-34, ISSN 0026-6493-82-0001-0198.

BUCZACKI, S., *Best Fuchsias*, Hamlyn, London, 1999, ISBN 0-600-59672-9.

BUTLER, L. A., *Fuchsias in Australia*, Guyra Publishing, South Yarra, Australia, Undated, ISBN 0-909921-00-8.

CÉSAR, J., *Les Fuchsias*, Dargaud, Neuilly-sur-Seine, France, 1981, ISBN 2-205-01840-X.

CLAPHAM, S., *Fuchsias for House and Garden*, David & Charles, Newton Abbot, Devon, 1982, ISBN 0-7153-8217-9.

CLARK, D., *Fuchsia*, Hamlyn, London, 1997, ISBN 0-600-59140-9.

CLARK, D., *Fuchsias for Greenhouse and Garden*, Collingridge Books, Twickenham, Middlesex, 1987, ISBN 0-600-35177-7.

CLARK, D., *The Hardy Fuchsia Guide*, Oakleigh Publications, Monkwood, Hampshire, 1990, ISBN 0-9510578-7-1.

CLARK, D., *The Fuchsia Guide*, Oakleigh Publications, Monkwood, Hampshire, 1985, ISBN 0-9510578-4-7.

CLARK, D., *The Oakleigh Guide to Fuchsias*, Oakleigh Publications, Monkwood, Hampshire, 1985, ISBN 0-9510578-0-4.

CLARK, J. R., *Fuchsias*, Century Hutchinson, London, 1988, ISBN 0-7126-2386-8.

CLARK, J. R., *Fuchsias, Their Care and Cultivation*, Cassell, London, 1990, ISBN 0-304-34007-3.

COOKE, B., *Fabulous Fuchsias*, Lorenz Books, London, 1998, ISBN 1-85967-433-X.

DALE, A. D., *An Illustrated Guide to Growing Fuchsias*, Grange Publications, Ormskirk, Lancashire, 1986, ISBN 0-9511617-0-9.

DARLINGTON, C. D., and JANAKI AMMAL, E. K., *Chromosome Atlas of Cultivated Plants*, George Allen & Unwin, London, 1949.

DARLINGTON, C. D., and LA COUR, L. F., *The Handling of Chromosomes*, George Allen & Unwin, London, fifth edition 1969.

DE GRAAFF, H., *Fuchsias*, Rebo Productions, The Netherlands, 1997, ISBN 1-9010-94-73-1.

DREYER, G., *Mein Fuchsienbuch*, Pauli-Balleis-Verlag, Nurnberg, Germany, 1986, ISBN 3-89078-008-3.

EWART, R., *Fuchsia Lexicon*, Blandford Press, Poole, Dorset, 1982, ISBN 0-7137-1078-0.

EWART, R., *Fuchsias*, Ward Lock, London, 1990, ISBN 0-7063-6872-X.

EWART, R., *The Fuchsia Grower's Handbook*, Blandford Press, London, 1989, ISBN 0-7137-1712-2.

FEßLER, A., *Fuchsien Für Haus und Garten*, Kosmos, Stuttgart, Germany, 1980, ISBN 3-440-04820-9.

FOGG, W., *Begonias and Fuchsias*, Foyles, 1958.

GAUCHER, M., *Les Fuchsias d'ombre et de lumière*, La Maison Rustique, Paris, France, 1979, ISBN 2-7066-0097-7.

GODLEY, E. J., 'Breeding Systems in New Zealand Plants 2', *New Zealand Journal of Botany* 1, 1963, pp 48-52.

GODLEY, E. J., and BERRY, P. E., 'The Biology and Systematics of *Fuchsia* in the South Pacific', in *Annals of the Missouri Botanical Garden*, Vol.82, 1995, pp 473-516.

GOEDMAN-FRANKEMA, M., Botanische *Fuchsia's*, Uitgeverij Terra, Zutphen, The Netherlands, 1992, ISBN 90-6255-486-5.

GORER, R., *The Development of Garden Flowers*, Eyre & Spottiswoode, London, 1970, ISBN 413-27070-X, pp 148-55, Plates V, VI, 27, 28, 29, 30, 31.

GOULDING, E. J., *Fuchsias, a Guide to Cultivation and Identification*, Bartholomew, Edinburgh, 1973, ISBN 0-85152-909-7.

GOULDING, E. J., *Fuchsias, The Complete Guide*, Batsford, London, 1995, ISBN 0-7134-6948-X.

GUBLER, C., *Growing Fuchsias*, Aura Books, Godalming, Surrey, 1994, ISBN 1-85833-162-5.

HEINKE, R., *Fuchsien so gedeihen und bluhen sie am besten*, Grafe und Unzer, Munchen, Germany, 1989, ISBN 3-7742-2487-0.

HOSHINO, T., and BERRY, P. E., 'Observations on Polyploidy in *Fuchsia* Sections *Quelusia* and *Kierschlegeria* (Onagraceae)', *Annals of the Missouri Botanical Garden*, Vol.76, 585-592, 1989, ISSN 0026-6493.

JENNINGS, J., and MILLER, V., *Growing Fuchsias*, Croom Helm, London, 1979, ISBN 0-85664-890-6.

JOHNS, E. A., *Fuchsias of the 19th and early 20th Century*, British Fuchsia Society, 1997, ISBN 0-901774-15-4.

LAW, D., *Growing Fuchsias*, Kangaroo Press, Kenthurst 2154, Australia, Reprinted 1987, ISBN 0-86417-024-6.

LAWRENCE, W. J. C., *Practical Plant Breeding*, George Allen & Unwin, London, 1937.

LAWRENCE, W. J. C., and NEWELL, J., *Seed and Potting Composts*, George Allen & Unwin, London, Revised Third Edition 1948.

LEE, W., *Fuchsias for Greenhouse and Garden*, Littlebury Co. Ltd., Worcester.

LINSENMAIER, W., *Insects of the World*, McGraw-Hill, New York, U.S.A., 1972, Library of Congress no 78-178047-07-037953.

MANTHEY, G., *Fuchsien*, Verlag Eugen Ulmer, Stuttgart, Germany, 1983, ISBN 3-8001-6348-9.

MANTHEY, G., *Schone Fuchsien*, Verlag Eugen Ulmer, Stuttgart, Germany, 1989, ISBN 3-8001-6395-0.

MATHEW, B., *The Year Round Bulb Garden*, Souvenir Press, London, 1986, ISBN 0-28562-787-2.

MIDGLEY, K., *Garden Design*, Pelham Books, London, 1987 edition, ISBN 0-7207-1685-3.

MIKOLAJSKI, A., *Fuchsias*, Lorenz Books, London, 1997, ISBN 1-85967-387-2.

MINISTRY OF AGRICULTURE, FISHERIES AND FOOD, *Windbreaks for Horticulture*, Booklet 2280, Revised Edition 1985.

MUNZ, P. A., *A Revision of the Genus Fuchsia (Onagraceae)*, Johnson Reprint Corporation, New York, U.S.A., Reprinted 1970, ISBN 0-85409-393-1.

MYERS, D., *Fuchsias and Bedding Plants*, Parragon Books, Bristol, 1996, ISBN 0-75251-584-5.

NEDERLANDSE KRING VAN FUCHSIAVRIENDEN. *Fuchsia's hebben en houden*, Gottmer, Haarlem, The Netherlands, 1985, ISBN 90-257-1898-1.

NEDERLANDSE KRING VAN FUCHSIAVRIENDEN, *Het Niewe Fuchsia Handboek*, Kosmos, Utrecht, The Netherlands, 1995, ISBN 90-215-2520-8.

NIJHUIS, M., *1000 Fuchsias*, Batsford, London, 1994, ISBN 0-7134-7587-0.

NIJHUIS, M., *500 More Fuchsias*, Batsford, London, 1996, ISBN 0-7134-7941-8.

NIJHUIS, M., *Fuchsias, The Complete Handbook*, Cassell, London, 1994, ISBN 0-304-34387-0.

NIJHUIS, M., *Fuchsia's om ons heen*, Gottmer, Haarlem, The Netherlands, 1988, ISBN 90-257-2112-5.

NIJHUIS, M., *Fuchsia's van stek tot stam*, Gottmer, Haarlem, The Netherlands, 1986, ISBN 90-257-1964-3.

NIJHUIS, M., and DE GRAAFF, H., and VAN WIJK, A., *Fuchsia's uit Nederland*, Gottmer, Haarlem, The Netherlands, 1990, ISBN 90-257-2276-8.

PLUMIER, P. C., *Nova Plantarum Americanum Genera*, 1703.

PORCHER, M. F., *Le Fuchsia, histoire et culture*, Connaissance et Mémoires Européennes, France, 1996, ISBN 2-909-112-41-1.

PROUDLEY, B. & V., *Fuchsias in Colour*, Blandford Press, Poole, Dorset, 1975, ISBN 0-7137-0754-2.

PROUDLEY, B. & V., *How to Grow Fuchsias*, Blandford Press, Poole, Dorset, 1983, ISBN 0-7137-1376-3.

PUTTOCK, A. G., *Lovely Fuchsias*, John Gifford, London, 1959, SBN 70710190-5.

PUTTOCK, A. G., *Pelargoniums and Fuchsias*, Collingridge, London, 1959.

RUSSELL, E. W., *Soil Conditions and Plant Growth*, Longman Press, Harlow, Essex, Ninth Edition 1961, ISBN 0-582-44677-5.

SAUNDERS, E., *Wagtails Book of Fuchsias Vol 1*, E. R. M. Saunders, Henfield, Sussex, 1971.

SAUNDERS, E., *Wagtails Book of Fuchsias Vol 2*, E. R. M. Saunders, Godalming, Surrey, 1972.

SAUNDERS, E., *Wagtails Book of Fuchsias Vol 3*, E. R. M. Saunders, Godalming, Surrey, 1973.

SAUNDERS, E., *Wagtails Book of Fuchsias Vol 4*, E. R. M. Saunders, Godalming, Surrey, 1976.

SAUNDERS, E., *Wagtails Book of Fuchsias Vol 5*, Wagtails Fuchsia Publications, Lechlade, Gloucestershire, 1987.

SCHNEDL, E. and H., *Wildformen Der Fuchsien*, Austria, 1997, ISBN 3-95-00696.

SCHURR, A. and R., *Fuchsien*, West Germany, 1988, ISBN 3-7724-1176-2.

SHARP, W., 'Fuchsia Rust', in *British Fuchsia Society Annual*, 1973, pp 35-6.

SHERMAN, W., 'Towards an Understanding of Moisture', in *British Fuchsia Society Annual*, 1981, pp 67-9.

SWEETMAN, T., *Fuchsia Growing*, Procumbens Publishing, New Zealand, 1991, ISBN 0-477-01464-X.

THE NATIONAL FUCHSIA SOCIETY, *The New A to Z on Fuchsias*, The National Fuchsia Society of America, 1976.

The Times Atlas of the World, 1990, ISBN 0-7230-0346-7.

THORNE, T., *Fuchsias for all Purposes*, Collingridge, London, Revised 1964.

TOMLINSON, V., *Growing Fuchsias in South Africa*, Khenty Press, Natal, South Africa, Revised 1978, ISBN 0-86876-004-8.

TOOGOOD, A., *Practical Fuchsia Growing*, Crowood Press, Marlborough, Wiltshire, 1992, ISBN 1-85223-632-9.

TRAVIS, S., 'Fertility, Polyploids and Genetics', in *The Fuchsia Annual*, The British Fuchsia Society, 1974.

VAN DER LAAN, J. E., *Fuchsia's het hele jaar door*, Thieme, Zutphen, The Netherlands, 1974, ISBN 90-03-94681-7.

VAN VEEN, G., *Winterharde Fuchsia's*, J. H. Gottmer, Harlem, The Netherlands, 1992, ISBN 90-257-2471-X.

WADDINGTON, A., and SWINDELLS, P., *The Fuchsia Book*, David & Charles, Newton Abbot, Devon, 1988, ISBN 0-7153-9076-7.

WALKER, G. and A., *A Colour Guide to Fuchsias*, G. A. Walker, Ormskirk, Lancs.

WALKER, G. and A., *A Second Colour Guide to Fuchsias*, G. A. Walker, Ormskirk, Lancs.

WALKER, G. and A., *A Third Colour Guide to Fuchsias*, G. A. Walker, Ormskirk, Lancs., ISBN 0-9511617-5-X.

WELLS, G., *Fuchsias*, Royal Horticultural Society, Wisley, Surrey, 1972, ISBN 900-62919-3.

WELLS, G., *Fuchsias*, Cassell, London, Revised 1985, ISBN 0-304-31084-0.

WILKINS, M., *Plantwatching*, Macmillan, London, 1988, ISBN 0-333-44503-1.

WILSON, S. J., *Fuchsias, a Complete Guide to their Propagation and Cultivation for House and Garden*, Faber & Faber, London, 1965.

WOOD, W. P., *A Fuchsia Survey*, Ernest Benn Ltd., London, 1950.

List of Gouldings Fuchsia Raisings (1981–2001)

1 Lady Ramsey (1981) = Coquet Dale x Estelle Marie

2 Linda Goulding (1981) = Coquet Dale x Estelle Marie

3 Playford (1981) = Coquet Dale x Estelle Marie

4 Charlie Gardiner (1982) = Coquet Dale x *F. fulgens* var. *rubra grandiflora*

5 Bealings (1983) = Bobby Shaftoe x Coquet Dale

6 Camelot (1983) = Lady Ramsey x Norman Mitchinson

7 Excalibur (1983) = Coquet Dale x High Peak

8 Florence Mary Abbott (1983) = Lady Ramsey x Norman Mitchinson

9 Galahad (1983) = High Peak x High Peak

10 Lancelot (1983) = Playford x Citation

11 Mordred (1983) = High Peak x Coquet Bell

12 Nimue (1983) = Estelle Marie x High Peak

13 Pamela Knights (1983) = Lady Ramsey x Coquet Dale

14 Tom Knights (1983) = Estelle Marie x Coquet Dale

15 Constable Country (1984) = (Estelle Marie x Lye's Unique) x Annabel

16 Dedham Vale (1984) = (Estelle Marie x Lye's Unique) x Annabel

17 Harvest Glow (1984) = (Estelle Marie x Lye's Unique) x Annabel

18 Hay Wain (1984) = (Estelle Marie x Lye's Unique) x Annabel

19 Grace Durham (1984) = Lady Ramsey x Norman Mitchinson

20 Lemacto (1984) = Yellow foliage sport off Camelot

21 Linet (1984) = (Estelle Marie x Lye's Unique) x Annabel

22 Sir Alfred Ramsey (1984) = (Estelle Marie x Lye's Unique) x Annabel

23 Tolemac (1984) = Variegated foliage sport off Camelot

24 Willie Lott (1984) = (Estelle Marie x Lye's Unique) x Annabel

25 Brighton Belle (1985) = Thalia x Lye's Unique

26 Continental (1985) = Coquet Dale x Snowfire

27 Easterling (1985) = Annabel x (Estelle Marie x Lye's Unique)

28 Fenman (1985) = Flirtation Waltz x Pink Flamingo

29 Flying Scotsman (1985) = Coquet Dale x Snowfire

30 Golden Arrow (1985) = *F. fulgens* var. *gesneriana*

31 Hessett Festival (1985) = Coquet Dale x Snowfire

32 John Maynard Scales (1985) = Thalia x *F. fulgens* var. *gesneriana*

33 Mancunian (1985) = Igloo Maid x Annabel

34 Orient Express (1985) = Thalia x Lye's Unique

35 Peter Crooks (1985) = Thalia x Lye's Unique

36 Barry Sheppard (1986) = Thalia x *F. fulgens* var. *gesneriana*

37 Carnoustie (1986) = (Coquet Dale x Snowfire) x (Coquet Dale x Snowfire)

38 Gleneagles (1986) = (Coquet Dale x Snowfire) x (Coquet Dale x Snowfire)

39 Letts Delight (1986) = Blush of Dawn x (Rambling Rose x Cloverdale Jewel)

40 Muirfield (1986) = (Coquet Dale x Snowfire) x (Coquet Dale x Snowfire)

41 Royal and Ancient (1986) = (Coquet Dale x Snowfire) x (Coquet Dale x Snowfire)

42 Squadron Leader (1986) = Unknown

43 St Andrews (1986) = (Coquet Dale x Snowfire) x (Coquet Dale x Snowfire)

44 Sunningdale (1986) = Thalia x *F. fulgens* var. *gesneriana*

45 Troon (1986) = (Lady Ramsey x Caroline) x (Annabel x unknown seedling)

46 Wentworth (1986) = *F. fulgens* var. *rubra grandiflora* x Mrs W. Rundle

47 Gondoliers (1987) = Unknown

48 Grand Duke (1987) = Unknown

49 Hilda Fitzsimmons (1987) = Unknown

50 Hilda May Salmon (1987) = Unknown

51 Iolanthe (1987) = Unknown

52 Jean Dawes (1987) = Unknown

53 Mikado (1987) = Unknown

54 Our Ted (1987) = Thalia x Thalia

55 Patience (1987) = Unknown

56 Ruddigore (1987) = Unknown

57 Alde (1988) = *F. fulgens* x Lye's Unique

58 Blythe (1988) = Coquet Dale x Unknown

59 Brian Stannard (1988) = Estelle Marie x Applause

60 Celebration (1988) = Coquet Dale x Unknown

61 Deben (1988) = Estelle Marie x Gay Parasol

62 Ernie Bromley (1988) = Hawkshead x Troon

63 Finn (1988) = Waveney Sunrise x Eusabia

64 Gipping (1988) = (Lady Ramsey x Annabel) x Troon

65 Harry Lye (1988) = Unknown

66 Lark (1988) = Unknown x Lye's Unique

67 Little Ouse (1988) = Coquet Dale x Unknown

68 Orwell (1988) = Coquet Dale x Unknown

69 Achilles (1989) = Unknown

70 Ajax (1989) = Unknown

71 Altmark (1989) = Unknown

72 Buenos Aires (1989) = Unknown

73 David Ward (1989) = Coquet Dale x Eusabia

74 Dorothy M. Goldsmith (1989) = Dusky Beauty x Unknown

75 Exeter (1989) = Unknown

76 Graf Spee (1989) = Unknown

77 Jim Dowers (1989) = Unknown

78 Montevideo (1989) = Unknown

79 Natalie Jones (1989) = Unknown

80 River Plate (1989) = Unknown

81 Misty Morn (1990) = Unknown

82 Dreamy Days (1990) = Unknown

83 Harnser's Flight (1990) = Unknown

84 Sunlight Path (1990) = Unknown

85 Wagoner's Way (1990) = Unknown

86 Ann Roots (1991) = Unknown

87 Diann Goodwin (1991) = Unknown

88 Plumb-bob (1992) = Unknown

89 Gold Foil (1993) = Yellow foliage sport off Celebration

90 Barry M. Cox (1994) = Florentina x Continental

91 Becky (1994) = Satchmo x Christina Becker

92 Congreve Road (1994) = Satchmo x Unknown

93 Dorrian Brogdale (1994) = Unknown

94 Eve Hollands (1994) = Bealings x Gerharda's Aubergine

95 Jennifer Haslam (1994) = Satchmo x Christina Becker

96 Joan Young (1994) = Conspicua x Ann Roots

97 Lee Anthony (1994) = Thalia x Dancing Flame

98 Tear Fund (1994) = Conspicua x Cheers

99 Audrey Booth (1995) = Citation x Cheers

100 Colin Chambers (1995) = Malibu Mist x Florentina

101 Evelyn Stanley (1995) = Alice Hoffman x Cheers

102 Norfolk Ivor (1995) = Graf Spee x Christina Becker

103 Raymond Scopes (1995) = Alice Hoffman x Cheers

104 Thumbelina (1995) = Lechlade Tinkerbell x Wapenveld's Bloei

105 Brian A. Mcdonald (1996) = Unknown

106 Eira Goulding (1996) = Unknown

107 Gwendoline (1996) = Unknown

108 John Boy (1996) = Unknown

109 Marjory Almond (1996) = Unknown

110 May Rogers (1996) = Unknown

111 Spellbinder (1996) = Little Witch x Baby Chang

112 Wilfred C. Dodson (1996) = Unknown

113 William Jay (1996) = Unknown

114 Gwen Wallis (1997) = Ruby Wedding x Bella Rozella

115 Popely Pride (1997) = Plumb-bob x Bella Rozella

116 Ralph Oliver (1997) = Unknown

117 Ralph's Delight (1997) = Blush of Dawn x Bella Rozella

118 Ron Chambers Love (1997) = Plumb-bob x Bella Rozella

119 Anne Strudwick (1998) = Plumb-bob x Bella Rozella

120 Betty Jean (1998) = Dawn Carless x Bella Rozella

121 Byron Rees (1998) = Cheers x Bella Rozella

122 Jack Rowlands (1998) = Dawn Carless x Bella Rozella

123 June Spencer (1998) = Toos x Aalt Groothuis

124 Patricia Joan Yates (1998) = Miss Debbie x Marcus Graham

125 Sonia Ann Barry (1998) = Delta's Bride x Aalt Groothuis

126 Timothy Titus (1998) = Thalia x Vuurwerk

127 Wally Yendell (1998) = Blush of Dawn x Cheers

128 Brian Kimberley (1999) = Thalia x (Thalia x *F. apetala*)

129 Capt. Al. Sutton (1999) = Scarborough Rosette x Ovation

130 Forfar's Pride (1999) = Scarborough Rosette x Ovation

131 Giovanna & Wesley (1999) = Blush of Dawn x Bella Rozella

132 Lavender Ann (1999) = Malibu Mist x Supersport

133 Monica Dare (1999) = Thalia x Vuurwerk

134 Reinholt Leuthardt (1999) = Thalia x Vuurwerk

135 Tom Coulson (1999) = Plumb-bob x Cheers

136 William Grant (1999) = Scarborough Rosette x Ovation

137 Alison Ruth Griffin (2000) = Miss Debbie x Marcus Graham

138 Ben Jiggins (2000) = Malibu Mist x Supersport

139 Daryn John Woods (2000) = Thalia x *F. juntasensis*

140 Kelly Stableford (2000) = Unknown

141 Pride of Ipswich (2000) = Delta's Bride x Aalt Groothuis

142 Suffolk Punch (2000) = Scarborough Rosette x Ovation

143 Alison Woods (2001) = (Delta's Bride x Aalt Groothuis) x (Estelle Marie x Aalt Groothuis)

144 John Shead (2001) = Thalia x Unknown

145 Kevin R. Peake (2001) = Wally Yendell x Giovanna & Wesley

146 Mary Shead (2001) = Blush of Dawn x Love's Reward

147 Robert J. Pierce (2001) = Estelle Marie x (Jeeves x Hathor)

List of other Fuchsias released by Gouldings Fuchsias (1984–2001)

1. Waveney Valley (Burns 1984)
2. Waveney Unique (Burns 1985)
3. Melissa Heavens (Heavens 1986)
4. Waveney Sunrise (Burns 1986)
5. Breckland (Heavens 1987)
6. H.M.S. Victorious (Sheppard 1987)
7. Look East (Heavens 1987)
8. Lunteren Sun (Appel 1987)
9. Sportsknight (Newstead 1987)
10. Bedfords Park (Rout 1988)
11. Michael (Barker 1988)
12. Alan's Joy (Rudd 1989)
13. Piquant Pixie (Whiting 1989)
14. Lunters Klokje (Appel 1990)
15. Fuchsiarama '91 (Stannard 1991)
16. Grange Farm (Sheppard 1991)
17. Ken Goldsmith (Stannard 1991)
18. Larksfield Skylark (Sheppard 1991)
19. Sophie Claire (Stannard 1991)
20. Alton Water (Ransby 1992)
21. Edwin J. Goulding (Stannard 1992)
22. Piper's Vale (Stannard 1992)
23. Sophie's Surprise (Stannard 1992)
24. Brian C. Morrison (Stannard 1993)
25. Chantry Park (Stannard 1993)
26. Christine Shaffery (Shaffery 1993)
27. Drifter (Stannard 1993)
28. Grand Duchess (Stannard 1993)
29. Irene L. Peartree (Peartree 1993)
30. Millrace (Stannard 1993)
31. Ploughman (Stannard 1993)
32. Poacher (Stannard 1993)
33. Rodeo (Stannard 1993)
34. Roos Breytenbach (Stannard 1993)
35. Twink (Stannard 1993)
36. Vivienne Davis (Stannard 1993)
37. Dawning (Shaffery 1994)
38. Snow Goose (Shaffery 1994)
39. Cornelia Smith (Smits 1995)
40. Christine Bamford (Carless 1996)
41. Aalt Groothuis (Beije 1997)
42. Beryl Shaffery (Shaffery 1997)
43. Dorothy Hanley (Carless 1997)
44. Hobo (Carless 1997)
45. Mrs Janice Morrison (Beije 1997)
46. Scarlet O'Hara (Shaffery 1997)
47. Fulpila (Beije 1998)
48. Kath van Hanegem (Carless 1998)
49. Martin's Cinderella (Beije 1998)
50. Musi (De Boer 1998)
51. Priscilla Spek (Beije 1998)
52. Richard John (Wye 1998)
53. Straat Napier (De Boer 1998)
54. Susan Diana (Wye 1998)
55. Taco (de Boer 1998)
56. Jan S. Kamphuis (Beije 1999)
57. Martin's Choice (Beije 1999)
58. Martin's Double Delicate (Beije 1999)
59. Matthew Morrison (Beije 1999)
60. Obcylin (Beije 1999)
61. Georgie Girl (Kimberley 2000)
62. Karin van der Sande (Beije 2000)
63. Lord Jim (Dobson 2000)
64. Martin's Tiny (Beije 2000)
65. Rianne Foks (Beije 2000)
66. Summer Daffodil (De Graaff 2000)
67. Bessie Kimberley (Kimberley 2001)
68. Dymph Werker van Groenland (Beije 2001)
69. Irving Alexander (De Boer 2001)
70. Martin's Inspiration (Beije 2001)
71. Martin's Umbrella (Beije 2001)

Specialist Societies across the World

Note: Internet and e-mail information is increasingly available. Much of this is out of date and of questionable value. Key entry points to each country for further information are all that are given here.

Australia
Australian Fuchsia Society
The Secretary,
P.O. Box 97,
Kent Town,
South Australia 5071,
Australia.

Austria
Austrian Fuchsia Society
(also ÉuroFuchsia)
Hans & Elizabeth Schnedl,
Wienerstaße 216,
A-8051 GRAZ,
Austria.

Belgium
Belgian Fuchsia Societies
Oscar Defue,
De Vlaamse Fuchsia-Vrienden,
Hoge Akker 25,
B-2930 BRASSCHAT,
Belgium.

Greta De Wachter,
Secretary De Vrije Fuchsiavrienden,
Botermelkstraat 29,
B-9100 St. Niklaas,
Belgium.

Michel Cornet,
Les Amis du Fuchsia,
Rue du Moulin 24,
B-6230 PONT-A-CELLES,
Belgium.

Britain
British Fuchsia Society
Peter Darnley,
British Fuchsia Society,
P.O. Box 1068,
Kidderminster,
DY11 7GZ,
England.

Canada
Canadian Fuchsia Society
Lorna Herchenson,
Corresponding Secretary,
British Columbia Fuchsia & Begonia Society,
2402 Swinburne Avenue,
North Vancouver, B.C.,
Canada, V7H 1L2.

France
French Fuchsia Society
Suzanne Néttilard,
Fuchsia Section of National Horticultural Society of France,
24 rue Ferdinand Jamin,
F-92340 Bourg le Reine,
France.

Germany
German Fuchsia Societies
Reinhold Leuthardt,
Mozartstrasse 23,
D-59227 AHLEN/WESTF,
Germany.

Waltraud Strumper
Teichstrasse 29,
D-37085 GÖTTINGEN,
Germany.

Ireland
Irish Fuchsia Society
Joyce McMaster,
Secretary of The Irish Fuchsia Society,
70 Tullynagardy Road,
Newtownards,
Ireland.

Italy
Italian Fuchsia Society
Pietro Bonati,
President, Italian Fuchsia Association,
via S. Filippo 13,
13501 PIELLA,
Italy.

The Netherlands
Dutch Fuchsia Society
J. C. Makkinje,
Secretary, Dutch Fuchsia Society,
Gratamastraat 28,
3067 SE ROTTERDAM,
The Netherlands.

New Zealand
Ted & Alison Sweetman,
National Fuchsia Society of New Zealand,
18 Churton Drive,
Wellington 4,
New Zealand.

Northern Ireland
Yvonne Caldwell,
22 Wandsworth Road,
Bangor,
Northern Ireland.

Norway
Norwegian Fuchsia Society
Bjørg Linbye,
Secretary, Norwegian Fuchsia Society,
Rustadv,
2830 Raufoss,
Norway.

South Africa
South African Fuchsia Society
Roos Breytenbach,
P.O. Box 537,
Alberton 1450,
South Africa.

Jan Wiggleslinkhuizen,
Secretary, The Western Cape Fuchsia Society of South Africa,
Box 53,
Bloubergstrand 7436,
South Africa.

Sweden
Swedish Fuchsia Society
Agneta Westin,
Östermalmsgatan 68,
114 50 Stockholm,
Sweden.

Switzerland
Swiss Fuchsia Society
Vreny Schleeweiss,
Fuchsia Society of Switzerland,
Gruebweg 163,
CH-4451 Wintersingen,
Switzerland.

USA
American Fuchsia Society,
County Fair Building,
9th Avenue & Lincoln Way,
San Francisco,
California 94122,
United States of America.

National Fuchsia Society,
11507 East 187th Street,
Artesia,
California 90701,
United States of America.

Zimbabwe
Zimbabwe Fuchsia Society
Fuchsia Society of Zimbabwe,
PO Box GD 115,
Greendale,
Harare,
Zimbabwe.

Fuchsia Index

Glossary

Antipetalous: Inserted opposite the insertion of the petals.

Apetalous: A flower without petals; without a corolla.

Axil: The angle between the upper surface of a leaf stalk, flower or branch, and the stem or axis from which it arises.

B-9: Internodal reduction agent based on daminozide.

Banker: Of reliable high quality; one of the most consistent show winners.

Bicoloured: Flowers with a clear contrast in colour between the tubes and sepals, and the corolla. 'Finn', with its red corolla and white tubes and sepals, is a good example.

Binomial nomenclature: The two-part system of naming species. The first part is the name of the genus to which the species belongs. The second distinguishes the species from others in the same genus; for example, *Fuchsia triphylla*.

Bract: Leaves that are modified and much reduced in size; they may be little more than scales. They are usually on the ends of fuchsia branches and branchlets. *F. simplicicaulis* carries them once flowering starts.

Bracteate: A plant that possesses bracts.

Chelated: Fully soluble; absorbable.

Chlorophylls: Green colourants present in plant tissue that contain magnesium and are contained in chloroplasts. They trap blue and red light (energy) and are responsible for photosynthesis.

Chloroplasts: Green plastids that contain chlorophyll. They are responsible for photosynthesis and are found in leaf cells and green stems.

Circadian rhythms: Cyclical actions most often associated in fuchsias with daylight and darkness. Seasonal swings also perform this cycle.

Connate: The fusion between two opposite leaves (through which a stem appears to pass).

Coriaceous: Leathery.

Corymbose: Shaped like a corymb; of branches as well as inflorescences.

Corymbs: The arrangement of the inflorescence in which different parts originate along a main axis. Inferior pedicels are longer than the upper ones so that all flowers are carried at about the same level.

Cultivar: In cultivation; a cross; not a species.

Cylindrical-fusiform: Cylindrical in shape and possibly slightly tapered. Having partially fused sepals.

Diapause: Period of suspended or retarded development in some insects.

Dicotyledons: A class of plants that has two or more seed leaves.

Dioecious: A separate class or order of plants in which unisexual flowers of the same species are produced on distinct individuals.

Divaricating: Branching or spreading widely from a point or axis.

Elliptic: An oval shape, with pointed or rounded ends.

Emasculation: To remove the male parts.

Epipetalous: Having stamens inserted upon petals.

Epiphytic: Like an epiphyte: attached to other plants for support but obtaining no nutrients from them.

Etiolation: The blanching of leaves and lengthening of stems that occurs when plants are grown in the dark or in heavy shade.

Facultative: A plant that can live under a variety of different conditions, for example, as an epiphyte or growing in the ground.

Fasciation: The growing together, or fusion, of different parts or a plant, for example, flowers and leaves.

Funnelform: Funnel-shaped; a hollow cone.

Fusiform: Tapering at each end; spindle-shaped.

Gene: A unit of inheritance; a length of DNA in a chromosome that codes for a particular characteristic.

Genetic pool: Sometimes 'gene pool': all the genes present in a population.

Genus: The group name given to all the species of one family, e.g. *Fuchsia*.

Gigantism: Massive and abnormal enlargement; usually, but not always, relates to flowers.

Glabrous: Smooth; without pubescence.

Gland-serrate: Having leaf serrations tipped with glands.

Gynodioecious: Having female and hermaphrodite flowers separately on distinct individuals of a species of plants.

Herb: A plant without a woody stem.

Hermaphrodite: Of flowers that have both male and female parts.

Hybrid: Offspring of two species, subspecies or varieties.

Hypanthium: The outer parts of a flower that form a protective tube and attract pollinators to the stigma.

Inflorescence: Of flowers: usually arranged around a single axis, as in *F. paniculata*.

Internodes: The parts of the stem between nodes.

Lance-elliptic: Broader than lance- or spear-shaped, and more narrowly tapered at one end than the other.

Lanceolate: Narrowly tapering like the head of a spear.

Liana: A woody perennial climber.

Linear-lanceolate: More narrowly tapered than lanceolate.

Micropropagation: Propagation, usually under sterile conditions, using minute sections of tissue from plants.

Multiflowering: Carrying more than a single bloom in each leaf axil; for example, 'Linda Goulding'. Not applied to *triphylla* types.

Mutation: A change in sequence of material in chromosome chains that results (in fuchsias) in changes in foliage or flower.

Mycelia: Thread-like; usually of fungi (singular-mycelium).

Obconic: Cone-shaped with the tapering end at the point of attachment.

Oblanceolate: Broader and rounder at the apex, and tapering at the base.

Oblong-ovate: Rather longer than ovate and wider than lanceolate; more narrowly tapered at one end than the other.

Obovate: More broadly rounded than spatulate. Narrowest where the leaf joins the pedicel.

Orbicular-ovate: Part way between orbicular and ovate, being broader than the latter.

Ovate: Of leaves, looking like a flattened egg and pointed at the narrowest end.

Panicles: A branched inflorescence consisting of a number of racemes.

Pansy-flowered: Upward-pointing, saucer-shaped blooms. Petals have different colours at the centre and the periphery.

Peripheral: On the outside or periphery; of flowers carried on the ends of branches.

Petaloids: Diminutive petals; within the main petals; for example, on 'Excalibur'.

Pheromones: Chemicals with sexually attractive scents usually undetected by humans. Produced by insects such as moths to attract mates in the dark.

Photosynthesis: The process by which the chlorophyll in chloroplasts uses the sun's energy to generate carbohydrates from carbon dioxide and water.

Phototropism: The plant's response to light by moving in relation to light. Shoots and leaves are positively phototropic. Roots are usually negatively phototropic or have no response.

Pilose: Hairy.

Pubescent: A covering of down or short hairs.

Quarternate: When leaves are carried four to a node.

Raceme: An inflorescence with a central axis that bears flowers along its length.

Recurved: Bent backwards; usually of sepals.

Reflexed: Synonymous with recurved.

Relative air humidity: The relationship between air temperature and humidity levels. Relative air humidity drops as temperatures rise unless more water is added in compensation.

Scandent: Of fuchsias that would normally be unable to raise themselves above the ground when they climb or are supported by other plants.

Sclerotized: Hardened.

Sessile: Stalkless and attached directly at the base.

Species: The smallest unit of classification. Individuals in a species are assumed to have emanated from a single original genetic source and are sexually compatible with each other.

Subcylindric: Like a small cylinder.

Subdioecy: Having partial dioeciousness. This may be the case with *F. procumbens*.

Suberect: Partially or sometimes erect; usually of flowers.

Subracemosely: Having small or partial racemes of flowers.

Subrhombic: Small and quadrangular but not square; usually of leaves.

Subshrub: Rather more herbaceous than shrubby; without woody stems rising from ground level.

Subspecies: A partially differentiated group within a species.

Subterminal: Before the end; usually on branchlets.

Terminal: At the extremity or end of a branch.

Ternate: Arranged in threes; of leaves or blooms at a joint.

Toggle ties: Ties that fasten round plant stems and supporting canes in a figure-of-eight fashion; a single toggle tie has a loop on either side of a restricting band.

Trace elements: Those elements required by a plant in minute amounts; for example, molybdenum.

Triphylla: Like *F. triphylla*, with terminal racemes of long, tapered flowers.

Villous: Covered with long, weak hair.

Whorls: A set of appendages that are arranged in a circle around a single axis. A ring of leaves or flowers.

General Index